COMPUTER GLOSSARY
FOR
STUDENTS AND
TEACHERS

by

Larry C. Schmalz
Charles J. Sippl

FUNK &
WAGNALLS
LIBRARY OF
COMPUTER
SCIENCE

Funk & Wagnalls
New York

ACKNOWLEDGMENT: Reference source for the terms and definitions in this glossary is "Computer Dictionary and Handbook" published by Howard W. Sams & Co., Inc., 4300 West 62nd Street, Indianapolis, Indiana 46268. It is available through book stores, electronic parts distributors, or directly from the publisher.

Larry C. Schmalz received his Bachelor of Arts Degree in Quantitative Methods from the California State College at Fullerton and worked on the staff for the City of Anaheim and functioned as a Systems Analyst in the redesigning of the Public Utilities Computer Information System.

Charles J. Sippl has taught a variety of Computer, Management, and Mathematics courses at several California colleges and universities. His Bachelor of Science Degree in Finance is from the University of Wisconsin, Master of Arts in Economics from the University of Miami. He has written extensively in the computer field over the past ten years and has lectured nationwide on computer industry structure and financial topics.

Library of Computer Science

Computer Glossary for Students and Teachers
Beginning Computer Glossary for Businessmen
Computer Glossary for Accountants and Bankers
Computer Glossary for Engineers and Scientists
Computer Glossary for Medical and Health Sciences
Computer Glossary for Production Automation

PREFACE

The other day on the University of California, Irvine Campus we heard a student remark, "Computers are BIG in Anthropology". On the UCLA campus, a very common greeting from one professor to another is, "Hi, what have you got going on the computer these days". On the Cal State, Fullerton Campus it seems that most of the Quantitative Methods, Statistics, and Accounting students are constantly carrying around stacks of punched cards or computer printouts of problems and assignments. The great majority of Engineering and Math students are loaded with computer courses. Graduate Library Science students almost weep about the new additions of still more computer systems courses. What does all this mean to students and teachers? It's simple enough! It is almost impossible to escape the computer and the required knowledge concerning its operations or applications in practically any of the college disciplines — even Music, Art and the Social Sciences.

And that's what this Computer Glossary is all about. In order to understand and retain many of the rather heavy lectures relating to computer capability and utility, the great majority of students (and teachers) really need either a pre-knowledge of computer terminology or a quick and handy reference to explanations of computer concepts and equipment. And most students are not happy about lugging too many thick books around to classes which contain extensive descriptions and analyses of coding, electronics, engineering, or computer mathematics. Our survey of many campuses has revealed an extensive and almost compelling need for low-cost, highly specific computer glossaries lucidly and clearly defining basic, modern computer equipment and operations terms and concepts.

This convenient book is one of a series of glossaries designed for specific disciplines and professions. It is the basic tool for all beginning students and alert teachers. Others in the series are developed as specialized computer reference tools for: Accountants and Bankers, Engineers and Scientists, Medical and Health Sciences, etc. And these fit the very particular needs of these students or professionals. All have appendices, as has this one, which relate to Impact Areas, Special Languages, or Basic Principles of the distinct computer knowledge required of the specialization the titles designate. The companion "updating" applications books are the latest reporting and analyses of computer capability in being "today", with descriptions of computer models and systems, purposes and current uses, and most importantly an impartial critique of the value of the results. These books are again, low-cost, compact and convenient with titles such as: Computer Applications in Education and Research; Computer Applications in Accounting and Auditing, in Medical and Health Sciences, etc.

The computer terms and definitions in these and other glossaries are selected from an information base of more than 25,000 computer concepts definitions and explanations. They are constantly updated, and the collection is steadily expanding with the addition of new inventions, applications, and innovations.

The computer IS here . . . and there . . . and there. Don't fight it! Stay WITH it!

Larry C. Schmalz
Charles J. Sippl

TABLE OF CONTENTS

HOW TO USE THIS BOOK

In the dictionary section of this book all terms of more than one word are treated as one word, regardless of spaces or punctuation. For example, "check indicator" appears between "check digits" and "checking program;" and "characters, alphameric" appears between "character recognition" and "character set." Abbreviations are also treated alphabetically; the letters "I/O" follow "inverter" rather than appearing at the beginning of the I's.

If you do not find a compound term under the first word, try the second word of the term. For example, "parallel access" may be found under "access, parallel."

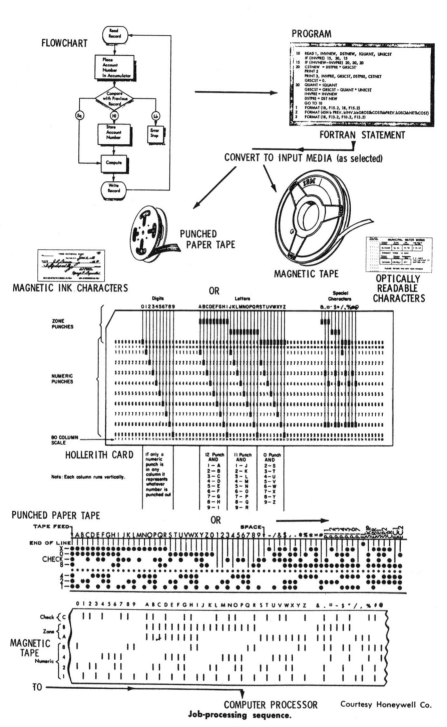

Job-processing sequence.

Courtesy Honeywell Co.

TERMS & DEFINITIONS

A-address—That portion of the instruction code which indicates the location of data to be processed.

A AND NOT B gate—A binary logic coincidence (two-input) circuit used to complete the logic operations of A AND NOT B, i.e., result is true only if statement A is true and statement B is false.

abacus—1. This device performs calculations by sliding beads or counters along rods. 2. An early (3000 B.C.) form of biquinary calculator.

ABA number—An abbreviation used as the coding number assigned to commercial banks to assist the process of clearing checks for the members and associates of the American Banking Association.

abort—A process designed to terminate the execution of a program when an irrevocable error, mistake, or malfunction occurs.

absolute address—1. The actual location in storage ot a particular unit of data; an address that the control unit can interpret directly. 2. A pattern of characters that identifies a unique storage location or device without further modification (synonymous with machine address).

absolute error—The magnitude of the error disregarding the algebraic sign, or if a vectorial error, disregarding its direction.

absolute instruction—A computer instruction which specifies completely a specific computer operation and which is also capable of causing the execution of that operation.

absolute language—1. A set of symbols, characters, or signs, and the rules for combining them, that conveys instructions or information to a computer. 2. A language for writing instructions in a form to be executed by the compiler; the language can be directly interpreted by the control section of the machine. 3. Information or data is expressed in code that can be read directly, used or written by the computer or peripheral machines without further processing.

absolute value—The ordering or ranking of numbers and values but disregarding the algebraic sign.

absolute-value computer—A computer that processes all data expressed in full values of all variables at all times (as contrasted with incremental computer).

absolute value sign—A specific sign using the symbol, $\|$, to indicate that the absolute value of a number is to be taken, i.e., the value of the number irrespective of the sign.

abstract—1. Short form or summary of a document. 2. To shorten or summarize a document.

abstract symbol—A specific symbol whose shape or pattern is not indicative of its meaning or use, and one which almost always requires definition for each particular set of applications.

ac analog computer—An analog computer where electrical signals are amplitude modulated suppressed carrier signals and where the absolute value of a computer variable is represented by the amplitude of the carrier and the sign of a computer variable is represented by the phase (0 to 180 degrees) of the carrier relative to the

1

reference ac signal.

access—The process of obtaining data from or placing data in storage.

access-coding, minimal—The reference of programming which is done in order to locate the data in such a manner as to reduce the access time and minimize the amount of time required to transfer words from auxiliary storage to main memory.

access, immediate—Pertaining to the ability to directly obtain data from, or place data in, a storage device or register without serial delay due to other units of data, and usually in a relatively short period of time.

access method—The software link between the program and the data that must be transferred into or out of memory by the program. It is defined by both the file structures and programming language elements involved.

access mode—In COBOL, the technique that is used to obtain a specific logic record from, or place a specific logic record into, a file assigned to a mass-storage device.

accessory—An additional part or an added feature which is designed to increase the function or add to the value or capacity of equipment without redesigning or altering the basic function of the equipment.

access time—1. Time interval between the instant at which information is called for storage and the instant at which delivery is completed, i.e., the read time. 2. Time interval between the instant at which data are ready for storage and the instant at which storage is completed, i.e., the write time.

accounting machine—A machine that reads information from one medium (e.g.,

cards, paper tape, and magnetic tape) and produces lists, tables, and totals on separate forms or continuous paper. Clarified by tabulating equipment.

accounting overhead—Concerns specific costs not directly attributable to productive work but which are instead allocated or spread over the entire production costs to develop accuracy of detail for total cost projections.

accumulating reproducer—A piece of equipment that reproduces punched cards and has limited additional capabilities of adding, subtracting and summary punching.

accumulator—1. A part of the logical-arithmetic unit of a computer. It is used for intermediate storage, to form algebraic sums, or for other intermediate operations. 2. The zero-access register (and associated equipment) in the arithmetic unit in which are formed sums and other arithmetical and logical results; a unit in a digital computer where numbers are totaled, i.e., accumulated. Often the accumulator stores one quantity and upon receipt of any second quantity, it forms and stores the sum of the first and second quantities. See: register.

accumulator register—That part of the arithmetic unit in which the result of an operation remains, and into which numbers are brought from storage, and from which numbers may be taken for storage.

accuracy—A measurement of freedom from error as related to programs, operations, machine capability, and most often expressed as a percentage of perfection. See: double-precision.

accuracy, conformity—This concept includes simple and combined conformity

2

errors as well as hysteresis and repeatability errors. The units being used are to be stated explicitly. It is preferred that a + and/or − sign precede the number or quantity. The absence of a sign infers a + sign. It can be expressed in a number of forms.

accuracy control characters—A specific character designed with a function to control a given block of data, to indicate if the data are in error, to indicate if they are to be disregarded or whether they can or cannot be represented on a particular device.

accuracy-control system—A system of error control and detection.

acquisition and control system, data—The system is designed to handle a wide variety of real-time applications, process control, and high-speed data acquisition. Each system is individually tailored with modular building blocks that are easily integrated to meet specific system requirements. A large family of real-time process input/output devices is included, such as analog input, analog output, contact-sense, and contact-operate as well as data processing I/O units, such as magnetic tape, disk storage, line printer, graph plotter, card and paper tape. Input and output data are received and transmitted on either a high-speed cycle steal basis or under program control depending on the intrinsic data rate of the I/O device.

acquisition, data—1. Various data and information are acquired by the DA system, converted into digital information, and printed to provide: (a) operating records for accounting and supervisory purposes, or (b) a record of experimental data in process research. 2. Operations in the marketplace consist of data collection, data reduction, and digital test control applications in scientific/engineering environments. In addition, there is a market for data collection and reduction applications in remote business operations (manufacturing plants and retail outlets, warehouses, sales offices, etc.) This latter type of system can provide the complete, timely information about a firm's overall operations that is required for accurate cost control and informed management decisions. It can reduce the number of times and places at which data must be manually handled and transcribed thereby cutting clerical costs and error rates.

acronym—The word formed from the first letter or letters of the words in a name, term, or phrase; e.g., SAGE from Semi-Automatic Ground Environment, and ALGOL from ALGOrithmic Language.

action—Relates to activity or processing activity steps, operations, etc.

active file—A file which is being used to which entries or references are made on a current basis.

activity—1. A general term which indicates that a record in a master file is being used, altered, or referred to. 2. A measure of the changes made concerning the use of files of data; e.g., the part of the file or the number of records. 3. A structural variable whose level is to be computed in a programming problem.

activity level—That value which is taken by a structural variable in an intermediate or final solution to a programming problem.

actual coding—Same as absolute coding.

actual instruction—Presumptive instructions or unmodified instructions are altered in a prescribed way by means of part of a stored computer program available for this purpose, to produce the complete instruction actually executed and called the effective or actual instruction.

actual time—Relating to the performance of computing during the specific time in which the related process, event, problem, or communication is taking place, i.e., the computing must be fast enough, during the process of the happening of the event for the results of this computing to influence the related process or result.

adapting—Concerns the ability of a system to change its performance characteristics in response to its environment.

addend—The number or quantity to be added to another number or quantity (augend) to produce the result (sum).

adder, analog—Related to a specific amplifier (analog computer) with output voltage which is the weighted sum of the input voltages. The weights correspond to the positional significance of a given numbering system and would be proportional to the conductances of the circuit elements in the input leads.

addition—In data processing, that function of combining quantities according to various circuitry designs with specific machine rules regarding changes in values and types of carryover operations.

addition table—The core storage area that holds a table of numbers which are used during the table-scan concept of addition.

addition, zero access—The development of addition by adding a number to another number already stored in an accumulator, thus forming the sum in the same accumulator. Consequently, the sum is available for the next operation and no access time is required for the addend or storage of the sum. The term is incorrectly applied because this is accomplished during the addition process in most computers.

address—1. A label, name, or number identifying a register, location, or unit where information is stored. 2. The operand portion of an instruction. 3. In communications, the coded representation of the destination of a message. 4. To call a specific piece of information from the memory or to put it in the memory. Types: absolute, effective, immediate, indirect, direct, level, instruction, machine, multiple, symbolic, and third-level address.

addressable register—A specifically designed temporary storage unit or device represented by particular storage location numbers.

address comparator—A device used for verifying that the correct address is being read. The comparison is made between the address being read and the specified address.

address, dummy—An artificial address utilized for illustration or instruction purposes.

addressed memory—Memory sections that contain each individual register.

address format—The arrangement of the address parts of an instruction. The expression "plus-one" is frequently used to indicate that one of the addresses specifies the location of the next instruction to be executed, such as one plus one, two plus one, three plus one, four plus one.

address generation—The generation of numbers or symbols by means of instructions in a program. These symbols are then used to form an address.

4

address, index—A particular address to which indexing is applied before or during the execution of an instruction.

address, indirect—1. An address that specifies a storage location whose content is either an indirect address or another indirect address. 2. A single instruction address that is at once the address of another address. The second address is the specific address of the data to be processed. This is classified as single-level indirect addressing. But, the second address could also be indirect, which is then second-level indirect addressing. This same process could develop third, fourth, fifth, and other levels of indirect addressing.

addressing, direct—A technique for specifically citing an operand in the instruction by the operand's location in storage. The direct address is the number representing the storage location.

addressing, implied—The addressing method or procedure used in computers which have variable instruction formats, and in which instrutions having zero address instruction format refer automatically to the location following that affected by the last instruction executed, i.e., stepped addressing.

address, machine—An absolute, direct, unindexed address expressed as such, or resulting after indexing and other processing has been completed.

address modification—1. The process of changing the address part of a machine instruction by means of coded instruction. 2. A change in the address portion of an instruction or command which, if the routine containing the instruction or command is repeated, the computer will go to a new address or location for data or instructions. 3. A process used to obtain the address of the effective memory location, starting from a given reference address value in an instruction word.

address, one—Same as single address.

address register—Register in which an address is stored.

address, three—A method of specifying the location of operands and instruction in which the storage location of the two operands and the storage location of the results of the operations are cited, and in which the location or address of the next instruction to be executed is also to be specified; e.g., addend, augend, and sum addresses all specified in one instruction word.

address, two—An instruction that includes an operation and specifies the location of an operand and the result of the operation.

add time (in microseconds)—The time required to acquire from memory and execute one fixed-point add instruction using all features such as overlapped memory banks, instruction look-ahead and parallel execution. The add is either from one full word in memory to a register, or from memory to memory; but not from register to register.

add-to-storage concept—The process which immediately enters the final sum of the accumulator into the computer memory.

adjacency—1. Relates to character recognition and printing conditions. Reference lines designate spacing between two consecutive characters. 2. A condition in character recognition in which two consecutive characters, either printed or handwritten, are closer than the specified distance.

Administrative Terminal System (ATS) IBM—The Administrative Terminal

System (ATS) developed by IBM. One of the remote computer systems text editing systems as follows: Text preparation and manipulation is an application particularly suited for on-line operations. ATS represents a good example of text-processing system. ATS is an operational system in use by several organizations and is offered on a subscriber basis, thus making it generally available. ATS is a time-sharing system capable of servicing up to 40 terminals. An extended system can also carry out simple background programs—normal peripheral input/output programs, such as card-to-tape and tape-to-printer. The functions which a user may perform at an ATS terminal may be categorized into the following groups: entry of text; printing of text; storing of documents; correction and modification of text; message transmission; simulated keypunching; and simple calculation.

administrative data processing—An expression usually meaning business data processing such as the recording, classifying or summarizing transactions activities, events, etc., usually of a financial nature or the collection, retrieval, or control of such items.

ADP (Automatic Data Processing)—1. This acronym pertains to equipment such as EAM (Electronic Accounting Machines) and EDP (Electronic Data Processing) equipment units, or systems. 2. Data processing performed by a system of electronic or electrical machines so interconnected and interacting as to reduce to a minimum the necessity for human assistance or intervention.

ADPE—Abbreviation for Automatic Data Processing Equipment.

ADPS—Abbreviation for Automatic Data Processing System.

agenda—The set of control-language statements used to prescribe a solution path or run procedure; an ordered list of the major operations constituting a procedure for a solution or computer run (this usage corresponds roughly to the ordinary "agenda" for a meeting).

agendum—The body of code called for execution by a control-language statement (agendum call card).

agendum call card—A single agendum name with its parameters punched on one card in a stylized form; one item of the agenda—a control-language statement calling for the execution of the named agendum. A set of agendum call cards is used to control a linear programming system, thus forming an agenda.

algebra, Boolean—1. An algebra named for George Boole. This algebra is similar in form to ordinary algebra, but with classes, propositions, on-off-circuit elements, etc., for variables rather than data values. It includes the operators **and, or, not, except, if, then.** 2. A binary system of algebra; hence, a useful tool for logical analysis of binary computers. Has been instrumental in the development and design of original computer units and continues to be useful not only for students in developing binary concepts, but also for continuous technological research. 3. The logic and functions constructed from two-valued variables: truth/falsity; go/no go; zero/one; yes/no. Set algebra, class algebra, and propositional calculus are similar math systems used in computer switching theory and computer design. See: gates (decision elements).

algebraic expression—A statement expressed in various symbols, signs, and

6

abbreviations following mathematical rules and syntax to designate variables, constant, functions, and rules.

algebraic language—1. A language which uses symbols and letters, both Greek and English, to express relationships, variables, constants, parameters, operators, operands and mathematical or logical relationships. Each algebra has its own set of rules and is designed to delineate situations, relationships, operations and equalities and inequalities.

algebraic oriented language—An incorrect name for ALGOL.

ALGOL—1. ALGOrithmic Language. A data processing language used to express problem-solving formulas for machine solution. 2. ALGebraic Oriented Language (some authors). The international procedural language. 3. An arithmetic language by which numerical procedures may be precisely presented to a computer in a standard form. This language is intended not only as a means of directly presenting any numerical procedure to any suitable computer for which a compiler exists, but also as a means of communicating numerical procedures among individuals. The language itself is a result of international cooperation to obtain a standardized algorithmic language. The International Algebraic Language is the forerunner of ALGOL.

algorithm—1. A fixed step-by-step procedure to accomplish a given result; usually a simplified procedure for solving a complex problem, also a full statement of a finite number of steps. 2. A defined process or set of rules that leads and assures development of a desired output from a given input. A sequence of formulas and/or algebraic/logical steps to calculate or determine a given task;

processing rules.

algorithmic language—A language used to solve problems in a finite number of steps, and thus, procedure-oriented and designed for clarity and precision for expression and communication of mathematical solutions using well-defined rules.

algorithmic routine—That type of program or routine which directs a computer specifically toward a solution of a problem in a finite number of distinct and discrete steps as contrasted to trial-and-error methods, i.e., heuristic methods or routines.

algorithm translation—1. A specific, effective, essentially computational method for obtaining a translation from one language to another. 2. Various sets of rules, specific methods or procedures are used to obtain translations from one language to various others. Oftentimes this is done by the computer using computational methods to solve the algorithm.

alias—A label which is an alternate for something of the same nature or type for which it is being used, i.e., a synonym. Various primary or secondary names are used in computer slang such as red tape, GIGO, kludge, etc., which may be aliases for the basic or primary term.

allocate—The assignment of storage locations to the main routines and subroutines, thereby fixing the absolute values of any symbolic address.

allocation and loading program—Relocatable binary elements produced by compilation are linked together for execution or for future use by an allocation program which is resident in the system at all times. An extensive selection of subroutines is directly available from the system library, enabling the allocator to incorporate them dynamically as the compiled elements are being constructed into a program. The relocatable element is the common-denominator output of processors, allowing applications to be programmed in several different languages, compiled, and properly linked at execution time.

allocation, dynamic-storage—Each time a subroutine is called using this feature, the unique storage area for that subroutine is assigned to the first storage available. Thus, all subroutines called on the same level will share the same storage area. This results in a significant storage saving in many cases. In addition, a recursive subroutine call is possible because a new storage area is assigned each time a subroutine is entered. This feature, together with in-line symbolic coding, provides real-time capability.

all-purpose computer—A computer combining the specific talents heretofore assigned solely to a general-purpose or special-purpose computer (scientific or business).

alpha—1. The first letter of the Greek alphabet, and thus, a symbol representing first. 2. An abbreviation for Alphanumeric. 3. A feature of representation of data in alphabetical characters in contrast to numerical.

alphabetic code—A system of alphabetic abbreviations used in preparing information for input to a machine; e.g., Boston, New York, Philadelphia, and Washington may in alphabetical coding be reported as BS, NY, PH, WA. (contrasted with numeric code.)

alphabetic word—A computer word is a character string or group of characters in number adjacency, and an alphabetic word consists only of letters.

alphameric—The contraction of alphanumeric or alphabetic-numeric.

alphameric code—Same as code, alphanumeric.

altering—An operation for inserting, deleting or changing information.

alternate routine—Assignment of a secondary communications path to a destination if the primary path is unavailable.

ambiguity—Having more than one meaning or interpretation. In computer processing, ambiguity is often the result of changes of state in various systems.

amphibolous—Pertaining to ambiguity; uncertainty; doubtfulness.

amplifier—An unidirectional device that is capable of putting out an enlargement of the waveform of the electric current, voltage, or power that is supplied to the input.

amplifier, high gain—A special voltage amplifier in analog computers having the characteristic of arbitrary feedback. Same as D.C. Amplifier.

amplifier, sign-reversing—An amplifier whose output voltage is equal in magnitude to the input voltage but opposite in sign.

analog comparator—Performs range checking on digital values developed by the ADC (analog-to-digital converter). The high and low limits are selectively obtained from the processor-controller (P-C) for those values to be checked. When values are determined to be out-of-limit, then an interrupt informs the P-C. Only one P-C cycle is required for each value to be limit checked. (IBM)

analog computer—A computer that represents variables by physical analogies.

8

Thus, any computer that solves problems by translating physical conditions such as flow, temperature, pressure, angular position, or voltage into related mechanical or electrical quantities and uses mechanical or electrical-equivalent circuits is an analog for the physical phenomenon being investigated. Generally, it is a computer that uses an analog for each variable and produces analogs as output. Thus, an analog computer measures continuously, whereas a digital computer counts discretely.

analog device—See analog computer.

analog divider—A unit with two input variables and one output variable which is proportional to the quotient of the input variables, provided that all the variables are within the operating range of the unit. An analog multiplier unit can be used in the feedback path of an operational amplifier to perform division. These two units combined become an analog divider.

analog interrupt mode—In reference to analog computing, in the hold mode, also called the freeze or interrupt mode, the computing action is stopped and all variables are held at the value they had when the computation was interrupted.

analog multiplier—The analog device which develops the analog product from two or more analog input signals, i.e., the output variable is proportional to the product of the input variables.

analog network—A circuit or circuits representing physical variables in such a manner as to permit the expression and solution of mathematical relationships between the variables, or to permit the solution directly or through electric or electronic means.

analog representation—A representation having discrete values but continuously variable.

analysis—The methodological investigation of a problem by a consistent procedure, with separation into related units for further detailed study.

analysis mode—A mode of operation in which special programs monitor the performance of the system for subsequent analysis. Program testing data or statistical data may be automatically recorded when the system is running in the analysis mode.

analysis, numerical—The study of methods of obtaining useful quantitative solutions to mathematical problems, regardless of whether an analytic solution exists or not, and the study of the errors and bounds on errors in obtaining such solutions.

analysis, statistical—One of the main four techniques of operations research. Data gathering, arranging, sorting, sequencing, and evaluating are all common statistical analysis and the three other techniques, linear programming, queuing theory, and simulation. Statistical analysis combines mathematical techniques and computer technology to handle a wide range of business and scientific problems wherever large amounts of information or data must be evaluated and analyzed.

analyst—An individual who is skilled and trained to define problems and analyze, develop, and express algorithms for their solution, especially algorithms that may be resolved and implemented by a computer.

analyst, computer applications—This job classification pertains to those employees who provide primarily software-oriented technical sales support to sales personnel in both pre-sale and post-sale situations.

analyst, programmer—Has capability in programming as well as analysis of problems, systems, and specific specialities as desired.

analyst, systems—1. A person who primarily designs information-handling processes which incorporate computer processing. The systems analyst is usually highly skilled in defining problems and developing algorithms for their solution. 2. Systems analysts are primarily concerned with the planning of new applications. The general title "systems analyst" is normally used interchangeably with "systems designer" for most levels. They are occasionally more specific titles. The following list is arranged in ascending order for responsibility: Research Analyst, Forms Designer, Procedure Analyst, Methods Analyst and Systems Consultant.

analyzer—A computer routine whose purpose is to analyze a program written for the same or a different computer. This analysis may consist of summarizing instruction references to storage and tracing sequences of jumps.

analyzer, differential—Refers to an analog computer used primarily for solving differential equations.

answering time—A data communications term which represents the measure of time which elapses between the appearance of a signal and the response made to it.

aperture—The opening or part of a card or mask or type of filter for allowing passage or viewing of portions of information.

application—The system or problem to which a computer is applied. Reference is often made to an application as being either of the computational type, wherein arithmetic computations predominate, or of the data-processing type, wherein data-handling operations predominate.

applications study—1. The development of the design and sequence of an integrated or specific system relating and ordering processes and equipment to perform individual and integrated data processing. 2. The detailed process of determining a system or set of procedures for using a computer for definite functions or operations, and establishing specifications to be used as a base for the selection of equipment suitable to the specific needs.

area, analysis—An area of core into which data required to monitor or debug programs are written. A log of interrupts, program identifications, or macro trace data are written in the analysis area.

area, input/output—A distinct storage area in a computer reserved for data or instructions received by or ready to be transferred from or to an external (peripheral) input or output device or to another specific section of storage, i.e., a storage working area.

area search—Examination of a large group of documents to select those that pertain to one group, such as one category, class, etc.

area, storage—A specifically designated location in various types of storage units, i.e., for programs, constants, input-output buffer storage, etc.

argument—1. The known reference factor necessary to locate the desired item (function) in a table. 2. A variable upon whose value the value of a function depends. The arguments of a function are listed in parentheses after the function name, whenever that function is used.

The computations specified by the function definition occur using the variables specified as arguments.

arithmetic address—Relates to specific locations which are used for the results of computations.

arithmetical operation—An operation completed according to arithmetical rules, i.e., the operands are the addend and augend, the result is the sum.

arithmetic expression—An expression containing any combination of data-names, numeric literals, and named constants, joined by one or more arithmetic operators in such a way that the expression as a whole can be reduced to a single numeric value.

arithmetic, fixed-point—1. A method of calculation in which operators take place in an invariant manner, and in which the computer does not consider the location of the radix point. This is illustrated by desk calculators or slide rules, with which the operator must keep track of the decimal point. Similarly with many automatic computers, in which the location of the radix point is the programmer's responsibility. (Contrasted with floating-point arithmetic.) 2. A type of arithmetic in which the operands and results of all arithmetic operations must be properly scaled so as to have a magnitude between certain fixed values.

arithmetic, floating point operation—In order to add two floating-point numbers, it is first necessary to equalize the exponents of the numbers. This is accomplished by shifting the mantissa of the smaller expression to the right the number of places that equals the difference of the two exponents. For example, in adding the floating-point decimal numbers 0.3×10^4 and 0.27×10^6, 0.3

$\times 10^4$ is written as 0.003×10^6 and then the two numbers are added which gives the results of 0.273×10^6.

$$
\begin{array}{l}
.3 \times 10^4 \\
+\ .27 \times 10^6
\end{array}
\ =\
\begin{array}{l}
.003 \times 10^6 \\
+\ .27\ \times 10^6 \\
\hline
.273 \times 10^6
\end{array}
$$

The same procedure is required for subtraction except that the subtrahend is subtracted from the minuend in the final step of the operation.

arithmetic instruction—The operator part of this instruction specifies an arithmetic operation: add, subtract, multiply, divide, powers, or square-root.

arithmetic operation—Any of the basic or fundamental operations of arithmetic; e.g., the binary operations of addition, subtraction, multiplication, division, negation and absolute value.

arithmetic unit—The portion of the hardware of a computer in which arithmetic and logical operations are performed. The arithmetic unit generally consists of an accumulator, some special registers for the storage of operands and results, supplemented by shifting and sequencing circuitry for implementing multiplication, division, and other desired operations.

armed interrupt—See disabled interrupt.

ARQ—An automatic system which provides error correction by utilizing a constant ratio code and a closed loop to request retransmission of mutilated characters as indicated by receipt of nonconstant ratio characters.

array—1. A series of items arranged in a meaningful pattern. 2. Usually the arrangement or positioning of the elements of an array in columns and rows provides for ease of computation in

11

matrix algebra or using other manipulative rules fixed to yield values as when arrays are used as operands, a new array is the result of executed operations.

artificial intelligence—1. Research and study in methods for the development of a machine that can improve its own operations. The development or capability of a machine that can proceed or perform functions which are normally concerned with human intelligence as learning, adapting, reasoning, selfcorrection, automatic improvement. 2. The study of computer and related techniques to supplement the intellectual capabilities of man. As man has invented and used tools to increase his physical powers, he now is beginning to use artificial intelligence to increase his mental powers. In a more restricted sense, the study of techniques for more effective use of digital computers by improved programming techniques.

artificial language—A language specifically designed for ease of communication in a particular area of endeavor, but one that is not yet natural to that area. This is contrasted with a natural language which has evolved through long usage.

ascending sort—A sort in which the final sequence of records is such that successive keys compare greater than, less than or equal to.

aspect card—A card on which is entered the accession numbers of documents in an information-retrieval system. Such cards often contain identity numbers of various documents or data elements and their relation to the problem or programmed concept. They are used for coordinate indexing, and accession numbers can be represented as holes or edge-punched cards.

assemble—1. To prepare an object language program from a symbolic language program by substituting machine operation codes for symbolic operation codes and absolute or relocatable addresses for symbolic addresses. 2. To integrate subroutines (supplied, selected, or generated) into the main routine, by adapting or changing relative and symbolic addresses to absolute form or incorporating, or placing in storage.

assembler program—The assembler is an assembly program for a symbolic-coding language. It is composed of simple, brief expressions that provide rapid translation from symbolic to machine-language relocatable-object coding for the computer. The assembly language includes a wide and sophisticated variety of operators which allows the fabrication of desired fields based on information generated at assembly time. The instruction-operation codes are assigned mnemonics which describe the hardware function of each instruction. Assembler-directive commands provide the programmer with the ability to generate data words and values based on specific conditions at assembly time.

assembler, symbolic—The symbolic assembler lets the programmer code instructions in a symbolic language. The assembler allows mnemomic symbols to be used for instruction codes and addresses. Constant and variable storage registers can be automatically assigned. The assembler produces a binary object tape and lists a symbol with memory allocations and useful diagnostic messages.

assembly—The act of translation of a source program written in a symbolic language into an object or target program in a machine language.

assembly language—1. A machine-oriented language for programming, such as ARGUS or EASY, which belongs to an assembly program or system. 2. In writing instructions using the assembly language, the programmer is primarily concerned with three fields: label field, operation field, and operand field. It is possible to relate the symbolic coding to its associated flowchart, if desired, by appending comments to each instruction line or program segment.

assembly language processor—A language processor that accepts words, statements, and phrases to produce machine instructions. It is more than an assembly program because it has compiler powers. The macro-assembler permits segmentation of a large program so that positions may be tested separately. It also provides extensive program analysis to aid in debugging.

assembly list—A printed list which is the by-product of an assembly procedure. It lists in logical-instruction sequence all details of a routine, showing the coded and symbolic notation next to the actual notations established by the assembly procedure. This listing is highly useful in the debugging of routines.

assembly routine—1. A procedure that directs the conversion of a program which is written in relative or symbolic form into a machine-language program, most often on an instruction-by-instruction design. 2. A computer program that operates on symbolic input data to produce from such data machine instructions by carrying out such functions as: translation of symbolic-operation codes into computer-operating instructions; assigning locations in storage for successive instructions; or computation

of absolute addresses from symbolic addresses. 3. An assembler generally translates input symbolic codes into machine instructions item for item, and produces as output the same number of instructions or constants which were defined in the input symbolic codes. (Synonymous with assembly program, and related to compiler.)

associative memories—With associative-memory capability, high-speed memory searches within computer are based on content or subject matter rather than being limited to locating data through specified "addresses."

associative storage—A storage system or device such that storage locations are identified by their contents. Such systems are often considered synonymous with parallel search and content-addressed storage.

assumed decimal point—The point within a numeric item at which the decimal point is assumed to be located. When a numeric item is to be used within a computer, the location of the assumed decimal point is considered to be at the right, unless otherwise specified in the appropriate record description entry. It does not occupy an actual space in storage, but it will be used by the computer to align the value properly for calculation.

asynchronous—1. Pertaining to a lack of time coincidence in a set of repeated events where this term is applied to a computer to indicate that the execution of one operation is dependent on the signal that the previous operation is completed. 2. A mode of computer operation in which performance of the next command is started by a signal that the previous command has been com-pelted. Contrast synchronous, characterized by a fixed time cycle for the execution of operations.

asynchronous computer—A computer in which the performance of each operation starts as a result of a signal either that the previous operation has been completed, or that the parts of the computer required for the next operation are now available. (Contrasted with synchronous computer.)

asynchronous operation—The method of processing in which one operation is completed before the next operation is initiated.

asyndetic—1. Omitting conjunctions and connectives. 2. Pertaining to a catalog without cross references.

atom—1. A term used in compiling techniques, denoting either an operator or an operand. 2. Smallest unit of a chemical element.

atomic symbols—In list processing languages, atomic symbols are sometimes referred to as atoms and may either be numeric or non-numeric. The external representation of a non-numeric atomic symbol is a string of letters or digits starting with a letter, such as AB5, or epsilon.

ATS—A popular and widely-used remote Administrative Terminal System, developed by IBM, which permits an individual at a terminal typewriter to communicate directly with the computer in the tasks of creating, editing, storing, printing or adding large volumes of textual information to an information base to thus avoid repetitive copying or unnecessary manual correcting, updating, expanding or editing.

attribute—An inherent characteristic that sets something apart from other things that do not have the specific characteristic. For data items, attributes could include the location, length, and type of data.

audio system—Relates to various types of special equipment which have capabilities of storing and processing data obtained from voice sources, either recorded or transmitted. Voice Answer Back systems are a type of audio output systems as a contrast.

audit—The operations developed to corroborate the evidence as to authenticity and validity of the data that are introduced into the data-processing problem or system.

augment—To increase a quantity to bring it to its full value.

AUTOCODER—An IBM programming language.

automata theory—The development of theory which relates the study of principles of operations and applications of automatic devices to various behaviorist concepts and theories.

automated management—All types of management completed with the aid of data processing equipment but usually depicted in more specialized terms as: Automated Production Management; Business Data Management; Automated Use Processing Management, etc.

automated production management—The management with the assistance or under the control of data processing equipment which relates to production planning, scheduling, design or change, and control (reporting) of output.

automated question answering, time sharing—It is desirable in a remote computer system to relieve the user of the need for digging through a set of manuals by providing him with a facility for answering

14

his questions from a bank of prestored questions. A good example of a question answering facility is found in the HELP subsystem of the XDS-940 Time Sharing System.

automatic carriage—A device on a printer that moves continuous-form paper under machine control.

automatic checking—Processors are constructed and designed for verification of information transmitted, computed, or stored. The procedure completed when all processes in the machine are automatically checked, or else the check is considered a partial verification. Partial checking concerns either the number or proportion of the processes that are checked, or the number and proportion of the machine units that are assigned to checking.

automatic computer—1. A computer configuration that includes a general-purpose stored-program digital computer often generally considered to be simply an electronic computer. 2. A computer that performs long sequences of operations without human intervention.

automatic control—Automatic devices regulate processes and calculations.

automatic data processing (ADP)—Data processing performed by a system of electronic or electrical machines so interconnected and interacting as to reduce to a minimum the need for human assistance or intervention.

automatic data-processing system—See automatic data processing.

automatic dictionary—The component of a language-translating machine that will provide a word-for-word substitution from one language to another. In automatic searching systems, the automatic dictionary is the component that sub-stitutes codes for words or phrases during the encoding operation. (Related to machine translation.)

automatic error detection—The program itself, or the program embedded in a more complicated system, is usually designed to detect its own errors, print them out with the cause and, if so designed, take steps to correct them.

automatic electronic data-switching center—A communications center designed for relaying digitized information through automatic electronic means.

automatic plotting—In many diverse areas of industry and science, a clear graphical representation of results is essential for rapid interpretation and evaluation of data. From weather mapping to business and stock market reports, from engineering design investigations to insurance actuarial graphs, in research laboratories and in computer laboratories, graphs of X vs. Y plots are required for summarizing and presenting information in concise form. This need has been further accentuated by modern high-speed computers. The rapid production of vast quantities of data by these machines requires especially fast and accurate plotting equipment.

automatic programming—1. A technique by which a machine converts the definition of the solution of a problem into a series of ordered procedures and operations that can be automatically coded. 2. The method or technique whereby the computer itself is used to transform or translate programming from a language or form that is easy for a human beging to produce, into a language that is efficient for the computer to carry out. Examples of automatic programming are compiling, assembling, and interpretive routines.

automatic programming language (APL)—A device, technique, or language permitting the computer to aid in doing part of the coding and programming.

automatic punch—A punch which automatically punches a card or tape, and moves it as necessary under control of electrical or electronic signals.

automatic recovery program—A program enabling a system to remain functioning when a piece of equipment has failed. The automatic recovery program often activates duplex circuitry, a stand-by computer, or switches to a mode of degraded operation.

automatic teaching—An educational application of the computer which involves an interplay between a student and a programmed set of messages that not only present material to be learned, but also test and assist the student's comprehension and allow him to proceed at his own pace. Also called computerized instruction.

automation—The generalized term used to convey the dedicated use or exploitation of automatic machines or devices designed to control various processes, such as: control of machines, machine tools, routine office procedures, accounting, and several thousand other applications.

autoplotter—A system designed to allow the user to automatically generate a variety of plotted information with a minimum of control in a wide variety of input and output formats. The requirements for use are a few control parameters that are similar to those that would be required for hard plotting. It will plot paragraphs, histograms, point and line graphs and many others.

auxiliary data—That data which is associated with specific data but which does not become or form a part of it, i.e., data which are not used in the computations, but are instead back-up, reference, or comment data.

auxiliary equipment—1. Various units or machines that are used in combination or conjunction with the computer but are not part of the computer itself, such as typewriters, sorters, tape readers, and others. 2. Operations considered not a part of processing, computing, or logic, but instead are mainly input and output operations, such as magnetic tape conversion, card punching, printing, reading, etc.

auxiliary operation—An operation performed by equipment not under constant control of the central processing unit.

auxiliary storage—Same as external storage.

availability—1. The ratio or percent of the time, during a certain period, that a piece of equipment is operating correctly, to the total time in that period. Also called operating ratio. 2. The ratio of total service time to the total of fault time, supplementary time, and serviceable time.

awareness, network—A condition in which the central processor is cognizant of the status of the network.

* _ * _ *

background processing—Work which is of a low priority and is handled by the computer when higher priority or real-time entires are not occurring. Batch processing such as inventory control, payroll, housekepping, etc., are often treated as background processing but can be interrupted on orders from terminals or inquiries from other units.

background program—A program that is not time-dependent. This program is of a lower priority than the foreground or main program and is at halt or standby while the main program runs.

back-up system—These systems combine several sophisticated error detection and correction techniques which spot and correct equipment and transmission errors.

backward read—A feature included in some magnetic-tape systems whereby the magnetic-tape units can transfer data to a computer storage while moving in a reverse direction. Normally used, if available, during the external sort phase to reduce rewind time.

balanced sorting—A technique used in a sort program to merge strings of sequenced data. The power of the merge is equal to T/2.

bank—An aggregation of similar devices (transformers, lamps, etc.) connected to each other and used in cooperation. In automatic switching, a bank is an assemblage of fixed contacts used to establish electric connections.

bank, data—As man and his order becomes more mechanized and more scientifically and socially aware of his fellow beings, the need for special purpose information banks increases. These banks are needed to furnish instant information for man on man or for man on some aspect of accumulated knowledge. The banks now include information on credit, reservations, and research projects. The information may be retrieved selectively or in mass.

banner word—The first word in a file record.

base—1. The number of characters for use in each of the digital positions of a numbering system. In the more common numbering systems the characters are some or all of the Arabic numerals as follows:

System Name	Characters	Radix
binary	(0,1)	2
octal	(0,1,2,3,4,5,6,7)	8
decimal	(0,1,2,3,4,5,6,7,8,9)	10

Unless otherwise indicated, the radix of any number is assumed to be 10. For positive identification of a radix-10 number, the radix is written in parentheses as a subscript to the expressed number, i.e., $125_{(10)}$ and $5_{(8)}$ (synonymous with base number and radix number). 2. A quantity used to define a system of representing numbers by positional notation.

base address—1. A number that appears as an address in a computer instruction, but which serves as the base, index, initial or starting point for subsequent addresses to be modified. (Synonymous with presumptive address and reference address.) 2. A number used in symbolic coding in conjunction with a relative address.

base notation—1. An annotation consisting of a decimal number, in parentheses, written as a subscript suffix to a number, its decimal value indicating the radix of the number; e.g., $11_{(2)}$ indicates the number 11 is in the radix of two; $11_{(8)}$ indicates the number 11 is in the radix of eight. 2. A number written without its radix notation is assumed in the radix of ten.

BASIC—Beginner's All-Purpose Symbolic Instruction Code. A procedure-level computer language that is well suited for time-sharing. BASIC, developed at

17

Dartmouth College, is probably one of the easiest computer programming languages to learn and master. These are attributes which have allowed BASIC to become instrumental in the spread of time-sharing to businesses that are not within the computer industry.

batch data processing—Computer processing in which similar input data items or problems are put in groups or "batches" for manipulating in single machine runs with the same program for economy and efficiency and as restricted by the particular computer's capability, i.e., a batch processing-only computer.

batch process—A sequential-processing procedure that uses an accumulation or set of units; this is in contrast to on-line processing, during which each unit of data or information is processed immediately at the time of presentation to the top of the processing sequence.

batch-processing interrupt—An outstanding feature of any real-time system is its capacity to process real-time and batch-processing applications concurrently. This real-time data processing innovation is made possible through a unique feature that permits remote external units with information of high precedence to interrupt computer processing. Whenever transaction data for a real-time problem are entered into a remote external unit, the computer's batch-processing program may be interrupted to permit handling of the high priority real-time transaction and the sending of processed results back to the external unit.

batch, remote—The method of entering jobs for the computer to perform through a remote terminal as opposed to normal batch processing, where inputting the job must take place in the computer center.

Bayesian statistics—Statistics which concerns estimates of (prior) probability distributions, as subsequently revised (posterity distribution) in order to incorporate new data by means of Bayes' equation.

BCD, Binary Coded Decimal—Numerical representation in which decimal digits are represented by binary numerals. The most common binary code is the 8-4-2-1. In binary coded decimal the decimal 14 would be 0001 0100.

BCO, Binary Coded Octal—In this system, binary numbers are used to represent octal digits of an octal number. In the common 4-2-1 octal code, 101 equals octal 5.

beginning file label—A label located at the beginning of a file describing the contents of the file.

beginning tape label—A description located at the beginning of a tape describing the tape's content.

bell character—A control character designed to activate a signal which calls for attention by humans for intervention.

benchmark—A point of reference from which measurements are based, timed, or judged as a type of standard and from which other moving points may be made.

benchmark routine—A set of routines or problems which will help determine the performance of a given piece of equipment.

bias—A sample is selected by a technique that in the long run would yield samples whose obtained measures differ systematically from the corresponding true measures, the sample drawn is thus the biased sample.

biased data—A distribution of records in a file which is nonrandom with respect to the sequencing or sorting criteria. Biased data affects sorting time, depending on the technique used during the first pass on the data.

bias testing—More often called marginal testing, it is a type of test often used as part of preventive maintenance or as an aid to debugging or diagnostics in which the operation of a piece of equipment is tested with its operating conditions altered or changed to decrease the safety margin against faults, i.e., it is used either to check the equipment for fixed margins or to measure what margins are really available.

billibit—One-thousand-million binary digits or one billion binary digits, i.e., a one-billion bit storage capacity. Same as kilomegabit.

billisecond—Same as nanosecond, one billionth of a second.

binary—1. Numbering system based on 2's rather than 10's which uses only the digits 0 and 1 when written. 2. A characteristic, property, or condition in which there are but two possible alternatives; e.g., the binary number system using 2 as its base and using only the digits zero (0) and one (1) (related to binary-coded decimal, and clarified by number systems).

binary card—The standard data processing card with data punched and in binary form, i.e., in column binary or row binary.

binary code—1. A system where the encoding of any data is done through the use of bits; i.e., 0 or 1. 2. A code for the ten decimal digits, 0, 1, . . ., 9 in which each is represented by its binary, radix 2, equivalent; i.e., straight binary.

binary-coded decimal notation—A technique for representing each figure in a decimal number by a four-figured binary number.

binary-coded octal—A system where binary numbers are utilized to represent the octal digits of an octal number.

binary deck—A deck of punched cards containing data, information and instructions in binary codes.

binary digit (bit)—1. A numeral in the binary scale of notation. This digit may be zero (0), or one (1). It may be equivalent to an on or off condition, a yes, or a no. Often abbreviated to (bit). 2. The kind of number that computers use internally. There are only two binary digits, 1 and 0, otherwise known as "on" and "off." Follow the table below by progressing geometrically per column right to left, and add the column values where one appears, i.e.; 7 is 1, 2, 4, 0, right to left.

COLUMN VALUES

		8	4	2	1
0	is	0	0	0	0
1	is	0	0	0	1
2	is	0	0	1	0
3	is	0	0	1	1
4	is	0	1	0	0
5	is	0	1	0	1
6	is	0	1	1	0
7	is	0	1	1	1
8	is	1	0	0	0
9	is	1	0	0	1

binary incremental representation—In this type of incremental representation, the value of an increment is confined to one of the two values plus one or minus one for each quantum step. The maximum positive rate of change is represented as a continuous string of plus ones, the maximum negative rate of change, conversely is a continuous string of minus ones, i.e., representation of changes in variables throughout the use of binary numbers.

binary logic—Digital logic elements which operate with two distinct states. The two states are variously called true and false, high and low, on and off, or "1" and "0." In computers they are represented by two different voltage levels. The level which is more positive (or less negative) than the other is called the high level, the other the low level. If the true ("1") level is the most positive voltage, such logic is referred to as positive true or positive logic.

binary mode—Operations using the number system with a base 2, allowing only the digits 0 and 1, in contrast to the decimal system of base 10 with digits 0, 1, 2..., 9 allowed.

binary number—A number, which usually consists of more than one figure, representing a sum in which the individual quantity represented by each figure is based on a radix of two. The figures used are 0 and 1.

binary operation—An particular operation which depends on the applications and the strict adherence to the rules of Boolean algebra, i.e., any operation in which the operands and results take either one of two values or states such as logic operations on single bits.

binary search—The procedure for finding an element of an order table by successively halving a search interval to then evaluate the remaining half where the element is known to exist.

binary zero—Contrasted to the only other binary representation, 1, binary zero represents the lack of magnitude, and is represented as the presence or absence of a punched hole in a card or tape, a metallic spot, a current or lack of it, a flip-flop, etc.

bionics—The system of applying knowledge gained from the analysis of living systems to the creation of hardware that will perform functions in a manner analogous to the more sophisticated functions of the living system.

biquinary—A representation in two-parts of a decimal digit consisting of a binary portion with values of 0 or 5, and a quinary portion with values of 0 through 4; e.g., the number 7 is coded as 12 which implies 5 and 2.

biquinary code—A code in two parts where each decimal digit is represented by the sum of the two parts, one of which has the value of decimal zero or five, and the other the values zero through four. The abacus and soroban both use biquinary codes. An example follows:

Decimal	Biquinary	Interpretation
0	0 000	0+0
1	0 001	0+1
2	0 010	0+2
3	0 011	0+3
4	0 100	0+4
5	1 000	5+0
6	1 001	5+1
7	1 010	5+2
8	1 011	5+3
9	1 100	5+4

biquinary number—A number which consists of a pair of figures representing a sum, in which the quantity represented by the left figure is based on the radix two, and the quantity represented by the right figure is based on the radix five. The figures 0 and 1 are used for the left figure, and 0, 1, 2, 3, and 4 are used for the right figure.

biquinary system—A numbering system utilizing the numerals 2 and 5 as base numbers, and alternately so, as represented by the design of the abacus. See: biquinary number.

bird, whirley—The slang reference or expression to designate disk-pack equipment.

bistable—1. Capability of assuming either of two stable states, hence of storing one bit of information. 2. Pertaining to devices capable of assuming either one or two stable states.

bit—1. Abbreviation of binary digit. 2. A single character in a binary number. 3. A single pulse in a group of pulses. 4. The smallest element of binary machine language represented by a magnetized spot on a recording surface or a magnetized element of a storage device. Whether the bit represents a 0 or a 1 is determined by ascertaining whether the magnetism was created by a positive or negative electrical charge.

bit, check—A binary check digit; often a parity bit (related to parity check and self-checking number).

bit density—A measure of the number of bits recorded per unit of length or of area.

bit location—A storage position located on a record which is capable of storing one bit.

bit pattern—A combination of n binary digits representing 2 to the n possible choices; e.g., a 3-bit pattern represents 8 possible combinations.

bit significance—The presence or absence of a bit in a certain location of an instruction word which designates the instruction to be of certain type, for example, zero vs. one-address instruction.

blank—1. A specific code character which indicates that no information is present.
2. A portion of a storage unit or medium in which there are no characters recorded.

blank character—Any character or characters that are used for a character space on an output medium.

blank instruction—A specific instruction commanding the computer to do nothing but to proceed in sequence to the next instruction. Such an instruction thus has no direct bearing on the program nor does it have any functional part of it. Such instructions are usually for programmer convenience; it could advance the counter; provide for future changes in the program. Same as: no-op, nothing, waste or skip instruction.

blank medium—Relates to various types of blank forms or media, i.e., on which data has been recorded only to establish a frame of reference to enable the medium to be used as a data carrier, such as, paper tape punched only with feed holes, etc.

blast—The release of various specified areas or blocks of either main or auxiliary storage no longer needed by an operational program. This type of program will execute a blast macro instruction which causes the control program to return the address of the area blasted to its list of storage available for use by future operational programs.

bleed—In optical character recognition, the capillary flow of ink beyond the original edges of a printed character.

blind (unblind)—The selective controlling of a transmission printer or reperforator. Example: used to prevent prices from typing on a receiving teletypewriter.

block—1. A group of consecutive machine words or characters considered or transferred as a unit, particularly with reference to input and output (contrast with record). 2. In real-time systems, blocks are used to describe input/output or working storage areas in main storage. A file storage block is often called a "physical record." 3. The set of locations or tape positions in which a block of words, as defined above, is stored or recorded. 4. A circuit assemblage which functions as a unit; e.g., a circuit building block of standard design, and the logic block in a sequential circuit.

block, analysis—A relocatable part of the computer storage in which program testing or statistical data are stored which can later be utilized to analyze the performance of the system. During program testing there may be an analysis block for each transaction in the system, and when the transaction leaves the system this block is dumped onto a file or tape.

block, control—A storage location which contains information in condensed, formalized form necessary for the control of a task, function, operation, or quantity of information.

blockette—A particular subdivision of a group of consecutive machine words transferred as a unit, particularly with reference to input and output.

block gap—The space and/or distance between particular blocks of data or instructions on a tape or other storage medium left blank in order to separate blocks of data. Insertion of such blanks by programmers or by automatic means are to fix block lengths. Tapes can be stopped, for example, or they can be brought up to standard speed again, within such gaps. Same as: interblock gap.

blocking—1. The combining of two or more numbers (records) into one block. 2. To efficiently decrease the number of starts and stops; a combining of two or more items or groups of items. Total number of records, words, or characters contained in one block.

block record—A distinct storage area of fixed size which usually contains a main memory or file storage; it is organized into such standard blocks to allow more flexibility in storage allocation and control. (Synonymous with physical record.)

block sort—1. Sorting of one or more of the most significant characters of a key to serve as a means of making workable sized groups from a large volume of records to be sorted. 2. Sorting by separation of the entire field on the highest order portion of the key, usually implying separate ordering of these segments and then adjoining the entire file.

block storage—A portion or section of storage usually within a storage area. A storage block is considered a single element for holding a specific or fixed number of words.

block structure—A technique allowing program segmentation into blocks of information or subroutines of a total program.

bonds register—A separate register which keeps track of deductions from pay for bond payment.

book—A particular large segment of memory most often used in virtual memory addressing.

bookkeeping operation—1. A computer operation that does not directly contribute to the solution; i.e., arithmetical, logical, and transfer operations used in modifying the address section of other instructions, in the counting cycles, and

22

in the rearrangement data. 2. Those internal operations that are necessary to process the data, but do not contribute to any final solution.

book message—A message to be sent to a list of two or more destinations.

Boolean algebra—1. An algebra named for George Boole. This algebra is similar in form to ordinary algebra, but with classes, propositions, on-off-circuit elements, etc., for variables rather than data values. It includes the operators AND, OR, NOT, EXCEPT, IF, THEN, etc. 2. The logic and functions constructed from two-valued variables: truth/falsity; go/no go; zero/one; yes/no. Set algebra, class algebra, and propositional calculus are similar math systems used in computing switching theory and computer design. See: gates (decision elements).

Boolean variable—The use of two-valued Boolean algebra to assume either one of the only two values possible. Examples: true or false; on or off; open or closed. Basically, all digital computers use the two-state or two-variable Boolean algebra in construction and operation.

bootleg program—A conventional routine or stop-gap program used to begin, capture, and process data in a specifically prescribed manner, usually to start or initiate the reading of a program by means of its own action.

bootstrap—A very common technique or procedure for initiating entry (reading) of programs, i.e., a machine routine whose first few instructions are sufficient to bring in or "pull," i.e., bootstrap the rest of the program into the machine. This may be accomplished by completing the first few instructions at the console if desired, or the bootstrap may be the first

few cards or inches of tape.

bootstrap loader—A subroutine which is usually automatic and built into the hardware of the computer, which is capable of initiating the reading of another subroutine whose first instructions are designed to bring in the rest of the subroutine and thus initiate the total program schedule.

bootstrap memory—A time-saving device built into the main computer, consisting of sixteen 30-bit words of wired storage. It is programmed (wired) to fit the specialized needs of various computer users. The program and words in the bootstrap memory cannot be altered by the computer but can be manually changed when necessary. The purpose of the bootstrap memory is to provide for the automatic reading of new programs into the computer, with protection against erasing its vital instructions (UNIVAC).

BOS—Basic Operating System: Disk oriented, this is a more powerful extension of tape basic programming support.

branch—1. Departure from the normal sequence of executing instructions in a computer (synonymous with jump). 2. A machine instruction that can cause a departure as in definition 1 (synonymous with transfer). 3. A sequence of instructions that is executed as a result of a decision instruction.

branch instruction—An instruction to a computer which enables the programmer to instruct the computer to choose between alternative subprograms, depending upon the conditions determined by the computer during the execution of the program (synonymous with transfer instruction).

branch, unconditional—An instruction

which switches the sequence of control to some specified location. (Synonymous with unconditional jump, and unconditional transfer of control.)

brush readers—A technique of reading characters in punch cards by interpreting the electronic signals as each row on the card passes between the brushes and the roller.

brute-force approach—To try to undertake with existing equipment the mass of problems that do not use precise computation or logical manipulations (as do accounting problems and scientific problems).

BTAM—An abbreviation for: Basic Telecommunications Access Method.

bubble sort—A sorting method which exchanges a pair of numbers if they are out of order at a particular time.

buffer—1. A word often implying buffer storage. 2. An isolating circuit used to avoid any reaction of a driven circuit upon the corresponding driving circuit. 3. The auxiliary data-storage device which holds data temporarily and which may also perform other functions in conjunction with various input/output machines. 4. A storage device used to compensate for a difference in rate of flow of data, or time of occurrence of events when transmitting data from one device to another. 5. An extremely temporary storage device of relatively small capacity capable of receiving and transmitting data at different rates of speed. Used as an equalizer when positioned between any set of components that operates at different speeds than the computer itself, such as a card reader and a card punch. 6. A logical OR circuit. 7. An isolating component designed to eliminate the reaction of a

driven circuit on the circuits driving it; e.g., a buffer amplifier. 8. A diode.

buffer, data—Same as: buffer

buffered computer—A computing system with a storage device permitting input and output data to be stored temporarily in order to match the slow speed of input/output devices with the higher speeds of the computer. Thus, simultaneous input/output computer operations are possible. A data transmission trap is essential for effective use of buffering, since it obviates frequent testing for the availability of a data channel.

buffering, exchange—A technique for input/output buffering which prevents or avoids the internal movement of data. Buffers are either filled, emptied, or actively in use, by an input/output device exchange buffering related to distinct areas set aside for work and for buffering.

buffer memory register—1. A register wherein a word is stored as it comes from memory (reading) or just prior to its entering memory (writing). See register. 2. The memory buffer serves as a buffer register for all information passing between the processor and the core memory, and serves as a buffer directly between core memory and peripheral equipment during data-break information transfers. The memory buffer is also used as a distributor shift register for the analog-to-digital converter.

bug—1. Any mechanical, electrical or electronic defect which interferes with, or "bugs up" the operation of the computer. It can also be a defect in the coding of the program. 2. A mistake in the design of a routine or a computer, or a malfunction. 3. A high speed telegraph key.

bulk storage—Storage of large volume capacity used to supplement the high speed storage which can be made addressable, such as disks, drums, or remain nonaddressable with magnetic tapes. Other names for this type of storage are external or secondary storage.

burst mode—A mode of communications between the processor and I/O devices. When a signal from an I/O device operating through the multiplexer channel indicates burst mode, the receiving unit continues to fetch bits until the unit is finished.

bus—1. A circuit used for transmitting data or power. Often one which acts as a common connection among a number of locations (synonymous with trunk). 2. A path over which information is transferred, from any of several sources to any of several destinations.

business-data processing—1. The almost boundless variety of commercial applications from actual transactions (in contrast to problem solutions). These processes involve and concern file processing, manipulations, and reporting, plus planning procedures for operating or quality control, capital, and project budgeting. 2. Data processing for business purposes; e.g., recording and summarizing the financial transactions of a business.

business machine—Customer-provided equipment used to connect common carrier's communications services for the purpose of data movement.

by-pass procedure—A procedure used to get the most vital information into the main computer when the line control computer fails. The few direct control lines into the main computer are frequently switched to maximize different terminal input. Teleprinters, paper tape punches, telephones, etc., are used to provide by-pass.

byte—1. Generic term indicating a measurable portion of consecutive binary digits; e.g., an 8-bit or 6-bit byte. 2. A sequence of adjacent binary digits operated upon as a unit and usually shorter than a word.

byte mode—An alternate mode of communications between the processor and I/O devices. The multiplexer channel accepts one character at a time from an input device unless the input/output unit itself signals burst mode. Byte mode allows the multiplexer channel to accept data from multiple low-speed devices simultaneously.

byte multiplexing—A process in which time slots on a channel are delegated to individual slow input/output devices so that bytes from one after another can be interlaced on the channel to or from main memory. Such a procedure is used on several IBM 360 and 370 systems.

byte storage—The IBM System 360 has expandable addressing capability. A byte is composed of eight bits plus a parity bit, and represents one alphabetic or special character, two decimal digits, or eight binary bits of information.

The availability of expandable bytes on one model provides even the smallest user with the ability to integrate communications network control and real-time data processing in the same processor, and, as a byproduct, run conventional programs during those time periods when real-time transactions are not being proposed. (IBM)

* _ * _ *

25

CAL–1. Conversational Algebraic Language. CAL is a general purpose language which is used extensively in time-sharing. CAL was developed at the University of California and is similar in usage to BASIC. 2. CAL resembles JOSS. It is primarily aimed at small numerical problems in a highly interactive environment. It relieves the user of all burdens of storage allocation for both programs and data and offers a problem-oriented language for conversational use (some computers).

calculating punch–A type of punched card device which reads data from cards and performs various arithmetic or logic operations as well. The results are then punched on another card, or if desired, on the same card.

calculator–1. A specific device designed to perform primarily arithmetic operations based upon data and instructions inserted manually or contained on punch cards. It is sometimes used interchangeably with computer. 2. A particular device for performing arithmetic usually requiring frequent manual intervention. Generally, a device or machine used to carry out logical and arithmetic digital calculations of any type.

calculus–Calculus is a particular branch of mathematics that deals with the nature and the forms of functions with the aid of symbols. Its objective is the laws of derivation from one form to another, and the application of these laws to other branches of mathematics, such as algebra, analytical geometry, trigonometry, etc. There are two branches of calculus: the ordinary calculus, that deals with determinate functions; and the calculus of variations of indeterminate functions. In the ordinary calculus, there are two different methods of deriving determinate functions from other determinate functions. These methods give rise to the division of the ordinary calculus into two parts, differential and integral calculus.

calculus, differential–1. Concerns that branch of (calculus) mathematics that deals with the amount of change in the function of a dependent variable per unit change in the independent variable. 2. Differential calculus is that branch of mathematics that derives one determinate function from another. If the original function is one of several variables, we may find the differential of the function with respect to each one of the variables that is, as though all of the other variables were constants. These differentials are called partial differentials.

calculus, integral–1. Relates to the specific mathematical method of finding the relation connecting finite values of variables, as x and y, from the relation connecting their differentials as dx and dy. 2. The integral-calculus objective is to find a differential function that will produce the given differential; such an expression is called the integral of the differential. 3. Integral calculus is the inverse of differential calculus. The process of finding the prime function or integral is called integration. Besides the method of finding the integrals of given differentials, the integral calculus is also applied to various branches of mathematics, as well as to almost every branch of natural philosophy and engineering.

call–The branching or transferring of control to a specified closed subroutine.

call direction code (CDC)–Concerns a specific identifying call, usually of two letters, which is transmitted to an outlying receiver and which automatically turns on its printer (selective calling).

call, subroutine—A set or list of characters used to initiate a subroutine and containing the parameters or serving to locate and identify the parameters required to execute the subroutine.

CAN—An abbreviation for CANCEL CHARACTER.

cancel character—Relates to a specific control character designed to indicate that the data with which it is associated are erroneous or are to be ignored.

capacity, computer—Usually concerns a specific span, dimension, or range of values in which a number (variable) can assume, and usually expressed within beginning and ending limits or using N, if such limits are unknown.

capacity, storage—A calculation of the number of elementary pieces of data that can be contained in a storage device (frequently defined in terms of characters in a particular code or words of a fixed size that can be so contained).

card—This term usually refers to the punched card which has been the mainstay of computer input in the past. Types: aspect, binary, control, document, duo-purpose, Hollerith, IBM, master, punched, and transition cards.

card, binary—The fundamental punched card containing binary numerals representing numbers, characters, or control symbols in columns and rows.

card, column-binary—A card in which the columns are contiguous components of a binary vector.

card, control—A particular card that contains input data or parameters for a specific application of a general routine.

card, Hollerith—A common name for the standard punched card, 3-1/4 by 7-3/8 inches, usually divided into 80 columns of 1 punch hole sites, i.e., a combination of punches in a column (zone and field) can represent letters, digits, or symbols. The card was named in honor of Dr. Herman Hollerith who invented it in 1889.

card image—1. A representation in storage of the holes punched in a card, where the holes are represented by one binary digit and the unpunched spaces are represented by the other binary digit. 2. In machine language, a duplication of the data contained in a punch card.

card input—1. The introduction of information to a processing unit with punched cards. 2. A data channel used to feed card information into a machine. 3. The data read from punched cards and fed into the computer.

card mode—The status of the computer while cards are being read or punched.

card-programmed computer—An older type or new "mini" sized computer which is limited in input operation in obtaining information from punched, wired or magnetic cards or as preprogrammed computers.

card punch—The specific unit of peripheral equipment for punching holes (data) into cards, such as hand punches, keyboard print-punches, high-speed punches, paper tape-to-card punches, magnetic tape-to-card conversion units.

card-punch buffer—A type of group parity check is performed on all data transmitted to the card-punch buffer. The correctness of the punching is checked by the circuitry built into the card punch. If for any reason the card punch does not punch (hopper empty, stacker full, misfeed, etc.) after receiving data from the buffer, it will enter an inoperative status.

card reader—This peripheral unit converts holes punched in cards into electrical impulses, and transmits the data to the memory of the computer for processing.

card reproducer—A device which reproduces a punch card by punching another similar card.

card systems—Systems having card equipment with no mass storage device have an operating system contained in binary card decks. The operator determines system operation. The binary decks are of two types—formatted binary and absolute binary. Formatted binary programs are loaded by the system loader. Absolute binary programs may be loaded by the monitor or by a "pre-set" operation.

card verifying—This is a means of checking the accuracy of key punching and is a duplication check. A second operator verifies the original punching by depressing the keys of a verifier while reading the same source data. The machine compares the key depressed with the hole already punched in the card.

carriage, automatic—A specific device that automatically controls the console typewriter to feed forms, paper, provide spacing, skipping, tabulating, and other operations to display information, program progress, and diagnostics.

carriage control tape—This tape contains the control codes related to the movement of the carriage of the printer and thus controls the vertical and horizontal positioning of the carriage as well as the paper feed unit.

carriage return character—A specific control character designed to cause a carriage return to be performed.

carrier system—A means of obtaining a number of channels over a single path by modulating each channel upon a different carrier frequency and demodulating at the receiving point, restoring the signals to their original form.

carrier, video—The carrier of a video, i.e., usually a televised signal.

carry—1. A signal, or expression, produced as a result of an arithmetic operation on one digit place of two or more numbers expressed in positional notation and transferred to the next higher place for processing there. 2. A signal or expression, as defined in (1) above, which arises in adding, when the sum of two digits in the same digit place equals or exceeds the base of the number system in use. If a carry into a digit place will result in a carry out of the same digit place, and the normal adding circuit is bypassed when generating this new carry, it is called a high-speed carry, or standing-on-nines carry. If the normal adding circuit is used in such a case, the carry is called a cascaded carry. 3. A signal or expression in direct subtraction, as defined in (1) above, which arises when the difference between the digits is less than zero. Such a carry is frequently called a borrow (related to borrow). 4. The action of forwarding a carry. 5. The command directing a carry to be forwarded.

carry time—The time required for transferring all the carry digits to higher columns and adding them for all digits in the number.

catalog—1. A list of items with descriptive data, usually arranged so a specific kind of information can be readily located. 2. To assign a representative label for a document according to a definite set of rules.

cataloged procedure—A group of control cards placed in a cataloged data set.

catastrophic errors—When so many errors have occurred that no more useful diagnostic information can be produced, this terminates the compilation.

cathode-ray tube (CRT)—1. An electronic vacuum tube containing a screen on which information may be stored by means of a multigrid modulated beam of electrons from the thermionic emitter storage effected by means of charged or uncharged spots. 2. Abbreviated as CRT. A vacuum tube in which a beam of electrons can be focused to a small point on a luminescent screen and can be varied in position and intensity to form a pattern. 3. A storage tube. 4. An oscilloscope tube. 5. A picture tube.

cathode-ray tube storage—1. Often this relates to the electrostatic storage characteristics of cathode-ray tubes in which the electron beam is used to sense the data. 2. The storage of data on a dielectric surface, such as the screen of a cathode-ray tube, in the form of the presence or absence of spots bearing electrostatic charges; these spots can persist for a short time after the removal of the electrostatic charging force. 3. A storage device used as in the foregoing description.

cell—1. The storage for one unit of information, usually one character or one word. 2. A location specified by the whole or part of the address and possessed of the faculty of store. Specific terms such as column, block, field, and location are preferable when appropriate.

center, data switching—1. Relates specifically to a location at which incoming data from one circuit is transferred to the proper outgoing circuit. 2. A location where an incoming message is automatically or manually directed to one or more outgoing circuits, according to the intelligence contained in the message.

center, store-and-forward switching—A message-switching center which is designed so that the message accepted from the sender, whenever he offers it, is held in a physical store and forwarded to the receiver, whenever he is able to accept it.

central computer, input/output—Relates to those communications which are between the central computer and the peripheral units of some computer systems that may be performed over all input/output channels. Each of the several channels allows bidirectional transfers of data and control signals between the central computer and the peripheral devices.

central control unit—The basic unit of the computer, often called the CPU, Central Processing Unit, which when receiving a complete instruction, stimulates the proper circuits to execute the instruction as it interprets it, while also directing the sequencing and timing of the operations.

centralization—The concentration of decision making in an organizational structure. Centralization frequently takes place to make optimum use of a computer based information system. Computers encourage centralization because centralized management can consider all the relevant data, whereas a fragmented system does not.

central processing unit (CPU)—1. The unit of a computing system which contains the circuits which control and perform the execution of instructions. 2. The central processor of the computer system. It contains the main storage, arithmetic unit, and special register groups.

central terminal unit (CTU)—This unit supervises communication between the teller consoles and the processing center and receives incoming messages at random intervals and stores them until the central processor is ready to process them. It returns the processed replies to the teller consoles which originated the transactions.

centrex—Concerns the central office-type telephone equipment which serves subscribers at one location on a PABX basis.

chad—That piece of material removed in punching a hole in perforated tape.

chadless paper tape—Perforated tape with the chad partially attached, to facilitate interpretive printing on the tape.

chad tape—Tapes which have been completely perforated.

chain—1. Any series of items linked together. 2. Pertaining to a routine consisting of segments run through the computer in tandem, only one segment being within the computer at any one time and each segment using the output from the previous program as its input.

chain printer—A high-speed printer in which the type slugs are carried by the links of a revolving chain.

chain search—A procedure in which a search key is used and is transformed to bring out an initial address. If the contents of the initial address contain the key matching the search key, the contents contain the sum or other information sought. If unsuccessful, another address is found in the contents, and the process is repeated until the item is found or the chain ends. Thus a chain search operates in a file of unordered but related or interconnected data.

channel—1. A path along which signals can be sent; e.g., data channel, output channel. 2. The portion of a storage medium which is accessible to a given reading station, e.g., track, band. 3. A unit which controls the operation of one or more I/O units. 4. One or more parallel tracks treated as a unit. 5. In a circulating storage, a channel is one re-circulating path containing a fixed number of words stored serially by word (synonymous with band). 6. A path for electrical communication. 7. A band of frequencies used for communication. Types: Data, input/output, and paper tape channels.

channel capacity—1. A measurement of the maximum number of binary digits or elementary digits to other bases which can be handled in a particular channel per unit time. 2. The maximum possible information-transmission rate through a channel at a specified error rate. The channel capacity may be measured in bits per second or bauds. (Related to bits rate and baud.)

channel controller—A device which provides an independent data path to storage and assures multiprocessor systems maximum availability, allowing each processing unit to have access to every channel in the system.

channel, input/output—Concerns that specific channel which permits simultaneous communications and independently so between various storage units or any of the various input or output units. Such a channel is the control channel for most peripheral devices and quite often performs various checks on data transfers such as validity checks, etc.

channelize—The procedure used to divide a communications circuit into several channels.

channel selector—The selector channel is designed primarily for such devices as tape units and disk files. When the selector channel is directed to make connection with one input or output unit, all other units on that channel are locked out until the first unit is released. The selector channel is capable of handling high-speed units overlapped with processing, so that a stream of data can be fed to storage while the processing unit is performing arithmetic or logic operations for another phase of the program.

channel status table (CST)—The channel status table (CST) is used by input/output drivers to wait until a specific channel is available prior to using it. CST is composed of separate entries for each channel available to the system. Each entry corresponds in order to the address of the channel, that is, entry 0 corresponds to channel 0, entry 1 to channel 1, etc. The size of the table varies according to the number of channels. Each CST entry is one 24-bit word of the following format: CS is the channel status—if CS is zero, the channel is busy. If CS is nonzero, the channel is free and CS is the number of words last transferred via the channel (some computers).

channel utilization index—The ratio of the information rate (per second) through a channel to the channel capacity (per second).

character—1. One symbol of a set of elementary symbols such as those corresponding to typewriter keys. The symbols usually include the decimal digits 0 through 9, the letters A through Z, punctuation marks, operation symbols, and any other single symbols which a computer may read, store, or write. 2. The electrical, magnetic, or mechanical profile used to represent a character in a computer, and its various storage and peripheral devices. A character may be represented by a group of other elementary marks, such as bits or pulses. Types: Control, floating, instruction, least significant, most significant, print control, and tape characters.

character adjustment—The address adjustment in which the literal which is used to modify the address has reference to a specific given number or group of characters.

character, check—1. One or more characters carried in such a fashion that if a single error occurs (excluding compensating errors) a check will occur, and the error will be reported. 2. A character used for the purpose of performing a check.

character, command—Characters, when used as code elements, can initiate, modify, or stop a control operation. Characters may be used, for example, to control the carriage return, etc., on various devices or complete devices or peripheral units themselves.

character crowding—The effect of reducing the time interval between subsequent characters read from tape, caused by a combination of mechanical skew, gap scatter, jitter, amplitude variation, etc. Also called packing.

character fill—To replace all data in a particular storage device or unit in a group of locations by bringing all the cells to a prescribed or desired state.

character instruction—Characters, when used as code elements, can initiate, modify, or stop a control operation. Characters may be used, for example, to control the carriage return, etc.

character, least significant—The character in the rightmost position in a number or word.

character mode (display)—This mode provides a rapid means for displaying alphanumeric characters. Three characters or symbols are contained in each 18-bit word with provision for a 128-character alphabet. Characters or symbols may be displayed in one of three sizes. The character generator is capable of performing carriage-return functions upon specific characterlike commands. Escape from the character mode is accomplished with another characterlike code. (DEC)

character, most significant—The character in the leftmost position in a number or word.

character printer—A printer in which only a single character is composed and determined within the device before printing.

character reader—A specialized device designed so that it can convert data (represented in one of the type fonts or scripts readable by human beings) directly into machine language. Such a reader may operate optically; or, if the characters are printed in magnetic ink, the device may operate magnetically or optically.

character reader, optical—A specific unit which reads numerical data printed in widely used tape styles on paper or card documents at the rate of up to 480 characters/second, and documents at 400 per minute. The printed data is automatically translated into machine language for direct input to the processor. (IBM)

character set—An agreed set of representations, called characters, are made to denote and distinguish data. Each character differs from all others, and the total number of characters in a given set is fixed; e.g., a set may include the numerals 0 to 9, the letters A to Z, punctuation marks and a blank or space.

character string—1. A group of characters in a one-dimensional array in an order due to the reference of relations between adjacent numbers. 2. A sequence or group of connected characters, connected by codes, key words, or other programming or associative techniques.

check—1. A means of verifying the accuracy of data transmitted, manipulated, or stored by any unit or device in a computer. 2. A process of partial or complete testing of the correctness of machine operations, the existence of certain prescribed conditions within the computer, or the correctness of the results produced by a program. These conditions may be automatically checked by the equipment or may be programmed. Types: parity, program, and redundancy checks.

check digits—Relates to one or several digits generated and carried in computer processes for ascertaining error and accuracy control of data in batch processing, in real-time, or in subsequent operations; i.e., often periodically regenerated and compared with the original data.

check indicator—A device which displays or announces an error has been made or a failure has occurred.

checking program—A specific type of diagnostic (error-discovering) program which examines programs or data for the most obvious mistakes as misspelling in keypunching, or miskeypunching but which does not cause execution of the program itself.

check, longitudinal parity—The data line terminal communications designed to generate a longitudinal parity count character as the data characters are being transmitted. This is essentially a count for even parity of all bits in each one of the bit levels for all data characters in the message. This same count is also generated for the bits of the data characters entering the data line terminal when it is receiving. The longitudinal parity count character generated by the magnetic tape terminal at the sending end follows immediately after the end of the block character, to be compared with the longitudinal parity count character generated at the computer.

check, odd-even—A type of summation check in which the binary digits in a character or word, are added, and the sum checked against a single, previously computed parity digit, i.e., a check tests whether the number of ones in a word is odd or even.

checkout—Concerns the specific use of diagnostic analyses or specific test procedures to various programs and equipment in order to make determinations as to the possible errors, mistakes, or malfunctions of equipment, programs, or communication devices.

check, parity—1. A check by summation in which the binary digits, in a character or word, are added, and the sum checked against a single, previously computed parity digit; i.e., a check tests whether the number of ones in a word is odd or even. (Synonymous with odd-even check, and related to redundant check and forbidden-combination check.) 2. Use of

a redundant and the least significant digit (called the parity digit) carried along as a check of a binary (machine) word. It is 1 if the total number of 1's in the machine word is odd, and 0 if the total number of 1's in the machine word is even, for the even parity check. The digit value is 0 for an odd number of 1's, and 1 for an even number of 1's when the odd parity check is used. See: odd-even check.

check, validity—1. A specific check related to the accuracy of character representation. 2. A checking technique based on known reasonable limits on data or computed results. For instance: a man cannot work 400 hours in one week, a month does not have 32 days, an hourly classified man very seldom has a net pay greater than $250.00 per week, etc. Also called a reasonableness check.

check word—A machine word is often used to represent a check symbol and this is appended and printed to the block thus signifying the check.

chips, transistor—A specific example is one in which the chips themselves are 28 thousandths-of-an-inch square. Some of the diodes can switch, or change their electronic state, in six nanoseconds (six billionths of a second). This is more than twice as fast as the fastest elements in previous computers. The reduced size and simplified design of the new transistors and diodes contribute to the increased speed and reliability of the circuits. The minute copper pellets, for example, replace whisker like wires more than one inch long that connect conventional transistors and diodes to circuit modules. The metal caps that protect conventional transistors are replaced by a glass film, 60 millionths-of-an-inch thick, that is deposited on more than a thousand chips at a time. Completed circuit modules are coated with plastic and mounted onto circuit cards. These, in turn, are plugged into larger cards and installed in various elements of the system equipment. Printed circuits on the larger cards eliminate much of the conventional wiring. (IBM)

circuit—1. A system of conductors and related electrical elements through which electrical current flows. 2. A communications link between several points.

circuit reliability—The calculation of the percentage of time the circuit meets arbitrary standards set by the user.

circular shift—A shift which is designed so that the digits dropped-off at one end of a word are returned to the other end in a circular fashion; e.g., if a register holds eight digits, 23456789, the result of a circular or cyclic shift two columns to the left would be to change the contents of a register to 45678923. (Synonymous with cyclic shift, end-around shift, logical shift, nonarithmetic shift, and ring shift.)

circulating memory—A register or memory consisting of a means for delaying the information (delay line) and a means for regenerating and reinserting it into the delaying means.

circulating register—A shift register in which the contents do a circular shift out of one end of the register only to reenter the other end as in a closed loop.

circulating storage—A storage device in which access to any given location is only possible at specific, equally spaced times, i.e., magnetic drums, delay lines, etc.

CIU—Computer Interface Unit. A CIU is a device which interfaces with the central processing unit and peripheral devices such as disks or printers.

class—A group of data or information with similar or same characteristics, and which is often a subdivision of a category.

classify—The arrangement of data into classes or groups according to a definite plan or method.

clear—To erase or return all registers and accumulators to zero in preparation for new entries, problems, input data, etc.

clerk, input preparation—In general, tasks are to prepare accurate and properly coded information which is to be input into the system. Usually keypunch operators prepare this type of information. The average speed for keypunch operators is approximately 10,000 strokes per hour. In addition to keypunch operators, verifiers are needed to insure the accurate preparation of the input into the machine.

clock—A timekeeping, pulse-counting, frequency-measuring or synchronizing device within a computer system. Such clocks are of various types as: real-time clock, which measures the past or used time in the same analogous scale as external events it will be used to describe; a master clock, which is the source of pulses required for computer operation; programmable clock, whose time values are transmitted into a clock register and which may be accessed as determined by clock instructions in the program.

clock counter—A memory location that records the progress of real-time, or its approximation, by accumulating counts produced by a (clock) count pulse interrupt.

clock, time-of-day—A measurement or recording of time in hours, minutes, seconds, over 24-hour range—from 0.1 second to 23:59:9; sends time to central processor upon command.

clock time, real-time—This built-in clock is used for a wide variety of program-timing purposes. It can be used to log the receipt times of periodic real-time input data. Each input message and its receipt time may be recorded together. This clock is also used in connection with the preparation of statistical and analytical reports dealing with the frequency of certain transactions.

closed loop—1. A group of instructions which are repeated indefinitely. 2. Pertaining to a system with feedback type of control, so the output is used to modify the input.

closed-loop control system—A specific control system which is designed with feedback characteristics.

closed shop—1. A computing installation at which members of a regular computing group perform all computer programming, coding, and operating functions. 2. The operation of a computer facility where programming service to the user is the responsibility of a group of specialists, thereby effectively separating the phase of task formulation from that of computer implementation. The "outside" programmers are not allowed in the computer room to run or oversee the running of their programs (contrasted with open shop).

closed subroutine—1. Specific type of a subroutine that is not stored in the main path of the routine. Such a subroutine is entered by a jump operation and provision is made to return control to the main routine at the end of the operation. The instructions related to the entry and re-entry function constitute a linkage. (Synonymous with linked subroutine.) 2. A frequently used subroutine which can be stored in one place and then connected to a routine using various linkages or calling sequences or commands, at one or more locations, i.e., when it is stored separately from the main routine, jump instructions from program control will fetch or call the beginning of this subroutine, and at its end, another transfer instruction will return it.

COAM equipment—Concerns that specific customer owned and maintained communication equipment connected to common-carrier lines. IBM terminals are a good example (even though not owned by the customer).

COBOL—1. COmmon Business Oriented Language. Generally regarded as a common procedural language designed for commercial data processing as developed and defined by a national committee of computer manufacturers and users. 2. A specific language by which business-data processing procedure may be precisely described in a standard form. The language is intended not only as a means for directly presenting any business program to any suitable computer for which a compiler exists, but also as a means of communicating such procedures among individuals.

code check—To isolate and remove mistakes from a routine.

code—1. A system of symbols for meaningful communication (related to instruction). 2. A system of symbols for representating data or instructions in a computer or a tabulating machine. 3. The translating and writing of information in the form of abbreviations and specific notation to develop machine instructions or symbolic instructions from the statement of a problem. 4. To express a program in a code that a specific computer was built or programmed to interpret and execute. Types: computer, direct, external device, forced, function, gray, hamming, Hollerith, illegal, instruction, line, machine, micro, mnemonic, numeric, object, operation, quibinary, relfected, skip, and unitary codes.

code conversion—A process for changing the bit groupings for characters in one code into the corresponding character bit groupings for a second code.

coded program—A program which has been expressed in the language or code of a specific machine or programming system.

code element—Concerns a discrete condition or event in a code, such as, stroke in a printed character.

code, input instruction—A code designed for the convenience of programmers which has mnemonic symbols or groupings which appear somewhat like the actual operations to be performed, i.e., MPY for multiply, etc. The computer then translates these into actual machine instructions for execution.

code line—Relates to a single specific instruction, usually written on one line, in a code for a specific computer to solve a problem. This instruction is usually stored as a whole in the program register of the computer while it is executed, and it may contain one or more addresses of registers or storage locations in the computer where numbers or machine words are to be obtained or sent, and one or more operations to be executed. (Synonymous with program line.)

code, Magnetic Ink Character Recognition (MICR)—In Magnetic Ink Character Recognition the special code is developed which consists of a set of 10 numeric symbols and four special symbols standardized as Font E 13B developed for the American Bankers Association. The characters are visually readable through the use of magnetic sensing heads in various types of magnetic ink recognition equipment. The special symbols mentioned above are: amount, dash, transit number and "on us".

coder—A person who prepares instruction sequences from detailed flow charts and other algorithmic procedures prepared by others, as contrasted with a programmer who prepares the procedures and flow charts.

coefficient—A number or factor put before and multiplying another.

coefficient matrix—A specific matrix of left-side coefficients in a system of linear operations. It is to be distinguished from the matrix obtained by appending the right side, which is called the augmented matrix of the system. It may be thought of as including a full set of logical vectors to convert inequality constraints to equations, and in the case of the modified simplex array it also contains the objective function coefficients.

collate—1. To merge two or more ordered sets of data, or cards, in order to produce one or more ordered sets which still reflect the original ordering relations. The collation process is the merging of two sequences of cards, each ordered on some mutual key, into a single sequence ordered on the mutual key. 2. To produce a single sequence of items, ordered according to some rule (i.e., arranged in some orderly sequence), from two or more ordered sequences. The final sequence need not contain all of the data available in the original sets. If, for example, two sets of items are being matched, items that do not match may

36

be discarded. See merge.

collating sorting—A sort which uses a technique of continuous merging of data until one sequence is developed.

collator—1. A device designed to compare data from two decks of punched cards and to sequence check them, merge them, and/or select cards from them based on this data. 2. A device used to collate or merge sets or decks of cards or other units into a sequence. A typical example of a card collator has two input feeds, so two ordered sets may enter into the process, and four output stackers, so four ordered sets can be generated by the process. Three comparison stations are used to route the cards to one stacker or the other on the basis of comparison of criteria as specified by plugboard wiring.

column—1. A character or digit position in a positional-information format, particularly one in which characters appear in rows, and the rows are placed one above another; e.g., the rightmost column in a five decimal place table, or in a list of data. 2. A character or digit position in a physical device, such as punch card or a register, corresponding to a position in a written table or list; e.g., the right-most place in a register, or the third column in an eighty-column punch card.

column binary—A code used with punch cards in which successive bits are represented by the presence or absence of punches on contiguous positions in successive columns as opposed to rows. Column-binary code is widely used in connection with 36-bit word computers where each group of 3 columns is used to represent a single word.

combinational logic element—A device designed so that at least one output channel and one or more input channels, are characterized by discrete states, such that the state of each output channel is completely determined by the contemporaneous states of the input channels.

command chaining—The execution of a sequence of I/O commands in a command list, under control of an IOP, on one or more logical records.

command code—1. The portion of a computer instruction that signals the computer to perform a specific action. 2. The part of a computer instruction word which specifies, in coded form, the operation to be performed.

command control program—A program that handles all commands addressed to the system from the user-consoles. These commands would include requests to log in or out, a request to use the edit program, requests to have a program placed on the run queue, requests to load a program, etc. (DEC)

command language—1. The language which is recognized by the executive and utilized to issue control commands to the system. 2. A source language which is usually structured with procedural instructions. Such a language has capabilities for causing the execution of many functions, most of which are basic or used repetitively.

command mode—When no program is active at a given terminal, that terminal is in the command mode; and, conversely, when a user enters a command statement, he will destroy the active image of his program.

comment—Relates to various types of expressions which serve to identify or explain one or more steps in routines but whose words have no effects on the execution of such routines or programs.

common area—FORTRAN programs and other programs may specify that data storage is to occupy a common area. This allows programs to share temporary storage, and FORTRAN-coded programs to communicate with assembly-coded routines by using a common data storage. The system loader automatically allocates common area when it is loading programs. Common storage occupies the same memory space during execution as the system loader does when loading programs. This allows effective utilization of memory storage, since the space taken up by the loader can be used by the programs during execution.

Common Business Oriented Language—See COBOL.

common field—A field accessible to two or more routines.

common hardware—Such items are usually expendable items such as plugs, sockets, bolts, etc., and are items commonly used to construct or repair machines or components.

common language—1. A technique which reduces all information to a form which is intelligible to the units of a data processing system. 2. A language or macro code which can be read or written by many different machines or by various groups of users. 3. A single code used by devices—typewriters, calculators, transmitters, and others—manufactured by different companies.

common machine language—A machine sensible information representation common to a related group of data processing machines.

common software—Programs or routines which usually have common and multiple applications for many systems, i.e., report generators, sort routines, conver-

sion programs which can be used for several routines in language common to many computers.

common storage—Various COBOL programs can be chained (an executive function), and intermediate data results can be maintained between programs using the common storage provision of some versions of COBOL.

communication channel—Voice, mail, messenger, telephone, telegraph, microwave, teletype, and other media are available for transmitting business data over short or very great distances, i.e., a Telpak or microwave channel is a communication channel with data transmission rates up to 100,000 characters per second.

communication link—The physical means of connecting one location to another for purposes of transmitting and receiving information.

communications and inquiry systems—Systems are now provided for diversified on-site and long-distance inquiry and data-communications networks. Centralized records and data-processing operations can be tied in with information sources at remote locations, and will provide instant on-line response to interrogations and data from a large number of inquiry stations. Communication networks may include up to 5,985 standard teletype stations and up to 120 electric-typewriter stations (some computers).

communications control, ESI—A feature of several systems that provides communications control for many systems is ESI (externally specified index). ESI makes it possible to handle a substantial number of communications lines through a single computer channel, using buffers in memory. This buffer control permits other transactions to run without interruption. Communications instructions that involve other memory areas interrupt other programs for a minimum period of time, measured in microseconds, because subsequent instructions are in a "ready" position at all times. Real-time circuitry provides tight, accurate operations in rapid succession, handling a vast number of instructions in real-time, communications, and batch-processing modes simultaneously, or with logical priorities.

communications input/output control system (CIOCS)—A communications IOCS that allows the customer's problem program to communicate with remote terminals in the same general manner in which the program utilizes basic IOCS to communicate with magnetic tape or other standard I/O devices.

communications multiplexer, priority—In many systems the communication multiplexer contains priority logic which enables it to determine, on a priority basis, which CLT (communications line terminal) in the subsystem should be serviced first. Thirteen microseconds elapse from the time the communication multiplexer is freed from its previous CLT, by receiving either an input-acknowledge or an output-acknowledge signal from the central processor, until it is able to make the next input-data request or output-data request. During this 13-microsecond interval, the communication multiplexer must analyze the status of all CLTs in the subsystem, determine which CLT requesting service is connected to the highest number multiplexer position, and perform all of the necessary switching to permit the data transfer. (UNIVAC)

communication software—Sets of software

specifically designed for monitoring communication activities include the following routines: Interrupt—Upon a program interrupt, this routine directs data transfer between the communication control unit and the central processor and then returns control to the main program; Message Queuing—Controls the order in which messages are stored, processed, and transmitted; Error Control—Corrects errors in messages received from other communication stations.

communications system—A computer system which handles on-line real-time applications. A typical communication system would consist of the following: A teletype, visual display, or audio answerback device connected to an ordinary telephone line through a communication multiplexer, a device which converts the keyed-in characters to electronic pulses for transmission over the telephone line. An interface device in the computer center translates these pulses into binary code and delivers the character to computer storage. After receipt of the entire message, the central computer searches or stores the requested information and sends back the appropriate response.

communications terminal module controller (CTMC)—The communications terminal module controller functions as the link between the processor and the CTM's and CLT's (communication line terminal). A CTMC can handle 16 CTM's; this means that a maximum of 32 inputs and 32 outputs can be handled by a single CTMC.

The CTM's may request access to the central processor via the communications terminal module controller in random sequence. The CTMC automatically assigns priority among CTM's requesting access and identifies to the central processor the particular CTM granted access. This process is automatic and self-controlled on the system through externally specified indexing (ESI) on each I/O channel. (UNIVAC)

communication subsystem—In some systems the standard communication subsystem enables the real-time system to receive and transmit data via any common carrier in any of the standard codes and at any of the standard rates of transmission, up to 4800 bits per second. It is a communication system that can receive data from or transmit data to low-speed, medium-speed, or high-speed lines in any combination. The subsystem consists of two principal elements, the Communication Line Terminals (CLT's), which make direct connection with the communication facilities, and the communication multiplexer through which the CLT's deliver data to and receive data from the central processor. A communication multiplexer may be connected to any general purpose computer channel, or two or more multiplexers may be connected to two or more channels. If required, a number of multiplexers may be connected through a scanner selector to the same general purpose channel. The total number of multiplexers which can be connected to a general purpose channel is dependent on the number and speed of the communication systems linked to the multiplexers by their CLT's. (UNIVAC)

community automatic exchange (CAX)—A small dial telephone office serving an individual community.

commutative operation—Concerns a specific type of dyadic operation in which the order of the operands is immaterial, i.e., the dyadic operator X is commutative if and only if $X(A,B) = X(B,A)$.

commutator—The electronic circuit which is designed to act as an intermediate link between the accumulator and drum storage.

compacting, storage—Certain hardware features make feasible the dynamic relocation of programs residing in the central storage; a necessity in order to provide an effective multiprogramming environment. The storage assigned is returned to the pool of the available central storage at program termination. Storage compacting is initiated if, and only if, a requirement exists for contiguous storage, and compacting can meet this requirement.

compaction—A series of techniques used for the reduction of space, bandwidth, cost, transmission, generating time, and the storage of data. These techniques are designed to eliminate repetition, remove irrelevancies, and employ special coding techniques.

comparator—1. Device used to compare two different transcriptions of the same information to verify the accuracy of transcription, storage, arithmetic operation, or other processes, in which a signal is given dependent on some relation between two items; i.e., one item is larger than, smaller than, or equal to the other. 2. A form of verifier. 3. A circuit that compares two signals and indicates agreement or disagreement; a signal may be given indicating whether they are equal or unequal.

compare—1. To determine whether a particular quantity is higher, equal to, or lower than another quantity, or to determine whether one piece of data is exactly like another. 2. To examine the representation of a quantity to discover its relationship to zero, or to examine two quantities usually for the purposes of discovering identity or relative magnitude.

compare and print—A specified number of records from each of two tapes are compared, record for record, with all nonidentical records printed in either alpha-numeric or octal mode.

comparing unit—1. An electromechanical device used to compare two groups of timed pulses and signals, either identity or nonidentity. 2. Comparing is the automatic checking of cards on a match or nonmatch basis. With this machine, feeding, punching, and segregating are controlled by comparing cards from two separate files for a match or nonmatch condition. Comparison of both alphabetical and numerical data may be made on selected columns or fields, or on entire cards.

compatibility—The quality of an instruction to be translatable or executable on more than one class of computer.

compatibility test—Specific tests run to check acceptability of both software and hardware as a system, i.e., to test component workability.

compatible—That particular characteristic of a device, program, etc. which makes it acceptable to a computer or another device such that it can perform operations or functions intended for execution, operation and thus connection with other devices or computers, i.e., a suitable tape width, similarity of operating speeds, etc.

compatible hardware—Components, peripheral equipment, or other devices which can be used on more than one system with very little or no adjustment.

compatible software—Languages which can be used on more than one computer system.

compile—1. The conversion of relatively machine-independent source program into specific machine language routines. 2. To produce a machine language routine from a routine written in source language by selecting appropriate subroutines from a subroutine library, as directed by the instructions or other symbols of the original routine, supplying the linkage which combines the subroutines into a workable routine, and translating the subroutines and linkage into machine language. The compiled routine is then ready to be loaded into storage and run; i.e., the compiler does not usually run the routine it produces.

compiler—1. A program-making routine which produces a specific program for a particular problem by determining the intended meaning of an element of information expressed in pseudocode, selecting or generating the required subroutine, transforming the subroutine into specific coding for the specific problem, assigning specific storage registers, etc., and entering it as an element of the problem program, maintaining a record of the subroutines used and their position in the problem program and continuing to the next element of information in pseudocode. 2. A computer program more powerful than an assembler. In addition to its translating function which is generally the same process as that used in an assembler, it is able to replace certain items of input with series of instructions, usually called subroutines. Thus, where an assembler translates item for item and produces as output the same number of instructions or constant which were put into it, a compiler will do more than this. The program which results from compiling is a translated and expanded version of the original. (Synonymous with compiling routine, and related to assembler.)

compile routine—An executive routine that, before the desired computation is started, translates a program expressed in pseudocode into machine code (or into another pseudocode for further translation by an interpreter). In accomplishing the translation, the compiler may be required to adapt or to specialize the instructions.

compiler, Programming Language/1 (PL/1)—In many systems a compiler is provided in the special support system for use in compiling object programs from source programs written in PL/1. This language has some features that are characteristic of FORTRAN and also incorporates some of the best features of other languages, such as string manipulation, data structures, and extensive editing capabilities. The PL/1 compiler translates a PL/1 program to a machine-usable (binary) language as do other compilers, i.e., FORTRAN compilers. The new programming language for the special support system provides the facilities for the operating system. This new language is designed to provide the programmer with a flexible problem-oriented language for programming problems that can best be solved using a combination of scientific and commercial computing techniques.

compiler system, FORTRAN—In most systems the FORTRAN compiler system consists of two basic elements: a source language (FORTRAN IV) whose structure closely resembles the language of mathematics, and a compiler which translates the statements and formulas written in the source language into a machine-language program.

compiling computer—The computer which is designed to be used to translate a particular program into the machine language of another computer; such a computer is often called the source computer and the computer for which the translation (compiling) is being done is called the target or object computer.

compiling program—A unique but basic translating program designed to transform, to assemble, or to structure programs expressed in other languages into same or equivalent programs expressed in terms of the particular computer language for which that particular machine was design. Compiling programs or compilers most often include assemblers (or programs) as well as diagnostic and generating programs within them. The computer which is using the compiling program or compiler is called the source computer or compiling computer, and the computer in which the program is used or to be used is called the object computer or target computer. The occasion or run of compilation or translation is called the compiling phase while the use of the newly translated program is the run. Time to translate is compile duration.

complement—1. A quantity expressed to the base N, which is derived from a given quantity by a particular rule; frequently used to represent the negative of the given quantity. 2. A complement on N, obtained by subtracting each digit of the given quantity from N−I, adding unity to the least significant digit, and performing all resulting carrys; e.g., two's complement of binary 11010 is 00110; the tens complement of decimal 456 is 544. 3. A complement on N−1, obtained by subtracting each digit of the given quantity from N−1; e.g., the ones complement of binary 11010 is 00101; the nines complement of decimal 456 is 543. (Synonymous with radix-minus-1 complement, and radix complement.)

complete instruction—A specific instruction designed to take in a complete computer operation including the execution of that operation.

complex decision making simulation—A specific system designed to permit the man to make certain decisions which are difficult to define sufficiently rigorous for incorporation into the computer-based portion of the model.

component—A basic part or an element.

composite card—A card, often multipurpose, which contains data needed in the processing of various applications.

compress—The process for reduction of some parameter of a signal, such as bandwidth, amplitude variation, duration, etc., but with the preservation of the basic information content and purpose.

compute mode—Also known as the operate mode; the input signals are connected to the computing units (analog computers), including integrators for the generation of the solution.

computer—A device capable of accepting information, applying prescribed processes to information, and supplying the results of these processes. It usually consists of input and output devices, arithmetic, storage, communications units and a control unit. Types: absolute, value, all-purpose, analog, buffered, general-purpose, hybrid, incremental, parallel, second generation, serial, slave, target, and third generation computers.

computer-aided instruction (CAI)—An educational concept which places the student in a conversational mode with a computer which has a preprogrammed study plan. The programmed course selects the next topic or phase of study according to previous responses from the student, allowing each student to progress at a pace directly related to his learning capability.

computer application—The problem, task, or routine to be completed or solved by the computer system such as: library search, management science model, inventory control reporting, banking operation and other applications.

computer center, closed shop—A set of rules which usually relate to computer centers whose personnel alone are allowed to program and operate the computing equipment, excluding all other personnel, i.e., programs written by others are to be run, compiled, checked, etc. by inside personnel only and not outside programmers or personnel. Often the term also relates to centers which do not use outside service or temporary people.

computer code—1. A system of combinations of binary digits used by a given computer (synonymous with machine code). 2. Repertory of instructions.

computer configuration—The particular set of equipment so connected to form a single computer center or system for various computer runs. Such configurations may vary as almost any system man's imagination: mainframes of various sizes, speeds, and architecture, store units of a hundred varieties,

43

peripheral equipment in almost endless variety.

computer-dependent language—1. A group of languages designed for interpretation and use by a machine, without a translation being necessary. 2. A system designed for expressing information that is intelligible to a specific machine; e.g., a computer or class of computer. Such a language may include instructions that define and direct machine operations, and information to be recorded or acted upon by these machine operations. 3. That specific set of instructions expressed in the number system basic to a computer, together with symbolic operation codes with absolute addresses, relative addresses, or symbolic addresses. (Synonymous with machine language; clarified by language; related to object language; and contrasted with problem-oriented language.

computer-independent language—A programming language which is not a computer language, but one which requires translation or compiling to any one of a variety of computer languages. The language which is a particular language of that machine or one which has compilers for translating to its own machine language.

computer instruction code—An instruction code designed for specific computers, i.e., the machine language.

computer instruction set—A particular set of computer instructions which usually require no compiling and work directly to and within the computer.

Computer Interface Unit (CIU)—A CIU is a device which interfaces (matches and connects to) a central processing unit and/or peripheral devices such as discs, printers, and terminals.

computerized microfilm—A specific type of microfilm which is produced from magnetic tapes. Special equipment is used for this conversion activity.

computer language—A programming procedure or language in which instructions are computer instructions only, i.e., a machine language as contrasted to a problem-oriented language which must be compiled to a computer language before a machine can use it directly.

computer learning—1. That process by which a computer modifies programs according to its own memory or experience, i.e., changes of logic paths, parameter values. An example is the now famous chess-playing computer. 2. In process-control, an analog computer can alter its parameters by a continuous process according to temperatures, or other gauge reports it receives. Examples are adaptive autopilots for aircraft, which explore different alternatives.

computer logic—The logical operations of the computer, consisting entirely of five operations—add, subtract, multiply, divide and compare. This simple processing logic is enough to allow the computer to accomplish its entire potential of tasks when properly programmed.

computer network—1. Basically, two or more interconnected computers with advantages of permitting geographical distribution, and thus economy, of computer operations. Such a network also permits parallel processing, usually time-sharing, combinations of send-receive communications, multipoint remote entry and output, locally controlled and maintained data banks, and switching centers, reducing the necessity for centralized facilities. 2. The multiple connection of computers so that individual machines can either operate independently on their own programs or operate cooperatively on portions of a single large program. Ultimately, there is likely to be a nationwide public utility network of computers which will at all times provide subscribers with computational capability specifically tailored to the limitations of the problem at hand. The subscribers pay only for the actual time and capacity used on each problem.

computer, off-line—Relates to specific equipment system or set of programs which are not under the direct control of the central processor or specifically to a computer which is not actively monitoring or controlling a process or operation. Also relates to a computer operation completed while the computer is not monitoring or controlling a process or operation.

computer, on-line—Usually operations which relate to equipment or a computer which is actively monitoring or controlling a process or operation, i.e., a computer operation performed while the computer is monitoring or controlling a process or operation.

computer operation—One of many predetermined sets of operations which the computer is designed to perform directly, i.e., a jump, transfer, an addition, etc.

computer program—A plan, routine or set of instructions for solving a problem on a computer, as contrasted with such terms as fiscal program, military program, and development program.

computer programming language—The machine language that the computer was designed to understand. This is contrasted with compiler systems such as FORTRAN or COBOL.

computer science—The entire spectrum of theoretical and applied disciplines connected with the development and application of computers. Contributions have come mostly from such fields as mathematics, logic, language analysis, programming, computer design, systems engineering, and information systems.

computers, hybrid—By combining analog computer speed, flexibility, and direct communication capability with digital computer memory, logic, and accuracy, the special integrated hybrid computer has introduced a new dimension in engineering, scientific, and business technology, i.e., the power to attack every aspect of a problem with the computational capability suited to the task. Dynamic simulation and high-speed differential-equation solution may be performed on the analog side; static and algebraic computations may be handled on the digital side. Overall computational economy and efficiency are thereby maximized.

computer storage—Often called computer or automatic storage, it is a designed part of the automatic data processing system or hardware and may be controlled automatically or without the need for human intervention.

computer system—Generally regarded as a system which consists of one or more central processing units, input/output devices, and other peripheral hardware that is related and interconnected, and capable of simultaneous operation: A computer system is often referred to as a computer.

computer word—A series, set, or group of 1's and 0's grouped into units, intelligible to the computer, and representing alphabetic, numeric, and special characters.

Many computer systems, at the programmer's discretion, can act on part of a word while leaving the rest of the word intact for future use.

concordance—An alphabetic list of words and phrases appearing in a document, with an indication of the place where those words and phrases appear.

concurrent—Occurrence of two or more events within the same time period, i.e., two computers operating simultaneously.

concurrent computer—A specifically designed computer which executes two or more instructions simultaneously, for example, read, search, compute. Such action is program controlled in some cases, but is built-in or automatic depending upon the specific purpose for which the mainframe was designed.

concurrent control system—In many systems this relates to an environment allowing for the concurrent operation of many programs; it allows the system to react immediately to the inquires, requests and demands of many different users at local and remote stations; it allows for the stringent demands of real-time applications; it is able to store, file, retrieve, and protect large blocks of data; and it makes optimum use of all available hardware facilities, while minimizing job turn-around time.

Only through central control of all activities can this environment of the combined hardware and software systems be fully established and maintained to satisfy the requirements of all applications; this responsibility for efficient flexible, centralized control is borne by the executive system. The executive system controls and coordinates the functions of this complex internal environment, and be presenting a relatively simple interface to the programmer, allows him to use the system easily, while relieving him of concern for the internal interaction between his program and other coexistent programs.

concurrent processing—1. The ability to work on more than one program at a time. This is a valuable feature of the new large-scale computer systems. The result is a better utilization of time by taking full advantage of the high speed of the central processor. 2. Concerns the processing of more than one independent task simultaneously by a single computing system involving interlaced time-sharing of at least one section of hardware, which is generally the control unit and memory-address register or the multiplexing unit, for selecting individual control units and memory-address registers for each task.

condensed instruction deck—The card output from an assembly program in which several instructions per card are punched in machine language. Input to the assembly program may consist of one instruction per card; thus, the name condensed is used for output.

conditional—Subject to various constraints; e.g., results of comparisons made during the program or subject to human intervention.

conditional branch—An instruction which is interpreted as an unconditional transfer if a specified condition or set of conditions is satisfied. If the condition or conditions are not satisfied, the instruction causes the computer to proceed in its normal sequence of control. A conditional transfer also includes the testing of the condition (synonymous with conditional jump, and related to branch).

46

conditional expression—An expression in the COBOL language, which has the particular characteristic that, taken as a whole, it may be either true or false, in accordance with the rules.

conditional jump—A specific instruction which will basically depend upon the result of some arithmetical or logical operation or the state of some switch or indicator as to whether or not that instruction will cause a jump or skip to another preset instruction.

conditional transfer—A procedure designed to copy, exchange, read, record, store, transmit, or write data or to change control or jump to another location according to a certain specified rule or in accordance with a certain criteria.

configuration—A group (configurization or set) of machines that are interconnected and are programmed to operate as a system.

congestion—A specific condition that is developed when a sufficient number of calls arrive at the various communications input stations of a network that are excessive for the network capacity or capability for handling in a particular time allotment or that condition which arises when arriving "traffic" exceeds the number of "servers".

conjunction—The logical operation which makes use of the AND operator or logical product. The conjunction of two variables, or expressions, may be written as A · B, A ∩ B, or just plain AB. These may also be described as an intersection when using Venn diagrams. (Related to AND operator, AND gate, and contrasted with disjunction.)

consistency check—A process designed to verify that a piece of data is consistent with the rules prescribed for its handling.

console—1. The "operator" unit of a computer containing the control keys and certain special devices. They unit may contain the start key, stop key, power key, sense switches, etc., as well as lights which display the information located in certain registers. 2. A portion of the computer which may be used to control the machine manually, correct errors, determine the status of machine circuits, registers, and counters, determine the contents of storage, and manually revise the contents of storage.

console display—1. A visual display unit which provides a "window into the computer." It can display a message of thousands of characters of information, or tables, charts, graphs and the lines and curves of drawings as a series of points. A "light pen" (stylus), available with the display, can detect information that has been displayed on the screen and enable the operator to change information under program control. 2. There are binary displays on many computer operator's consoles. One display bit indicates the memory work parity; other display bits may indicate:
1. The next instruction.
2. The contents of any memory location.
3. The contents of the accumulator.
4. The contents of index registers.
5. The status of the traps.
When the computer halts, the display register will indicate the next instruction word, while a register will contain the address of the halt instruction that stopped the computer. To display anything else, the appropriate push-button display switch must be pressed.

console typewriter (monitor)—The console typewriter is a standard feature of the computer. The primary function of the typewriter is to monitor system and program operations. Such system conditions as Add Overflow, Exponent Overflow, etc. and program conditions as Syntax Error, Symbol Length, Integer Size, etc. are brought to the operator's attention via the typewriter. The typewriter may also be programmed to request information from the operator. The typewriter may also be used to enter programs and data into the central processor and to type out the results in lieu of other peripheral equipment specifically designed for these functions.

constant instruction—1. An instruction not intended to be executed as an instruction, i.e., it is usually written in the form of a constant. (Related to dummy instruction.) 2. That series of steps performed in processing of an instruction word, i.e., transfer from storage, interpretation, decoding, checking, etc.

constant(s)—1. The quantities or messages which will be present in the machine and available as data for the program, and which usually are not subject to change with time. 2. A character or group of characters usually representing a value, key or standard, used by the computer to identify, locate, measure, or test in order to make a decision.

content—Data, characters, words, or other units which are held specifically addressable in some storage unit are said to be its content.

context—Words of text that occur just before and just after a particular group of words.

contiguous—Adjoining or adjacent.

continuation card—A punched card which continues data that has been started on a previous card. This is allowed in many compilers such as FORTRAN.

continuous forms—Any of many types of source information, for character recognition, that is contained in reel form such as cash register receipts.

continuous processing—The technique of constantly processing input items. This is sometimes referred to as on-line or real-time processing and is contrasted to batch processing.

continuous simulation—The type of simulation which may be represented by continuous variables. The system is therefore suitable for representation by a set of differential equations. These may be further classified as linear or nonlinear. Example: missile flights.

continuous system diagnosis, time-sharing—Relates to a specific and very useful technique which can be easily included in a time-shared system to carry out more or less continuous system diagnosis. A collection of diagnostic tasks are permanently placed in the task queue with only a low priority assigned to them. Whenever the queue of user "ready" tasks is empty, the system selects and runs one of these test programs sending the results to a special monitor console. Normal preventive maintenance similarly can be interlaced with user tasks eliminating the need for shutting down the entire system at periodic intervals.

contour analysis—A reading technique, in optical character recognition, which uses a roving spot of light to trace the outline of a character by bouncing around the edges. This system is usually used for handwritten material because of the nonstandardized appearance of the input. The result of the contour tracing is compared to a complete character set within a library in an attempt to determine which character has been traced.

control—1. The part of a digital computer or processor determining the execution and interpretation of instructions in proper sequence, including the decoding of each instruction and the application of the proper signals to the arithmetic unit and other registers in accordance with the decoded information. 2. Frequently, it is one or more of the components in any mechanism responsible for interpreting and carrying out manually initiated directions. Sometimes it is called manual control.

control board—This concerns early computers, and relates to a removable plugboard or panel which contained the electrical jacks or connecting devices or terminals for various internal circuits which permitted external wiring for control of operation and equipment operations.

control card—A card which contains input data or parameters for a specific application of a general routine. Such cards are punched (coded) to cause segregation of various groups of cards, to cause changes in or startups of computer or peripheral machine operations.

control carriage tape—Pertains to a paper or magnetic tape that contains punches (coded) for peripheral machine operations as: vertical spacing, start of page, first and last line of printing, and other functions.

control character—A character whose occurrence in a particular context initiates, modifies, or stops a control operation; e.g., a character which controls carriage return.

control computer—A computer which, by means of inputs from and outputs to a process, directly controls the operation of elements in that process.

control console—The control console of the electronic data-processing system is designed to enable the operator to centrally control and monitor all processing functions. The panel is designed for efficient supervision and provides what is necessary for the operator, as the needs of the service engineers often have been placed within individual components of the system.

An electric typewriter provides direct communication with the processor memory. Data can be entered into the memory through the typewriter keyboard. The processor can transmit data to the typewriter for output through the typewriter printer. Thus, through the console typewriter, the operator can interrogate the memory, input programs and enter instructions to modify a program (some computers).

control data—The items of data, one or more of which are used to select, execute, identify or modify another routine, record, file, operation or data value.

control desk—That desk-like console or group of panels from which operators or service personnel actually control the computing system or use to communicate with it.

control field—A constant location where information for control purposes is placed; i.e., in a set of punch cards, if columns 79 and 80 contain various codes which control whether or not certain operations will be performed on any particular card, then columns 79 and 80 constitute a control field.

control function—An operation to control a device, i.e., the starting or stopping of a carriage, or a font change, rewind, transmission reading. Operation control symbols are not regarded as control operations, however.

control group—The number of people from one on up required to spend their full time in decision making when a system is being programmed. The group reads, modifies, evaluates, monitors the developing program and then approves the changes necessary as they occur to prevent the build-up of a queue of work.

control instructions—The instructions in this category are used to manipulate data within the main memory and the control memory, to prepare main memory storage areas for the processing of data fields. Also used to control the sequential selection and interpretation of instructions in the stored program.

control language, linear programming—The language used to prescribe the course of linear programming run on a computer. The language consists mainly of verbs (agendum names), which call in a body of code (program or subroutine) embodying the desired algorithm for execution.

control logic—Generally this relates to the sequence of steps or events necessary to perform a particular function. Each step or event is defined to be either a single arithmetic or a single Boolean expression.

control loop—The path along which control affecting signals travel from the error detecting point, through the controller, and back to the error detecting point.

control number—This is the quantity or number (value) which must be the result of a process or problem in order to prove the accuracy of the process or problem.

control, numeric—A specific field of computer activity which centers around the control of machine tools by mechanical devices; e.g., a computer can control assembly-line tools for machining.

control panel—1. An interconnection device, usually removable, which employs removable wires to control the operation of computing equipment. The panel is used on punch-card machines to carry out functions which are under control of the user. On computers it is used primarily to control input and output functions. 2. A device or component of some data-processing machines, which permits the expression of instructions in a semifixed computer program by the insertion of pins, plugs, or wires into sockets, or hubs in the device, in a pattern to represent instructions, and thus making electrical interconnections which may be sensed by the data-processing machine (synonymous with plugboard and related to pinboard).

control procedure—A basic key to achievement of high operating efficiency in a computing or data-processing installation. This procedure must include many functions: administrative control of job schedules, workflow, and computer usage records; control over data and program libraries; control over computer operations; and control over the flow of programs and data within the computer system during job runs.

control program—A sequence of instructions prescribing the series of steps to be taken by a system, a computer, or any other device.

control punches—In the broadest sense, control punches are used to alter the performance of the program in some manner. For example, it is customary to

50

identify different types of cards with significant control punches, and to use these punches to route the program in different directions for the various types of cards. One example of this distinction might be to identify a header card with a 1-punch in column 1 and a detail card with a 3-punch in column 1.

control ratio—Concerns that specific limitation in the relationship between two quantities as expressed in direct or percentage comparison.

control register—A register which holds the identification of the instruction word to be executed next in time sequence, following the current operation. The register is often a counter incremented to the address of the next sequential storage location, unless a transfer or other special instruction is specified by the program (synonymous with program counter, and contrasted with program register).

control routine—1. A routine which controls loading and relocation of routines and in some cases makes use of instructions which are unknown to the general programmer. Effectively, control routine is part of the machine itself (synonymous with monitor routine, supervisory routine, and supervisory program). 2. A set of coded instructions designed to process and control other sets of coded instructions. 3. A set of coded instructions used in realizing automatic coding.

control sequence—The normal order of selection of instructions for execution. In some computers one of the addresses in each instruction specifies the control sequence, while in most other computers, the sequence is consecutive except where a transfer occurs.

control state (display)—In some systems all operating modes can specify that the display enter the control state in which 12-bit words are decoded as instructions to change display parameters, change mode, or change the address of access to the computer memory.

control statements—1. Statements which are used to direct the flow of the program, either causing specific transfers or making transfers dependent upon meeting certain specific conditions. 2. Instructions which convey control information to the processor, but do not develop machine-language instructions, i.e., symbolic statements.

control station—A switching network station directing operations such as polling, alerting, recovering, selecting control, tape sequence. Same as tape program.

control system—A system of the closed loop type in which the computer is used to govern external processes.

control tape—A paper or plastic tape used to control carriage operation of some printing output devices. It is also called carriage control tape.

control unit—1. A unit or portion of the hardware of an automatic digital computer that is designed to direct sequence of operations, interprets coded instructions, and initiates proper commands to computer circuits to execute instructions. 2. An auxiliary component of a computer located behind the "main frame" and other component equipment such as tape units, printers and card readers, for the purpose of controlling these components.

CONTRON—A FORTRAN process control language developed by Control Data Corp.

conventions—Standard and accepted procedures in programs and systems analysis.

The abbreviations, symbols, and their meanings as developed for particular systems and programs.

conversational programming—A technique used in instructing the computer to perform its operations, whereby common vocabulary can be utilized by the user to describe his procedures most accurately. If a statement cannot be understood by the computer, it asks the user for a clarified instruction. This conversational procedure continues until the user has selected the series of statements in the proper sequence which will solve his problem. Conversational programming saves the user the inconvenience of having to study other programming languages extensively before he can solve his problem.

conversion—1. The process of changing information from one form of representation to another; such as, from the language of one type of machine to that of another, or from magnetic tape to the printed page (synonymous with data conversion). 2. The process of changing from one type of equipment to another, or from one data-processing method to another, i.e., conversion from punch-card equipment to magnetic-tape equipment.

conversion file—The transformation of parts of records, customer account records, employee records and the like from their original documents into magnetic files by the computer.

conversion mode—Communication between a terminal and the computer in which each entry from the terminal elicits a response from the computer and vice versa.

conversion routine—A flexible and generalized program which can be used by a programmer to change the presentation of data from one form to another; such as from card to disk.

converter—A device which converts the representation of information, or which permits the changing of the method for data processing from one form to another; i.e., a unit which accepts information from punch cards and records the information on magnetic tape, and possibly including editing facilities.

converter, tape-to-card—A device which is designed to convert information directly from punched or magnetic tape to Hollerith cards.

converter, tape-to-tape—A device designed to change from one form of input/output medium or code to another; i.e., magnetic tape to paper tape (or vice versa), or eight-channel code to five-channel code, etc. They handle the allocation and protection of main storage blocks, the interval timer, error diagnostic routines, and checkpoint procedures.

coordinate retrieval—A term which is generally used to describe the basic principles of various punched-card and mechanized information retrieval systems which involve the multi-dimensional analysis of information and coordinate retrieval. In concept coordination, independently assigned concepts are used to characterize the subject contents of document, and the latter are identified during searching by means of either such assigned concepts or a combination of the same.

copy and correct—A process in which a designated record is copied from one tape to another with specified corrections. In manipulating magnetic tapes, either a record-counting method or a file-identification method may be employed. The file option provides added convenience in that it permits operation over a entire tape or file, rather than over a specified number of records.

core—A configuration of magnetic material which is placed in a spatial relationship to current-carrying conductors, and whose magnetic properties are essential to its use. It is used to concentrate an induced magnetic field as in a transformer, induction coil, or armature, to retain a magnetic polarization for the purpose of storing data, or for its non-linear properties as in a logic element. It may be made of such material as iron, iron oxide, or ferrite, and in such shapes as wires, tapes, toroids, or thin film.

core bank—A stock of a specific number of core arrays and the associated electronics that make up a functional unit of digital computer memory.

core dump—A listing of the selected parts or contents of a storage device (synonymous with memory dump and memory printout).

core image—Relates to the images of ones and zeros as represented by polarized magnetic cores as formed or stored in other media. Each binary digit is represented as on or off in some media or by direction in magnetic type devices, or by magnetized spots on the surface of a magnetic storage drum.

core memory—A storage device composed of ferromagnetic cores, or an apertured ferrite plate, through which sense windings and select lines are threaded. See memory, and thin-film.

core storage—1. A form of high speed storage using magnetic cores. 2. A storage device in which binary data is represented by the direction of magnetization in each unit of an array of magnetic material, usually in the shape of toroidal

rings, but also in other forms, such as wraps on bobbins. 3. The funamental and most important storage of the central processing unit and usually of magnetic cores, each core of which is capable of storing one binary digit and which cores are uniquely arranged in matrices, arrays or stacks and on digit planes or work strings. Almost all core storage is high speed, random access, and expandable with high speed units or extra cores.

correction—Generally accepted to be a quantity (equal in absolute value to the error) that is added to a calculated or observed value to obtain the true value.

counter—1. A device for storing a number and allowing the number to be decreased or increased as directed by the instructions needed. An adding wheel or device. 2. A device, such as a register or storage location, used to represent the number of occurrences of an event.

counter, instruction—Concerns a specific hardware register which is used by the computer to remember the location of the next instruction to be processed in the normal sequence, but subject to branching, execute instructions and interrupts.

cpm—Cards per minute.

cps—Abbreviation for both "characters per second" and "cycles per second."

CPU—1. Central Processing Unit. The central processor of the computer system. This unit contains the main storage, arithmetic unit, and special register groups. 2. The principal unit of the computer which controls the processing routines, performs the arithmetic functions, and maintains a quickly accessible memory. It also contains the console in some computers.

critical path—The longest time path in a

project which has to be done as quickly as possible. Because the overall time required to complete the project cannot be less than that required along the critical path, it requires the most careful monitoring. Any delay along this path causes the project to be delayed, while minor delays along noncritical paths do not. See PERT.

crossfire—Relates to a type of interference from one telegraph circuit to another telegraph circuit or into telephone circuits.

cross-sectional testing—Relates to a series of tests required to obtain a representative sampling of system performance. These tests are usually one-pass tests such as an acceptance test.

CRT—See definition for cathode-ray tube.

cryotron—A device designed to utilize properties assumed by metals at near absolute zero temperature so that large current changes can be obtained by relatively small magnetic-field changes.

cryptographic crypto—Pertaining to equipment which transforms data to conceal its actual meaning, usually by secret code conversion.

current-instruction register—The control section register that contains the specific instruction that is currently being executed after it is brought to the control section from memory. Also called instruction register.

curve fitting—A specific representation usually on a cathode ray tube, of a curve by a mathematical expression or equation.

cybernetics—The field of technology involved in comparative study of the control and intracommunication of information handling machines and nervous sytems of animals and man in order to understand and improve communication.

cycle—1. To repeat a set of operations indefinitely, or until a stated condition is met. The set of operations may be subject to variation on each repetition, as by address changes obtained by programmed computation, or by use of devices such as index register. 2. An occurrence, phenomenon, or interval of space or time that recurs regularly and in the same sequence; i.e., the interval required for completion of one operation in a repetitive sequence of operations.

cycle, control—A particular cycle of the operation of a punch card machine's main shaft during which the feeding is stopped due to a control change, i.e., a choice is often given the user as to how many intercycles arise for a control change, which may or may not be determined within the machine.

cycle, major—1. Maximum access time of a recirculating serial storage element. 2. The time required for one rotation of a magnetic drum or of pulses in an acoustic delay line. 3. Several minor cycles.

cycle, minor—Refers to the time interval between the appearance of corresponding parts of successive words in a storage device which provides serial access to storage positions.

cycle, operation—Relates specifically to that portion of a machine cycle during which the actual execution of the instruction takes place. Some operations (e.g., divide, multiply) may need a large number of these operation cycles to complete the operation, and the normal instruction/operation alternation will be held up during this time. Also called execution cycle.

cycle, search—Concerns that specific

sequence of events or time interval needed for the occurrence of a fixed number of events required to complete a single search operation, such as carrying out a comparison.

cyclic redundancy check character—An operations character designed as a redundant character introduced for error detection purposes, in various modified cyclic codes.

cyclic storage—1. A storage unit which is designed to be accessable only at specific, and usually equally spaced times, such as magnetic drum storage or delay line storage . . . Often called circulating storage or dynamic storage. 2. A device or unit that stores information in a train or pattern of pulses, where the pattern of pulses issuing at the final end are sensed, amplified, reshaped and reinserted into the device at the beginning end.

cylinder concept—The concept, plan, or design that concerns data on all tracks above and below the one currently being used, is available by merely switching read/write heads. Allows access to large amounts of information with no extra movement of the access device.

* _ * _ *

D A—An abbreviation for differential analyzer.

data—In mathematics, a term used to express all the given quantities and elements of a proposition. In a problem, the data are given parts by means of which one is enabled to determine the unknown or required parts.

data acquisition—This technique consists of data collection, data reduction, and digital test control application in scientific/engineering environments. In addition, there are data collection and reduction applications in remote business operations (manufacturing plants and retail outlets, warehouses, sales offices, etc.). This latter type of system can provide the complete, timely information about a firm's overall operations that is required for accurate cost control and informed management decisions. It can reduce the number of times and places at which data must be manually handled and transcribed thereby cutting clerical costs and error rates.

data-acquisition system—A system used to gather data from multiple remote locations at a certain computing facility.

data base management—A systematic approach to updating, retrieval and storage of information stored as data items, usually in the form of records in a file, where many users, or even many remote installations, will use common data banks.

data buffer—A device for temporarily storing data and which is used to compensate for the difference between uneven rates of data flow from the slower input/output devices and the much faster internal memories of computers, i.e., buffers are designed to accept data at varying degrees of speed and retransmit data at varying degrees of speed, to thus more efficiently transfer information between two or more devices.

data cell—The smallest unit of data which cannot be further subdivided. Example: a magnetic bit.

data chaining—The gathering (or scattering) of information within one physical record, from (or to) more than one region of memory, by means of successive I/O commands.

data channel—The bidirectional data path

55

between the I/O devices and the main memory in a digital computer which permits one or more I/O operations to happen concurrently with computation.

data code—Sets of symbols which are used to represent various data items for data elements on a one for one basis. A single number or symbol might represent a particular week or month.

data collection system—A specific system designed to gather manufacturing information from electronic in-plant reporting stations and to transmit it directly to the computer system. The information is processed as it is received. Reports can be produced which indicate, for example, job cost or machine utilization. Information can enter the processor in several ways including punched card, plastic badge, keyboard or data cartridge. The latter logs production data on a pocket-sized recording device that the employee maintains at his work station.

data communications system—Usually a realtime system which is designed to act to establish compatibility between a teletype station and a computer system.

data control block—A control block combined with access routines for the purpose of receiving information required to store and receive data.

data link escape character—A data communications term representing a control character which when combined with one or more succeeding characters forms an escape sequence and the development of additional data communications control operations.

data logging—Relates to the logging or recording of data related to events which occur sequentially in time periods.

data net—A General Electric model which can be used for production control. A

message exchange which receives and transmits automatically. Another use is a data collection system for the purpose of transmitting data from a remote station to a central unit. Still another use permits an operator to dial and send perforated-tape data over a phone line.

data processing—1. Any procedure which is used for receiving information and producing a specific result. 2. Rearrangement and refinement of raw data into a form suitable for further use. 3. The preparation of source media which contain data or basic elements of information, and the handling of such data according to precise rules of procedure to accomplish such operations as classifying, sorting, calculating, summarizing, and recording. 4. The production of records and reports (synonymous with data handling). Types: automatic, batch, business, electronic, and industrial processing.

data processing (IDP), integrated—1. A system that treats as a whole all data-processing requirements to accomplish a sequence of data-processing steps, or a number of related data-processing sequences, and that strives to reduce or eliminate duplicating data entry or processing steps. 2. The processing of data by such a system in which all operations are in some way connected or associated with a computer.

data record—A record which contains the data to be processed by a program.

dataset—A circuit termination device which is used to provide interface between a circuit and terminal input/output equipment.

data set—A collection of similar and related data records that is recorded upon a computer readable medium such

as a data file. Interface of remote terminals to and from telephone lines.

data station—1. This unit has a broad range of operating characteristics and high speed; it can combine several input and output devices into a single console for use either on-line to a centralized computer system, or off-line for local data preparation. It can thus handle a variety of transmission applications, such as inquiries, field reporting, and data collection. The connected optical scanner can read documents encoded in a special bar code. As it scans, it transfers the encoded data to a buffer for direct transmission, or to punched tape for pretransmission editing. Various numbers of terminals include high- and medium-speed paper-tape punches and readers. The data station uses the ASCII (American Standard Code for Information Interchange) code for all transmission. Errors are detected by parity and channel-checking features. Through control programs in the remote computer, the data station can be turned on or off, specific peripheral units can be activated and deactivated, and full transmission cycles can be executed, including correction or retransmission. The computer system can thus time-share by running several programs simultaneously and independent of its core memory. (Honeywell) 2. Honeywell's data station is an all-purpose remote-communication terminal that can be used for a variety of applications involving direct, on-line transmission to and from the processor. The data station can transmit and receive data at the rate of 120 characters per second, regardless of the speeds of its peripheral devices. The data station is completely modular, permitting flexible

systems arrangements which involve several input and output devices. When it is not being used for actual on-line transmission, the data station can be used off-line for such activities as data preparation and editing.

data switching center—A location where an incoming message is automatically or manually directed to one or more outgoing circuits, according to the intelligence contained in the message.

data terminal—A group of devices with purposes of encoding, modulating, demodulating, decoding, etc., data between input/output devices, data transmission lines, networks or computer units or systems.

data, transaction—A set of data such as job number, quantity, price, etc., in a data processing area; a record of occurrence of a new event or transaction, in which the incidence of the data is essentially random and unpredictable. Hours worked, quantities shipped, and amounts invoiced are examples from, respectively, the areas of payroll, accounts receivable, and accounts payable.

data transcription—A standard process for copying information from one type of data transcribing media to a dissimilar type. Example: from magnetic tape to punched cards.

data transmission terminal installation—Installation composed of data-terminal equipment, signal-conversion equipment, and any intermediate equipment. Note: In some instances, the data-terminal equipment may be connected directly to a data-processing machine or may be a part of it.

data unit—A set of one or more related characters treated as a whole. Often used in place of fields to specify a particular unit of information.

data word—1. A word which may be primarily regarded as part of the information manipulated by a given program. A data word may be used to modify a program instruction, or may be arithmetically combined with other data words. 2. A data word often consists of 36 bits (or six 6-bit characters). Data is transferred on a word basis, 36 bits in parallel (some computers).

datum—Signifies a single computer word or unit of information.

DC1, DC2, DC3. . .etc.—Abbreviations for Device Control characters.

debug—1. To locate and correct any errors in a computer program. 2. To detect and correct malfunctions in the computer itself (related to diagnostic routine). 3. To test a program on a computer to discover if it works properly. If mistakes are revealed, they must be traced to their source and corrected.

debugging aids, reference—A set of routines providing a means of using the computer to assist the programmer in debugging his programs. Among the routines included are the following: (a) changed-word post mortem, a routine to compare the contents of program or data areas with a selected image area; (b) address reference search, a routine to detect all words in the computer memory which reference a particular address; (c) dump selected memory area, a routine to provide the contents of all locations within a specified memory area.

decimal notation—A number, usually of more than one figure, representing a sum, where the quantity represented by each figure is based on the radix of ten. The figures used are 0, 1, 2, 3, 4, 5, 6, 7, 8, and 9.

decision—1. Most often concerns a comparison to determine a verification concerning the existence or nonexistence of a given condition as a result of developing an alternative action. 2. The computer operation of determining if a certain relationship exists between words in storage or registers, and taking alternative courses of action. This is effected by conditional jumps or equivalent techniques. Use of this term has given rise to the misnomer "magic brain"; actually, the process consists of making comparisons, by use of arithmetic, to determine the relationship of two terms, e.g., equal, greater than, or less than.

decision elements, gates—A circuit having two or more inputs and one output. The output depends upon the combination of logic signals at the input.

decision table—1. Specifically developed and organized tabular representations of relationships between variables and parameters; sets of conditions, and ordering of actions or related sequences which make up sets of rules. 2. A tabulation or array of possible courses of action, selections, or alternatives which can be possible and thus considered in the analysis of various problems, i.e., a graphic aid to problem description, flow, and potential results, such as the purpose of a flow chart.

deck—A collection of cards, commonly a complete set of cards that have been punched for a definite service or purpose.

decode—1. To apply a code so as to reverse some previous encoding. 2. To determine the meaning of individual characters or groups of characters in a message. 3. To determine the meaning of an instruction from the set of pulses describing the instruction, command, or operation to be performed. 4. To translate coded characters to a more understandable form.

decryption—A procedure for the interpretation or deciphering of coded data.

degradation testing—Measurement of performance of a system at the extreme operating limits. Tests are performed to determine the gradual changes in performance characteristics.

delay—1. The length of time after the close of a reporting period before information pertaining to that period becomes available. Delay may also cover the time needed to process data, and to prepare and distribute reports. 2. The retardation of the flow of information in a channel for a definite period of time.

delay-line, magnetostrictive—One which utilizes the magnetostrictive property of materials. Magnetostriction is a property of materials causing them to change in length when they are magnetized.

delete character—A distinct operational character designed to be used to obliterate erroneous or undesired characters.

deleted representation—Similar to an erase character, i.e., a particular representation to which any other representation can be converted by almost any type of further operation or recording. In paper tape, which does not lend itself to erasure or deletions, deleted representation consists of a code hole in all of the code positions. Often called null representation. In graphics, the absence of information can be deleted representation.

demarcation strip—Usually a terminal board acting as a physical interface between the business machine and the common carrier. See interface.

density, storage—The amount of char-

acters stored per unit length or area of storage medium (for example, number of characters per inch of magnetic tape).

descending sort—A sort in which the final sequence of records is such that the successive keys compare "less than" or "equal to."

descriptor—1. A significant word which helps to classify the components of a document. 2. An elementary term, word, or simple phrase used to identify a subject, concept, or idea.

design, logic—The working relations specification between the parts of a system in terms of symbolic logic and without primary regard for its hardware implementation.

design, objective—The planned or projected performance goal or expectation based on or chosen prior to the developed operations. The technical estimates of performance requirements but awaiting confirmation, i.e., standards designed to be met.

design, systems—1. One which formulates and graphically describes the nature and content of input, files, procedures, and output in order to display the necessary connection processes and procedures. 2. The specification or design of the working relations between all the parts of a system in terms of their characteristic actions.

destructive read—The sensing of data using a process which inherently destroys (erases) the record of the data which has been read. In some core storage, reading is destructive, but such data is usually regenerated after each readout. In tapes, drums, disks, etc., reading is most often accomplished without destruction.

destructive readout—The act of retrieving information which is stored in memory by using a process which erases the contents of the cells whose contents are read out. Contrasted with a nondestructive readout in which the contents in memory are not erased.

detail card—A punched card which contains data which is a part of a total, i.e., an individual transaction card.

detail record—The distinct listing of data which is a unit part of a major classification of larger segments or a total classification of data.

device independence—The characteristic or capability of various devices, usually input/output units, to be addressed and operated independently and as disassociated with the characteristics of various associated devices within or outside a computing system.

Dewey decimal system—A classification system, developed by Mevil Dewey, to indicate the arrangement of books.

diagnostic—Concerns the detection, discovery, and further isolation of a malfunction or a mistake.

diagnostic check—A specific routine which is designed to locate a malfunction in a computer.

diagnostic function test (DFT)—A program to test overall system reliability.

diagnostics, system—A program resembling the operational program, rather than a systematic logical pattern program, which will detect overall system malfunctions rather than isolate or locate faulty components.

diagram—1. A schematic representation of a sequence of subroutines used to solve a problem. 2. A coarser and less symbolic representation than a flow chart, frequently including descriptions in English words. 3. A schematic or logical drawing showing the electrical circuit or logical

arrangements within a component.

diagram, run—A graphic representation of the files, transactions, information and data that are to be handled together under the program control to produce the newly updated files, list changes, or specific reports.

di-cap storage—A device that can hold data in the form of an array of charged capacitors, or condensers, and use diodes for controlling information flow.

dichotomy—A division into subordinate classes, i.e., all white and all nonwhite, or all zero and all nonzero.

dictionary, relocation (RLD)—1. The part of an object program that identifies all of the addresses of a program which must be changed when the program is to be relocated. 2. Part of a load module containing directions which enable a fetch program to properly initialize all relocatable address constants within the text section (TXT), by accounting for the actual starting address of the load module in storage and the incremental difference between the desired address and the initial address of the module.

differential—Either of a pair of symbols dy,dx associated with the functional relationship $y = f(x)$ in such a way that $dy/dx = f'(x)$ or $dy = f'(x)dx$. Therefore, it appears that when dy/dx is used as the notation for a derivative it may be treated as a fraction. While this gives consistent results in some circumstances, it is in general not true.

differential equation—An equation containing derivatives or differentials of an unknown function, i.e., the solution satisfies the equation identically throughout some interval of x. The general solution represents the set of functions that satisfy the equation. Related to

60

physical problems, the arbitrary constants are determined from additional conditions which must be satisfied. Most differential equations result from mathematical relations and descriptions of motion and change.

digital adder—A unit which can develop the representation of the sum of two or more numbers represented by signals applied to its inputs.

digital divider—A unit which can generate a quotient and a remainder from the representation of two numbers. (Compare with divider, analog.)

digital recording—As related to magnetic tape, a method of recording in which the information is first coded in a digital form. Most commonly, a binary code is used and recording takes place in terms of two discrete values of residual flux. In non-return-to-zero (NRZ) recording, the two values correspond to saturating the tape in opposite directions. In return-to-zero (RZ) recording, the tape is either saturated in one direction or is in a neutral or biased state. The most frequently used method is a form on non-return-to-zero recording in which a change in flux polarity represents a "one" and the absence of a change in flux during a bit interval indicates a "zero."

digital sort—An ordering or sorting first according to the least significant, followed by a resort on each next higher order digit until the items are completely sorted, most often used in punched card sorting.

digit, hexadecimal—A digit that is a member of the set of sixteen digits: 0 through 9 and then A, B, C, D, E, or F used in a numerical notation system using a radix of 16. Some systems use letters other than A-F for digits 10-15.

digit, least significant—The significant digit contributing the smallest quantity to the value of a numeral.

digit, most significant (MSD)—The leftmost nonzero digit, or the one which contributes the largest quantity to the value of a numeral.

digit, octal—A digit which is a member of the 8 digits of the octal system which consists of numerals 0 through 7, in a positional notation system with a radix of 8.

digit operation, serial—The one which can handle digits one following another regardless as to whether the bits can be handled in serial or parallel fashion.

digit punch—Relating to punched cards, a punch in any of the rows representing 0 through 9; the 0 punch also functions as a zone punch in alphabetic representation. Similar punches in paper or plastic tapes relate to other codes.

digit, significant—Designed to contribute to the precision of an accurate numeral. The number of significant digits is counted beginning with the digit contributing the most value, called the most significant digit, and ending with the one contributing the least value, called the least significant digit.

diminished-radix complement—A complement on $N-1$, obtained by subtracting each digit of the given quantity from $N-1$; e.g., the ones complement of binary 11010 is 00101; the nines complement of decimal 456 is 543.

diode—1. A device utilized to permit current flow in one direction in a circuit, and to inhibit current flow in the other direction. In computers, these diodes are primarily germanium or silicon crystals. 2. A vacuum tube with two active electrodes.

direct access—The ability to read or write information at any location within a storage device in a constant amount of time. Every site available for data storage on a direct access device is identified by its own unique numeric address.

direct access device—Same as a random access device or unit as differentiated from a serial access memory unit.

direct address—An address which indicates the location where the referenced operand is to be found or stored, with no reference to an index register or B-box (synonymous with first-level address).

direct code—A specific code that designates the use of actual computer command and address configurations.

direct control—When one unit of peripheral equipment is under control of another unit without human intervention, the controlling unit is then on-line to the second unit which is under direct control of the first. If human intervention is necessary the controlling unit is said to be off-line to the second, but the controlling unit has indirect control over the second unit while an operator acts as the link in the control sequence.

direct digital control—Control action in which control is obtained by a digital device which established the signal to the final control element.

director—Equipment in common-carrier telegraph message switching systems, used for making cross-office selection and connection from an input line to an output line equipment in accordance with addresses in the message.

direct output—Printed, visual, or communicated data which results from on-line output or output equipment, i.e., the final output is produced by equipment directly connected to the computer and directly under computer control as contrasted to printouts from generated tapes, etc., which are processed from stored equipment or off-line.

disabled interrupt—Most interrupts can be armed or disarmed. A specific armed interrrupt accepts and holds the interruption signal. A disarmed interrupt ignores the signal. An armed interrupt may be enabled or disabled. An interrupt signal for an enabled condition causes certain hardware processing to occur. A disabled interrupt is held waiting for enablement.

disaster dump—A dump or printout which occurs as a result of a nonrecoverable program error.

disc—A magnetic storage type in which the magnetic medium is on the surface of one or more rotating discs, the most modern of which are portable.

disk—A circular metal plate with magnetic material on both sides, continuously rotated for reading or writing by means of one or more read-write heads mounted on movable or fixed arms. Disks may be permanently mounted on a shaft, or as a package. They may be removable and others may be placed on the shaft.

disk file optimizer—Used to speed transfers between high-speed head-per-track disk files and the central system, the Burrough 6500 computer uses a block-multiplexing type system allowing blocks containing many bytes to be interleaved in the same way bytes are interleaved in a byte multiplexed system. A hardware device compares entries into a disk access request queue which shaft position registers, and the smallest difference is selected for the next access.

disk files—A type of storage medium consisting of numbers or disks which rotate;

each disk has a special coating for retaining stored information.

disk, magnetic—A distinct storage device on which information is recorded on the magnetized surface of a rotating disk. A magnetic-disk storage system is an array of such devices, with associated reading and writing heads that are mounted on movable arms. (Related to disk storage.)

disk operating system (DOS)—A more powerful twin of TOS, this is a versatile operating system for IBM System 360 installations having direct-access storage devices. This operating system supports almost every peripheral device available for System 360.

disk pack—A set of magnetic disks which have been designed so they can be placed in a processing device for reading and writing. Their design permits them to be interchanged with other disk packs.

disk storage—A type of storage in which information is recorded and stored on tracks of magnetic materials on rotating disks and read by magnetic heads.

display—Visible representation of data on a console screen in a printed report, graph or drawing which is subject to alteration by a light pen or "stylus."

display center—That selected position on a display screen for duplicating data or information to an advantage.

display console, CLT lines—Consoles often contain as standard equipment, a visual-display (cathode-ray tube) console to enhance operator-system communications. The advantages of a visual display to the operator are obvious and the possible display functions endless. The executive system will include a display of information from the run statement, operator requests associated with I/O interventions (printer interlocks, etc.)

and manually initiated CLT lines. The operator will have the option to request alternate information, such as backlog status. In the event that the available display area becomes filled up, the executive will defer lower-priority displays and compact or summarize displays.

display control—This unit permits up to eight display units to operate in an economical time sharing configuration. It has a keyboard which makes possible interpretive operations. Its function for a particular job is assigned by the computer program and the keys for that job are identified by removable illuminated overlays (IBM).

display CRT—This plots data point by point on a 16-inch cathode-ray tube in a raster 9-3/8 inches square having 1024 points on a side, and separate variables 10-bit X and Y coordinates. Includes program intensity control. Plotting rate is 35 microseconds per point. (DEC)

display station—Used to display alphameric information in a low-cost, efficient, and simple-to-use visual input/output system. It provides rapid man-machine communication by direct cable connection to the computer via a display control, or by remote transmission over telephone lines.

divider, analog—Composed of two input variables and one output variable which is proportional to the quotient of the input variables provided that all the variables are within the operating range of the unit. An analog multiplier unit can be used in the feedback path of an operational amplifier to perform division. These two units combined become an analog divider.

division—The parts into which a COBOL

63

program is organized. Identification division provides information to identify the source and object programs. Environment division specifies the equipment to use for translating and running a program. Data division contains entries to define the nature of the data to be processed. Procedure division consists of the processor program to be run with data.

documentation–1. The process of collecting, organizing, storing, citing and dispensing of documents or the information recorded in the documents. 2. The group of techniques necessary for the orderly presentation, organization, and communication of recorded specialized knowledge for maintaining a complete record of reasons for changes in variables. Documentation is necessary not so much to give maximum utility as it is to give an unquestionable historical-reference record.

document card–A card form used to prepare a document.

document, source–That document initially used by a data processing system and which supplies the basic data to be input to the data processing system. Many resulting errors are attributed to errors in the source document.

document transportation–The phase in the reading process in character recognition, which makes the effective delinery of the source document to the read station.

domain–The set associated with the variable is the domain. A set could be all real numbers, for example. The set on which the function is defined is the domain of the function.

dot printer–A type of stylus printer, i.e., the character being formed from a matrix

of points, as produced by the styli.

dot speed–Relates to telegraphic transmission speeds as measured in dot cycles per second.

double precision–Pertaining to a quantity having twice as many digits as are normally carried; i.e., a double precision number requires two machine words in a fixed-word machine.

double-precision arithmetic–Arithmetic used when more accuracy is necessary than a single word of computer storage will provide. Two computer words are used to represent one number.

double-precision operation–A specific type of operation in which two registers are considered as a 64-bit doubleword register containing a single quantity.

double punch–A term usually referring to more than one numeric punch in any one column of a Hollerith card.

doubleword command–A doubleword that contains detailed information concerning a portion of an input/output operation.

drive, tape–The mechanism that is designed to move magnetic or paper tape past sensing and recording heads and is usually associated with data processing equipment (synonymous to tape transport and tape feed, and related to tape unit, magnetic-tape unit, and paper tape unit).

drum, magnetic–A rapidly rotating cylinder, the surface of which is coated with a magnetic material on which information may be stored in the form of small polarized spots.

drum printer–A printing device consisting of a drum embossed with alphabetic and numeric characters. As the drum rotates, a hammer strikes the paper from behind at a time when the desired character(s) on the drum passes the line to be printed. The process continues until the line is finished.

drum storage—A random-access medium-sized storage device which can hold four million alpha-numeric characters or up to eight million digits, which can be retrieved at a rate of 1.2 million characters a second. Many units providing on-line storage for millions of alpha-numeric characters, can be linked to a processor.

(DSL) date-set label—A generic term covering DSCB's used for direct-access devices and the data-set labels used on sequential access devices.

DTR—An abbreviation for Distribution Tape Reel.

dual storage—These storage devices permit storage of logic of a particular programmer's own design as well as specific instructions and data, i.e., the programmer's instruction code is utilized to write a program of instructions.

dump—1. To accidentally or intentionally withdraw all power from a computer. 2. To record the contents of internal storage at a given instant of time, usually as an aid in detecting program mistakes or errors. 3. To print out or punch out a portion or all of the contents of the computer memory. 4. To transfer all or a part of the contents of one section of computer memory into another section of memory, or to some output device. Types: core, memory, programmed, reserve, and storage.

dump, memory—The procedure that lists the contents of a storage device, area, or selected parts of it. See: storage dumping.

dump, rescue—To record on magnetic tape the entire contents of the memory, which includes the status of the computer system at the time the dump is made. R dumps are made so that in the event of power failure, etc., a run can be resumed from the last rescue point (R point) rather than rerunning the entire program. (NCR)

duodecimal number system—1. A number system which uses the equivalent of the decimal number 12 as a base. 2. Preparing the number representation system with a radix of twelve. 3. Pertaining to a characteristic or property involving a selection, choice, or condition in which there are twelve possibilities.

duo purpose card—An Hollerith card containing information recorded on the card as well as the punched equivalent of such data. Such a card often serves as a source document for punching and is contrasted with a transcript card.

duplex computer—A pair of usually identical computers operating so that if and when one is shut down for maintenance, improvements, checkouts, etc., the other can operate without a reduction in capability of the total system. Use of each computer might alternate, to thus provide time for preventive maintenance, or one might run relatively low priority problems, or act as a slave to the other.

duplex system—Two computers used in special configuration, one is on-line while the other is standing by ready to be used if a malfunction of the on-line computer occurs. The stand-by computer is often used to complete off-line functions.

duplicating card punch—A unit which has an automatic-feed punch and which has in its card track a sensing station which each punched card passes after being punched. At the same time the following card is passing under the punch knives and the sensing station causes common data to be duplicated from each card to the following one.

dyadic operation—An operation performed on two operands.

dynamic—Pertaining to a quantity which is affected by time, energy or power, and therefore indicates a relatively transient or unstable condition.

dynamic accuracy—Accuracy determined with a time-varying output.

dynamic analysis—The study of control system performance with disturbance inputs affecting the controlled variable or in conditions which affect that variable.

dynamic error—The error or part of an error related to frequency such as the inadequate dynamic response of some computing device or unit. Similar to drift error.

dynamic memory—The storage of data on a device or in a manner which permits the data to move or vary with time, and thus the data is not always instantly available for recovery; i.e., acoustic delay line, magnetic drum, or circulating or recirculating of information in a medium.

dynamic program relocation—The moving of a partially executed program to a different location in main memory without detrimentally affecting its ability to finish its normal processing.

dynamic storage—1. Refers to mobility of stored data in time and space. Acoustic delay lines, in which stored data are constantly in motion relative to a storage medium and require continuous regeneration, are an example of a dynamic storage device. Magnetic-core storage, in which stored data are fixed in time and space, is an example of a static-stored device. 2. The storage of data on a device or in a manner that permits the data to move or vary with time, and thus the data is not always available instantly for recovery.

* — * — *

edge—Usually refers to a document reference edge or a stroke edge.

edit—To rearrange data or information. Editing may involve the deletion of unwanted data, the selection of pertinent data, the application of format techniques, the insertion of symbols such as page numbers and typewriter characters, the application of standard processes such as zero suppression, and the testing of data for reasonableness and proper range. Editing may sometimes be distinguished between input edit (arrangement of source data) and output edit (preparation of table formats).

editor program—Provides a means for manipulating the text of a named file on a micro tape or in the user area of the drum (corresponding to micro tape). This file may be used for the creation of text or for later use as data or as a program to be translated by the FORTRAN compiler, etc. The commands provided for the editor allows text to be created, deleted, or moved about.

editor, tape—A program used to edit, correct, and update symbolic program tapes using the computer and the teletype unit. With the editor in the core memory, the user reads in portions of his symbolic tape, removes, changes, or adds instructions or operands, and gets back a corrected symbolic tape. The user can work through the program instruction by instruction, spot-check it, or concentrate on new sections.

EDP system—An electronic data processing system is the aggregation of men, machines, and methods to perform data processing operations with a minimum of manual help.

education, simulation—The process which subjects the man to a complex environment similar to one in which he may wish to operate so that he may gain a feel of its dynamic behavior. Example: management games.

effective address—1. A modified address. 2. The address actually considered to be used in a particular execution of a computer instruction. 3. An address obtained by the combination of the contents of a specific index register with the address of an instruction. 4. The address used for the execution of an instruction. This may differ from that of the instruction in storage.

effective byte location—The actual storage location pointed to by the effective virtual address of a byte addressing instruction.

electronic data processing (EDP)—Data processing by way of electronic equipment, such as an internally stored program, electronic digital computer, or an automatic data processing machine.

electronic data-processing system—1. A machine system capable of receiving, storing, operating on, and recording data without the intermediate use of tabulating cards, and which also posesses the ability to store internally at least some instructions for data processing operations, and the means for locating and controlling access to data stored internally. 2. The general term used to define a system for data processing by means of machines utilizing electronic circuitry at electronic speed, as opposed to electromechanical equipment.

electrostatic printer—A device for printing an optical image on paper, in which dark and light areas of the original are represented by electrostatically charged and uncharged areas on the paper. The paper is dusted with particles of finely powdered dry ink and the particles adhere only to the electrically charged areas. The paper with ink particles is then heated, causing the ink to melt and become permanently fixed to the paper.

embossment—1. Usually a designed, engraved, or "raised up" deformation of the surface of a document. 2. As related to optical character recognition, the distance between the nondeformed part of a document surface and a specified point on a printed character.

emitter—A device, usually used on punched-card machines, to give timed pulses at regular intervals during the machine cycle.

empirical—The essence of scientific method, i.e., verifiable documentation from observations, experiments, evidence of a past recorded experience — without the use of theory or deduction.

emulation—A technique using software or microprogramming in which one computer is made to behave exactly like another computer.

emulsion-laser storage—A digital data storage medium which uses a controlled laser beam to expose very small areas on a photosensitive surface.

enabled—The condition of an interrupt level wherein the level is not inhibited from advancing from the waiting state to the active state, except for priority considerations.

encipher—Same as encode, i.e., the preparation of a routine in machine language often using several outputs from one input.

encode—1. To apply a code, frequently one consisting of binary numbers, to represent individual characters or groups of characters in a message (synonymous with encipher). 2. To substitute letters, numbers, or characters, usually to intentionally hide the meaning of the message except to certain individuals who know the enciphering scheme (synonymous with encipher).

end-around carry—The bit carried over from the high-order to the low-order position.

end-of-file—1. Automatic procedures to handle tapes when the end of an input or output tape is reached. A reflective spot, called a record mark, is placed on the physical end of the tape to signal the end. 2. Termination or point of completion of a quantity of data. End of file marks are used to indicate this point (synonymous with EOF).

end-of-medium character—A control character specifically designed to indicate either the physical end of the data medium or the end of the portion of the data medium upon which desired data is recorded.

end-of-text character—A data communications character designed to indicate the end of the text being transmitted.

end of transmission (EOT)—That particular character or sequence of characters which indicates termination of the sending process.

endorser—A particular feature now almost standard on most magnetic-ink character readers (MICRs) which is an endorsement record of each bank after the document has been read.

ENQ—An abbreviation for Enquiry Character.

entry—1. An input received from a terminal device. On receipt, an entry is placed by a control program in an entry block whose address is inserted in a list of entries awaiting processing. 2. A notation written in a stub of a row or in a cell of a decision table. Any row must be in the form of either a limited entry or an extended entry. 3. A statement in a programming system. In general each entry is written on one line of a coding form and punched on one card, although some systems permit a single entry to overflow several cards. 4. A member of a list.

environment—The elements and/or factors influencing or affecting the design and operation of a device or system.

equalizer—A modem or peripheral device designed to compensate for undesired levels of signal strength.

equipment—Types: auxiliary, off-line, on-line, peripheral, and tabulating.

equipment compatibility—That characteristic which allows one computer to accept and process data prepared by another computer without conversion or code modification.

equivalence—A logical operator having the property that if P is a statement, Q is a statement, R is a statement, then the equivalent of P, Q, R, is true if and only if all statements are true or all statements are false, they are otherwise false.

error—1. The general term referring to any deviation of a computed or a measured quantity from the theoretically correct or true value. 2. The part of the error due to a particular identifiable cause, e.g., a truncation error, or a rounding error. In a restricted sense, that deviation due to unavoidable random disturbances, or to the use of finite approximations to what is defined by an infinite series. (Contrasted with mistake.) 3. The amount that the computer or measured quantity differs from the theoretically correct or true value. 4. The amount of loss of precision in a quantity; the difference between an accurate quantity and its calculated approximation; errors occur in numerical methods; mistakes occur in programming, coding, data transcription, and operating; malfunctions occur in computers and are due to physical limitations on the properties of materials; the differential margin by which a controlled unit deviates from its target value.

error correction, programmer—When an error is detected from the results of a program, the programmer may initiate a print-out which traces step-by-step, or at a certain convenient interval, the operation of the program on actual data, or he may cause a program "dump" for analysis and correction.

error-detecting and feedback system—A system employing an error-detecting code and so arranged that a signal detected as being in error automatically initiates a request for retransmission of the correct signal.

error diagnostics, time sharing—In a remote system, it is highly desirable that a user's actions be closely monitored by the system, with errors in procedure or entry called to the user's attention as soon after commission as possible. The error message sent to an offending user should be provided whenever possible. Most systems developed to date have been delinquent in the error detection and diagnostic portions of system components.

error, loading—One found in the output of the computer which came about as a result of a change in value of the load which was supplied.

error, machine—Occurs when a deviation from correctness occurs in data due to an equipment failure.

error messages—Messages developed by a program to designate a variety of error types.

error, truncation—1. A specific error which results from the use of only a finite number of terms of an infinite series. 2. The approximation of operations in the infinite-serial calculus by a calculus of finite differences.

escape—The departure from one code or language to another code or language, i.e., the withdrawal from existing patterns.

ETB—An abbreviation for End of Transmission Block Character.

exchange—To interchange the contents of two storage devices or locations.

exchange, memory—1. The switching of the total contents of two storage devices or locations, such as, two registers. 2. A switching device capable of controlling and handling the flow or exchange of data between storage units or other data storage elements of a system.

Exchange-Oriented Memory—In the Burroughs B7700, an "exchange-oriented" system, any of up to 16 memory sections are available to up to 8 processing units; i.e., arithmetic or input/output processing. From some slower peripherals byte multiplexing is used to use single bytes or small groups of bytes, from a number of devices onto a single channel connected to a central system. Such bytes are dropped into preset time slots, and the system polls the peripheral devices attached to the channels in sequence to determine which is ready to transmit a byte.

EXEC—An abbreviation for Execute Statement.

execution instruction—The set of elementary steps carried out by the computer to produce the result specified by the operation code of the instruction.

execution time—1. The sum total of the amount of time required to complete a given command. 2. The portion of an instruction cycle during which the actual work is performed or operation executed; i.e., the time required to decode and perform an instruction (synonymous with instruction time).

executive—1. A routine that controls loading and relocation of routines and in some cases makes use of instructions which are unknown to the general programmer. Effectively, an executive routine is part of the machine itself (synonymous with monitor routine, supervisory routine, and supervisory program). 2. A set of coded instructions designed to process and control other sets of coded instructions. 3. A set of coded instructions used in realizing automatic coding. 4. A master set of coded instructions.

executive control system—Primary control of the executive system is by control information fed to the system by one or more input devices which may be either on-line or at various remote sites. The control information is similar in nature to present control-card operations, but allows additional flexibility and standardization.

executive instruction—Similar to supervisory instruction, this instruction is designed and used to control the operation or execution of other routines or programs.

executive system—1. An integrated collection of service routines for supervising the sequencing of programs by a computer. Operating systems may perform debugging, input-output, accounting, compilation, and storage-assignment tasks (synonymous with monitor system). 2. A fully integrated system that provides for concurrent operation of multiple programs, plus input-output, plus real-time control of a complete, on-demand computer network. The executive system also provides for automatic logging, simultaneously establishing an automatic and economical computer-accounting system and simplifying its maintenance.

executive system routine—A routine that automatically accomplishes the execution of program runs in compliance with a predetermined computer schedule. In this capacity, the executive routine extracts the programs that are to be executed, positions them in their operating locations, assigns input/output peripheral equipment, provides for the time sharing of several programs running concurrently, and provides special checking features for the job programs.

executive system utilities—Included within the utilities section of the executive system are diagnostic routines, program file manipulation routines, file utility routines, and cooperative routines for aiding the user in performing such functions as reading cards, printing line images on a printer, transferring files from device to device, and carrying out housekeeping functions required for file-residence on mass-storage devices.

exit—1. The time or place at which the control sequence ends or transfer out of a particular program or subroutine. 2. A way of momentarily interrupting or leaving a repeated cycle of operations in a program.

exit point—The instruction which transfers control from the main routine to the subroutine.

expected values—Basically, the summation of the products of all possible outcomes after each is multiplied by the probability that it will occur, and tables constructed to indicate these values.

expression—1. A valid series of constants, variables, and functions that may be connected by operation symbols and punctuated, if required, to cause a desired computation. 2. Any symbol representing a variable or a group of symbols representing a group of variables possibly combined by symbols representing operations in accordance with a set of definitions and rules.

external device code—In some systems most external devices are connected to the processor by a common cable that carries an external device address code and a code which specifies what operation is to be performed. Only that device whose address is on the lines will respond to an instruction on the common cable. No instruction will be initiated unless it is accompanied by a start signal. When a device recognizes its address and receives a start signal, it will start the essential information from the operation code in flip-flops and initiate the specified operation.

external device operation code—Relates to various bits of the EDCW (external device control word) which is the operation code that is sent to the external device to specify what operation is to be performed. The operation code is interpreted by the particular device that is addressed. The same operation code may have different meanings to different devices.

external error—Occurs if a file mark is read or an end-of-tape is sensed during a loading operation.

external labels—Relates to labels that are normally defined in the same program in which they are used as operands. However, it is possible to define a symbol in one program, use it in a program assembled independently of the first program, and then execute both programs together.

external reference—Usually concerns a distinct reference to a single variable from a range, or an item which is not defined in the particular program, segment, or subroutine. A linkage editor or a linking loader usually integrates various independently written routines which are united before execution. The assembler must be informed that an external symbol is being used to avoid an error condition.

external registers—Concerns registers, which are designed to be referenced by the program, and located in control storage as specific addresses. These are the locations (registers) which the programmer references when he desires that some sort of computational function be carried out.

external sort—Usually considered to be the second phase of a multipass sort program, wherein strings of data are continually merged until one string of sequenced data is formed.

extract instruction—An instruction that requests the formation of a new expression from selected parts of given expressions.

extrapolate—As regards curve characteristics, to extend a curve beyond the limits of known points by continuing the trend established over known points. As regards to statistical analysis, the extension of time-based data into future time-periods following trends, averages, or other measurements.

* _ * _ *

facility—Anything used or available for use in furnishing communication service. Commonly a general term for communication paths.

fading—Relates to the variation of radio-field intensity caused by changes in the transmission medium.

false add—This is addition without carries; the performance of a logic add.

false code—A character or combination of bits which is not accepted as a valid representation by the machine design or by a specific routine. False codes are commonly detected and used as an indication of machine malfunction.

fault—A physical condition that causes a device, a component, or element to fail to perform in a required manner, e.g., a short circuit, a broken wire, an intermittent connection.

feasibility study—1. Usually the initial procedures and criteria for determination of suitability, capability, and compatibility of computer systems to various firms or organizations. A preliminary systems analysis of potential costs savings from a higher level of operations and decision-making; problem-solving capacity as a result of computer procurement. 2. A study in which a projection of how a proposed system might operate in a particular organization is made to provide the basis for a decision to change the existing system.

feasible solution—A determined solution to the constraint equations in which all variables satisfy their sign restrictions.

feedback—The use of parts or all of the output of a machine, process, or system, as input for another phase, as when used for a self-correcting purpose. Such feedback systems or programs use the process of continual comparisons of output with input to make necessary corrections. The feedback system is considered self-correcting if it is a closed loop.

feedback control—A type of system control obtained when a portion of the output signal is fed back to the input in order to obtain a planned or desired branching effect.

feeding—A system used by character readers in character recognition, in which each individual input document is issued to the document transport at a predetermined and constant rate.

feeding, multiread—To feed punched cards in a way causing several fields of a single card to be sensed sequentially at successive revolutions of a card reader main shaft.

fibonacci series—A series of numbers used as part of a Fibonacci search and in which each integer is equal to the sum of the two preceding integers.

field—1. A set of one or more characters (not necessarily all lying on the same word) which is treated as a whole; a set of one or more columns on a punched card consistently used to record similar information. 2. A specified area of a record used for a particular category of data; e.g., a group of card columns used to represent a wage rate, or a set of bit locations in a computer word used to express the address of the operand. 3. The data which is contained in one or more adjacent core positions and which will be treated as a unit. A flag bit is used to designate the high-order position of the field.

field, data—An area located in the computer's main memory which contains a data record.

field, operation—That particular part of the instruction format which specifies the procedure or process which is to be performed.

field, signed—A field consisting of a plus or minus character coding over the unit's position to designate the algebraic sign of the entire number.

field, variable length—A data field that may have a variable number of characters. This requires item separators to indicate the end of each item.

file—1. A collection of related records treated as a unit; e.g., in inventory control, one line of an invoice forms an item, a complete invoice forms a record, and the complete set of such records forms a file. 2. The word file is used in the general sense to mean any collection of informational items similar to one another in purpose, form, and content. Thus, a magnetic-tape master file is a file. The term may also be applied to a punched-paper tape of input items, or if convenient, to a set of cards which is equivalent in nature to a magnetic or a paper tape. File may even be applied to an accumulation of information in the processor memory if the need arises to refer in a general way to this collection of data. Types: inactive mass storage, master, sequential, source, and transaction.

file addressing, disk—The operation which locates information on a random-access file.

file, dead—A file which is not in current use but which is retained.

file, follow-up—A file in which special matters are flagged for attention at the appropriate time.

file, logical—A data set that is composed of one or more logical records.

file-oriented programming—When I/O coding is simplified with the general file and record control program, programming is file-oriented rather than device-oriented. Information is requested in device-independent fashion.

file-oriented system—When reference to file storage is the principle or key basis of a system, it is considered to be file-oriented. Auxiliary storage used as fundamental or essential in many commercial systems might be file-oriented, while generally considered incidental in scientific systems.

file, program—A flexible, easily updated reference system designed for the maintenance of the entire software library.

file security—The relative privacy or inaccessibility of one's files from unauthorized users. As computers are used more and more frequently in the future as depositories of many kinds of information, file security will become an important legal issue.

file storage—Concerns a specific purpose type of storage designed to contain a master file, usually relatively large and uniformly accessible.

file, transaction—An applications file containing current information related to a data processing activity, and used to update a master file.

file, working data—Specific aggregations of data sets for definite usage. The file may contain one or more different data

73

sets. A permanent data file is one in which the data is perpetually subject to being updated; e.g., a name and address file. A working data file is a temporary accumulation of data sets which is destroyed (erased) after the data has been transferred to another form.

filler—In order to make some data processing items standard, such as a record, some portion of that item, called a filler, is used. Thus the standard size is achieved and the filler is not an essential part of the data involved.

filmorex system—A system, devised by Jacques Samain, for the electronic selection of microfilm cards. Each card has a microreproduction of the document or abstract and a field of twenty 5-digit code numbers giving the bibliographic reference and the subjects treated.

filter—1. A pattern of characters that is used to control the selection or elimination of portions of another pattern of characters. 2. A device or program that separates data, signal, or material in accordance with special criteria. 3. A machine word that specifies which parts of another machine word are to be operated on. Also called extractor or mask.

firmware—Software that is stored in a fixed (wired-in) or "firm" way, usually in a read-only memory. Changes can often only be made by exchanging the memory for an alternative unit.

first-level address—Same as direct address.

five-level code—A telegraph code that is designed to utilize five impulses for describing a character. Start and stop elements may be added for asynchronous transmission. A common five-level code is Baudot.

fixed point—1. A notation or system of arithmetic in which all numerical quantities are expressed by a predetermined number of digits, with the point implicitly located at some predetermined position (contrasted with floating point). 2. A type of calculation with integers only and without any decimal point or decimal portions.

fixed-point mathematics—A method of determining the assumed location of the radix point by placing a symbol at the point or by other rules and or conventions as predetermined.

fixed-point number—A number which is represented in fixed-point form in contrast to floating-point form. Example: FORTRAN variables.

fixed variable—1. Concerns a variable in a problem (logical, structural, primal, or dual) fixed at zero level for feasibility. 2. A variable to be bounded away from zero is sometimes "fixed" at its bound in a bounded variable algorithm so that the transformed variable associated with it is then feasible at zero level, thus permitting arbitrary upper and lower bounds.

flag—1. A bit of information attached to a character or word to indicate the boundary of a field. 2. An indicator used frequently to tell some later part of a program that some condition occurred earlier. 3. An indicator used to identify the members of several intermixed sets (synonymous with sentinel). 4. Any of various types of indicators used for identification, e.g., a wordmark. 5. A character that signals the occurrence of some condition, such as the end of a word. 6. A request for special handling, such as indirect addressing.

flat file—A file containing documents which are filed unfolded in a vertical, horizontal, or slanted position.

flip-flop—An electronic circuit having two stable states, two input lines, and two corresponding output lines such that a signal exists on either one of the output lines if, and only if, the last pulse received by the flip-flop can store one binary digit (bit) of information.

flip-flop storage—A bi-stable storage device which stores binary data as states of flip-flop elements.

floating point—A form of number representation on which quantities are represented by a number multiplied by the number base raised to a power; e.g., the decimal number 397 can be written as 3.97×10^2, or 0.397×10^3.

floating-point arithmetic (operation)—In order to add two floating-point numbers, it is first necessary to equalize the exponents of the numbers. This is accomplished by shifting the mantissa of the smaller expression to the right the number of places that equals the difference of the two exponents. For example, in adding the floating-point decimal numbers 0.3×10^4 and 0.27×10^6, 0.3×10^4 is written as 0.003×10^6 and then the two numbers are added which gives the results of 0.273×10^6.

$$\begin{array}{ccc} .3 \times 10^4 & & .003 \times 10^6 \\ +.27 \times 10^6 & = & +.27 \times 10^6 \\ \hline & & .273 \times 10^6 \end{array}$$

The same procedure is required for subtraction except that the subtrahend is subtracted from the minuend in the final step of the operation.

floating-point mathematics—An automatic method of determining the location of the radix point in values; such math is usually performed by using a signed mantissa times the radix, raised to an integral number, such as the decimal number 62.4 being equivalent to .624 times 10^2.

flowchart—1. A system-analysis tool that provides a graphical presentation of a procedure. Includes block diagrams, routine sequence diagrams, general flow symbols, and so forth. 2. A chart to represent, for a problem, the flow of data, procedures, growth, equipment, methods, documents, machine instructions, etc. 3. A graphical representation of a sequence of operations by using symbols to represent the operations such as compute, substitute, compare, jump, copy, read, write, etc.

flowchart, program—A visual representation of a computer problem in which machine instructions or groups of instructions are designated by symbols.

flow diagram—A chart consisting of various flow diagram symbols such as arrows, rectangular boxes, circles and other symbols used to graphically represent a procedure or pattern of computation and/or processing of the program.

flow diagram, data—Usually refers to a data flowchart.

font reticle—A system of lines forming various character outlines or dimensions in optical character recognition which are placed on the image of an input character and which determines whether that character conforms to the prescribed shape and range of dimensions. Other various outlines on the font reticle check for minimum space between lines and characters and also the maximum size of punctuation marks.

forced coding—Programming in such a way that minimum waiting time is required to obtain information out of storage, especially serial access storage (synonymous with minimum-latency programming).

foreground–A high priority program, process, or system part which is utilized immediately or when and where and as needed, but which still allows less critical or subsidiary programs to be processed in and as background tasks during the time when the priority programs are not being processed in the foreground. This is the basis of multiprogramming or foreground/background processing. Usually the foreground is a smaller, faster processing program which activates interrupts or suspensions of routines in the background processing to perform its tasks and then release the CPU back to the background processing. It is practical on smaller and medium computers for inquiry processing and to use slow peripheral equipment.

format–1. A predetermined arrangement of characters, fields, lines, punctuation, page numbers, etc. 2. A defined arrangement of words, totals, characters, stubs, and headings for a desired clear presentation of data or print-out, such as a profit and loss statement in a record.

FORTRAN–1. A programming system, including a language and a processor (compiler), allowing programs to be written in a mathematical-type language. These programs are subsequently translated by a computer (under control of the processor) into machine language. 2. FORmula TRANslator. A compiler language developed by the IBM Corporation, originally conceived for use on scientific problems but now widely adapted for most commercial problems as well.

FORTRAN language–Programs are written directly as algebraic expressions and arithmetic statements. Various symbols are used to signify equality, addition, subtraction, exponentiation, etc. Additional statements are provided to permit control over how the algebraic expressions and arithmetic statements are to be processed. These include transfer, decision, indexing, and input/output statements.

FORTRAN, real constants–A real constant is written with a decimal point, using the decimal digits 0, 1,...9. A preceding + or − sign is optional. An unsigned real constant is assumed to be positive. An integer exponent preceded by an E may follow a real constant. The exponent may have a preceding + or − sign. An unsigned exponent is assumed to be positive.

FORTRAN, real variables–A real variable consists of a series of not more than six alphanumeric characters (except special characters) of which the first is alphabetic but cannot be one of the integer indicators, i.e., I, J, K, L, M, or N.

forward scan–An editing operation which makes an output word conform to the control word by comparing positions from right to left and adding punctuation, such as decimals and dollar signs.

four address–1. Concerns a specific method of specifying the location of operands and instructions in which the storage location of the two operands and the storage location of the results of the operation are cited, and the storage location of the next instruction to be executed is cited. 2. Having the property that each complete instruction specifies the operation and addresses of four registers.

four-tape sorting–A type of merge sorting in which input data are supplied on two tapes and are sorted into incomplete sequences alternately on two output tapes. The output tapes are used for input on the succeeding pass, resulting in longer and longer sequences after each pass until the data are all in sequence on one output tape.

frame, main—The main part of the computer, i.e., the arithmetic or logic unit. The central processing unit (CPU).

frequency distribution—Usually concerns table showing the number of occurrences of each value displayed in an ordered array or pattern.

frequency, relative—A calculation of the ratio of numbers of observations in a class (subset) to the total number of observations or elements constituting a population, i.e., universal subset.

function—1. A special purpose or characteristic action. 2. The relation or association of one item from a set with each item from another set. 3. A means of referring to a type or sequence of calculations within an arithmetic statement.

functional symbols—A block diagram term representing the functional design, i.e., the practical specification of the working relations between all parts of a system, i.e., considering the logic design and the equipment.

function codes—Codes that appear in tape or on cards to operate machine functions, such as carriage return, space shift, skip, tabulate, etc.

function, control—Designed as an operation to control a device, i.e., the starting or stopping of a carriage, or a font change, rewind, transmission reading. Operation control symbols are not regarded as control operations, however.

function generator—A computing element designed with an output of a specified nonlinear function of its input or inputs.

Normal usage excludes multipliers and resolvers.

function key—A specific key on a keyboard (for example, CR, LF, LTRS, FIGS, etc.) which when operated, causes a receiving device to perform a certain mechanical function so that a message will be received in proper form.

function, objective—The independent variable function whose maximum or minimum is sought in an optimization problem.

* _ * _ *

game theory—A mathematical process, selecting an optimum strategy in the face of an opponent who has a strategy of his own.

Gantt chart—A chart of activity against time; such charts have historically been used to schedule or reserve resources for specific activities. Critical path method (CPM) and project evaluation and review techniques (PERT) are devices which have offered substantial improvement in scheduling and allocations.

gate—A combination logic element having at least one input channel.

gate, NAND—A logical operator having the property that if P is a statement, Q is a statement then the NAND of P.Q.R . . . is true if at least one statement is false, and false if all statements are true.

gates (decision elements)—A circuit having two or more inputs and one output. The output depends upon the combination of logic signals at the input.

generalized sort—A sort program which will accept the introduction of parameters at run time and which does not generate a program.

general program—A program, expressed in computer code, designed to solve a class of problems or specializing on a specific problem when appropriate parametric values are supplied (synonymous with general routine).

general-purpose computer—A computer designed to operate on a program of instruction for the purpose of solving many types of data processing problems rather than being designed to fulfill a single function or type of function. Contrasted with special-purpose computer.

generate—1. To construct a computer program by use of a generator. 2. To develop, or produce various required subroutines from parameters of outline skeleton coding.

generated, sort—A production program which was produced by a sort generator.

generating routine1. Generally concerns a compiling routine that is capable of handling less fully defined situations. 2. A generalized routine, such as a report generator, that accepts specifications and causes the processor to prepare a specific routine.

generation—Under control of parameters supplied to generator routines, a technique for producing a complete routine from one which is in skeleton form.

generation, third—Computers which use microcircuits and miniaturization of components, displaced vacuum tubes, to reduce costs, work faster, and increase reliability. The third generation of computers began in about 1964 and helped to foster the growth of time-sharing. There are "families" of third generation equipment, including IBM System 360, Honeywell's Series 200, NCR Century Series, GE's 400 and 600 lines, and RCA's Spectra 70. First genera-

tion computers used tubes (1954) and were made obsolete by second generation machines (1959-1960) which utilized transistors to increase speed and reliability and to decrease size and maintenance.

generator, random-number—A special machine routine or hardware designed to produce a random number or series of random numbers according to specified limitations.

generator, RPG—Most report program generators provide a convenient programming method for producing a wide variety of reports. These may range from a listing of a card deck or tape reel to a precisely arranged, calculated, and edited tabulation of data from several input sources.

geodetic systems—A computer application system used to reduce the costs of mining and drilling by performing seismographic studies by a computer. Geodesy is the branch of applied mathematics which determines the curvature, shape and dimensions of the earth. Computers are used for advanced geodetic survey work by mining companies to locate oil and ore deposits.

geometric solution—A specific graphic method of solving a linear programming problem, by plotting the half-planes determined by the constraints and the lines of constant value, for the function. Its use is usually restricted to problems with, at most, two structural variables.

get—To develop or make a record from an input file available for use by a routine in control of the machine.

giga—A prefix for one billion, i.e., 10^9, times a specific unit.

grammar—The word order in a communication or a portion of a communication.

graphic documentation—A process designed and developed for recording data on graphs and films.

graphics—The use of diagrams or other graphical means to obtain operating data and answers. The use of written symbols and visual displays.

graphic solution—A solution which is developed and obtained with graphs or other pictorial devices, as contrasted with solutions obtained by the manipulation of numbers.

gray code—1. Positional binary notation for numbers in which any two sequential numbers whose difference is 1 are represented by expressions that are the same except in one place or column, and in that place or column differ by only one unit. 2. A type of cycle unit-distance binary code.

grouping—A mass of data having common characteristics are arranged into related groups.

groupmark (GM)—In telegraphic usage, any indicator designed to signal the end of a word or other unit of data.

group printing—1. The function of a machine which does not print data from every card. Instead it summarizes the data contained in a group of cards and prints only the summarized total. 2. Printing one line of information for a specific group.

group theory—A study, in the mathematical sense, of the rules for combining groups, sets, and elements; i.e., the theory of combining groups.

* _ * _ *

half-adder—A circuit having two output points, S and C, representing sum and carry, and two input points, A and B, representing addend and augend such that the output is related to the input according to the following table:

INPUT		OUTPUT	
A	B	S	C
0	0	0	0
0	1	1	0
1	0	1	0
1	1	0	1

A and B are arbitrary input pulses, and S and C are sum without carry, and carry, respectively. Two half-adders, properly connected, may be used for performing binary addition and form a full serial adder.

half-subtracter—1. A specific logic element which consists of two inputs, a minuend and a subtrahend, and two outputs, the difference digit and the borrow digit, to be used in the digit position of the next higher significance. 2. A unit or device capable of representing the difference between two numbers, usually restricted to permitting the subtrahend to have only one non-zero digit.

half-word—1. A group of characters designed to represent half of a computer word for addressing purposes as a unit in storage. 2. A fixed group of bits which can be handled as a unit by the equipment and which is equivalent to two bytes.

halt instruction—Relates to a machine instruction that stops the execution of the program.

hamming code—One of the error-correction code systems in use today.

handling, interrupt—As an example, when an interrupt occurs, the control program saves the interrupted program's registers and status, and routes control to routines that handle the interrupt cause. When the interrupt is handled, the original program's registers and status are restored, and control is restored so that the original program continues as if no interrupt had taken place.

hard copy—1. Typewritten or printed characters on paper, produced at the same time information is copied or converted into machine language, that is not easily read by a human. 2. A printed copy of machine output in a visually readable form; e.g., printed reports, listings, documents, summaries, etc.

hardware—1. The electric, electronic, and mechanical equipment used for processing data consisting of cabinets, racks tubes, transistors, wires, motors, and such. 2. Any piece of automatic data processing equipment (slang).

hartley—A unit of information content equal to the information content of a message, a priori probability of which is one-tenth. Note: If, in the definition of information content, the logarithm is taken to the base ten, the result will be expressed in hartleys.

hash—1. Considered to be computer or program garbage specifically recorded on tapes to fill or comply with restrictions on conventions of starting procedures, block sizes, and others. 2. Same as garbage.

hash total—1. The development of a summation for purposes of verification of one or more corresponding fields of a file that would usually not be totalled. 2. A control developed from a specific number in each record processed that has no significance other than as a control. 3. A sum of numbers in specified fields of a record or of a batch of records used for checking purposes. No attention is paid to the significance of the total.

Examples of such numbers are customer numbers or part numbers.

header (message heading)—The initial characters of a message designating addressee, routing, time of origination, etc.

hertz—A unit of frequency equal to one cycle per second.

heuristic—1. A procedure or methodology designed to develop a plan or program that will obtain desired results or output as an improvement over current procedures and is satisfactory in relation to the constraints of time, cost, personnel and the limited use of the result. 2. Pertaining to exploratory methods of problem solving in which solutions are discovered by evaluation of the progress made toward the final result (contrast with algorithmic).

heuristic program—1. Usually concerns a set of computer instructions that simulate the behavior of human operators in approaching similar problems. 2. A routine by which the computer attacks a problem not by a direct algorithmic procedure, but by a trial and error approach frequently involving the act of learning.

hexadecimal notation—Notation of numbers in the base 16.

hexadecimal number—A number, usually of more than one figure, representing a sum in which the quantity represented by each figure is based on a radix of sixteen.

hierarchy, memory—A set of memories with differing sizes and speeds and usually having different cost-performance ratios. An hierarchy might consist of a very high-speed, small semiconductor memory, a medium-speed core memory and a large, slow-speed core.

high order—Pertaining to the weight or

significance assigned to the digits of a number; e.g., in the number 123456, the highest order digit is one; the lowest order digit is six. One may refer to the three high-order bits of a binary word as another example.

high punch—The 12, 11 and zero punch are zone punches, the 12 punch being the highest (vertically) on the standard punched card.

high-speed card reader—A reading device capable of being connected to a computer so as to operate on-line without seriously holding up the computer. A card reader reading more than 1,000 cards per minute would be called a high-speed reader. A reader that reads punched paper tape at a rate greater than 500 characters per second could also be called a high-speed reader.

hits—Momentary line disturbances which could result in mutilation of characters being transmitted.

hold instruction—A computer instruction which causes data called from storage to be also retained in storage after it is called out and transferred to its new location.

hold mode—An analog computing term used in the hold mode, also called the freeze or interrupt mode, the computing ac action is stopped and all variables are held at the value they had when the computation was interrupted.

Hollerith—The standard and widely used system of encoding alpha-numeric information onto cards; hence, Hollerith cards is synonymous with punch cards. Such cards were first used in 1890 for the U.S. Census and were named after Herman Hollerith, their originator.

Hollerith code—An alphanumeric punched card code invented by Dr. Herman Hollerith in 1889, in which the top three positions in a column are called "zone" punches (12, 11 and 0, or Y, X and 0, from the top downward), and are combined with the remaining punches, or digit punches (1 through 9) to represent alphabetic, numeric, and special characters. For example, A is a combination of a Y (12) and a 1 punch; and L is a combination of an X (11) and a 3 punch, etc.

host computer—A computer that is connected to a stored-program multiplexor and which is the base or independent computer upon which the multiplexor is dependent for certain vital functions as program read-in, etc. In an arrangement of this sort, the multiplexor could have stand-alone capacity in the event the host computer is not always available.

housekeeping—1. Pertaining to administrative or overhead operations or functions which are necessary in order to maintain control of a situation; e.g., for a computer program, housekeeping involves the setting up of constants and variables to be used in the program (synonymous with red tape). 2. A general term used to describe coding which reserves, restores, and clears memory areas.

housekeeping operation—A general term for the operation that must be performed for a machine run usually before actual processing begins. Examples of housekeeping operations are: establishing controlling marks, setting up auxiliary storage units, reading in the first record for processing, initializing, set-up verification operations, and file identification.

HT—An abbreviation for Horizontal Tabulation Character.

hybrid computer, problem analysis—Programs in the problem-analysis group help the hybrid programmer decide which parts of the problem to solve on a digital computer, and the mathematical technique that should be used. For example, multivariable function generation that may be difficult to perform on the analog computer is well suited to digital solution.

hybrid computers—By combining analog computer speed, flexibility, and direct communication capability with digital computer memory, logic, and accuracy, the integrated hybrid computer has introduced a new dimension in engineering, scientific, and business technology ... the power to attack every aspect of a problem with the computational capability suited to the task. Dynamic simulation and high-speed differential-equation solution may be performed on the analog side; static and algebraic computations may be handled on the digital side. Overall computational economy and efficiency are thereby maximized.

hybrid systems—The result of a number of efforts to utilize the best properties of both digital and analog computers by building hybrid systems. In the hybrid system, a digital computer is used for control purposes and provides the program, while analog components are used to obtain the continuous solutions.

* _ * _ *

IBM Administrative Terminal System (ATS)—A name which refers to a popular and widely-used remote Administrative Terminal System, developed by IBM, which permits an individual at a terminal typewriter to communicate directly with the computer in the tasks of creating, editing, storing, printing, or adding large volumes of textual information to an information base thus avoiding repetitive copying or unnecessary manual correcting, updating, expanding or editing.

IBM card—A type of paper card that may have information recorded on it by means of punched holes, and which may be read by a computer.

ICBS—An abbreviation for Interconnected Business System.

identifier—1. A specific symbol designed to identify or to indicate or to name a body of data. 2. A key.

idle time—The calculated time that a computer is available for use, but is not in operation.

illegal code—A code character or symbol which appears to be the proper element but really is not a true member of the defined alphabet or specific language. If forbidden patterns, characters, or symbols present themselves, they are judged to be mistakes or the results of malfunctions.

image processing system—An image processing system designed and built by the IBM Data Systems Division to specifications provided by GMR consists of: (a) a graphic console which includes a display tube, control buttons and lights, a card reader, an alphanumeric keyboard and a position indicating pencil; (b) an image processor which permits computer-controlled scanning of film images and computer-controlled recording on 35mm film; (c) a display adaptor unit.

immediate access—Pertaining to the ability to obtain data from or place data in a storage device or register directly, without serial delay due to other units of data, and usually in a relatively short period of time.

immediate access storage—A type of storage which is usually in several locations and has access time which is slight in comparison with operation time, i.e., very fast or real-time capabilities.

immediate address—The designation of an instruction address that is used as data by the instruction of which it is a part.

implicit computation—Refers to a computation which uses a self-nulling principle in which, for example, the variable sought first is assumed to exist, after which a synthetic variable is produced according to an equation and compared with a corresponding known variable and the difference between the synthetic and the known variable driven to zero by correcting the assumed variable. Although the term applies to most analog circuits, even a single Operational Amplifier, it is restricted usually to computation performed by (1) circuits in which a function is generated at the output of a single High-Gain dc Amplifier in the feedback path, (2) circuits in which combinations of computing elements are interconnected in closed loops to satisfy implicit equations, or (3) circuits in which linear or nonlinear differential equations yield the solutions to a system of algebraic or transcendental equations in the steady state.

imprinter—A device which causes the name and account number of a credit card holder to be transferred to the sales slip. Most credit cards show this information in raised, special type that can be automatically read from the sales slip by the computer.

incremental computer—Refers to a particular special-purpose computer that is specifically designed to process changes in the variables themselves, e.g., digital differential analyzer.

independent variable—A variable whose value is not a direct function of some other variable and does not depend on another variable. The independent variable is usually plotted as the abscissa (horizontal line) on an axis.

index—1. A table of computer words or fields containing addresses of records located in file storage. 2. An ordered reference list of the contents of a document, such as names, subjects, etc. 3. A symbol or number used to identify a particular quantity in an array of similar quantities; e.g., the terms of an array represented by x (1), x (2) . . . x (100) have the indexes 1, 2, . . . 100 respectively. 4. Pertaining to an index register.

index, file—A table of keyfields identifying the actual disk records in another permanent disk file.

indexing—1. The indexing method of random-access file organization in which a part of the file is set aside as an index in order to locate information in other parts of the file. 2. The mdofication of an instruction by the contents of an index register in order to obtain a new effective address. 3. The storing of copy in electronic form permits rapid and automatic indexing for information-retrieval purposes.

indicator—A device often used as a control unit when it is designed to determine the selection from alternative processes. It can be set into a prescribed state according to the results of a previous process. An example is an overflow indicator. The state of such indicators may be displayed on a control panel for the benefit of programmers and operators.

indirect address—A single instruction address that is at once the address of another address. The second address is the specific address of the data to be processed. This is classified as single-level indirect addressing.

indirect control—As contrasted with direct control, when one unit of computers is controlled by the other unit without human intervention, the first unit is said to be on-line to the second. If human intervention is necessary, the first unit is said to be off-line to the second and is under indirect control of the second while an operator is acting as a human link in the specific control chain.

industrial data processing—Data processing designed for industrial purposes, often numerical control (n/c).

industrial process control—Industrial processing applications are as wide and varied as the degrees of control that individual processes may require. Some general process-control application areas are precious metals production, cement production, environmental control, pilot plants, chemical processes, petroleum refining and many others. The data acquisition and control system provides maximum flexibility in the types of process data that it can accept, and the variety of output signals and data format that a computer may exercise.

information-feedback system—Refers to an error-control system which uses message feedback with reception of the erroneous group from the sending station.

inherent storage—A type of automatic storage which is designed to be the same as computer storage, automatic storage, etc. which is controlled automatically, i.e., without the intervention of humans, examples are internal or scratchpad storage in the CPU, Central Processing Unit.

inhibition rules—Priority and inhibition rules are usually designed to be implemented in the time-sharing hardware to resolve possible conflicts when two interrupts occur simultaneously or when a second interrupt occurs before a previous one is completely processed.

initialization—Concerns specific preliminary steps required before execution of iterative cycles to determine efficient start procedures. Usually a single, non-repetitive operation after a cycle has begun and/or until a full cycle is again begun.

initial program loader—Specific routines designed to load the initial section of an operating system or other programs and surrender control of the machine to the program loaded.

in-line data processing—Data processing in which all changes to relevant records and accounts are made at the time that each transaction or event occurs. The process usually requires random access storage.

input—1. Information or data transferred or to be transferred from an external storage medium into the internal storage of the computer. 2. Describing the routines with direct input as defined in (1), or the devices from which such information is available to the computer. 3. The device or collective set of devices necessary for input as defined in (1).

input, card—1. Refers to the introduction of information to a processing unit designed for punched cards. A data channel used to feed card information into a machine. 2. The data read from punched cards and fed into the computer.

input data—Various types of data upon which one or more of the basic processing functions are to be performed, such as coding, sorting, computing, summarizing and reporting, recording, and communications.

input device—The mechanical unit designed to bring data to be processed into a computer, e.g., a card reader, a tape reader, or a keyboard.

input equipment—1. Refers to the equipment that is used for transferring data and instructions into an automatic data-processing system. 2. The specific equipment by which an operator transcribes original data and instructions to a medium that may be used in an automatic data-processing system.

input/output—1. Commonly called I/O. A general term for equipment used to communicate with a computer. 2. The data involved in such communication. 3. The media carrying the data for input/output. 4. The process of transmitting information from an external source to the computer or from the computer to an external source.

input/output channel—A specific channel which permits simultaneous communications and independently so between various storage units or any of the various input or output units. Such a channel is the control channel for most peripheral devices and quite often performs various checks on data transfers such as validity checks, etc.

input/output control module (IOC)—In some systems the I/O control module provides control signals, parity checks,

time interface, and data transformations for I/O devices. It consists of an instruction register and associated decoding circuitry, a data register, and a manipulation register with associated timing circuits. Each control module is capable of controlling any standard device of the I/O complement. There can be as many simultaneous I/O operations as there are I/O control modules. The I/O exchange automatically connects control modules with any of the I/O devices on command from processor modules. The I/O control modules also provide interface with associated data-processing systems.

input/output control systems (IOCS)—A group of computer routines designed to automatically control the performance of input-output operations and direct other work or functions, such as, error correction, checkpoint, label processing, restart, and others.

input/output storage—A specific storage area in a computer reserved for data or instructions received by or ready to be transferred from or to an external (peripheral) input or output device or to another specific section of storage, i.e., a storage working area.

input/output table—A plotting device used to generate or to record one variable as a function of another variable.

input routine—1. A specific routine, sometimes stored permanently in a computer, designed to allow the reading of programs and data into the machine. 2. A routine which directs or controls the reading of programs and data into a computer system. Such a routine may be internally stored, wired, or part of a "bootstrap" operation and may perform housekeeping or system control operations according to rules.

85

inquiry—As related to computing, a designed request for specific information from storage; e.g., a request for the number of available airline seats or a machine statement to initiate a search of library documents.

instruction—A set of characters, together with one or more address (or no address), that defines an operation and which, as a unit, causes the computer to operate accordingly on the indicated quantities; a machine instruction to specific functions. Types: actual, arithmetic, blank, branch, control, direct, effective, execution, executive, extract, halt, hold, jump, machine, macro, programmed, and pseudo.

instruction address—The address of the storage location where the instruction word is stored. The next instruction to be performed is determined by the control program of the instruction addresses, and the machine control automatically refers to these addresses.

instruction characters—Characters, when used as code elements, can initiate, modify, or stop a control operation. Characters may be used, for example, to control the carriage return, etc.

instruction, check-indicator—A specific instruction designed to direct a signal device to be turned on to call operator's attention to the fact that there is some discrepancy in the instruction now in use.

instruction cycle—That series of steps performed in processing of an instruction word, i.e., transfer from storage, interpretation, decoding, checking, etc.

instruction, decision—An instruction which effects the selection of a branch of a program; e.g., a conditional jump instruction.

instruction, direct—An instruction which contains an operand for the operation specified by the instruction.

instruction, discrimination—A more acceptable term for conditional jump instruction or branch instruction. Also called decision instruction. Same as conditional jump instruction.

instruction, dynamic—The sequence of machine steps performed by the computer in a real-time or simulated environment.

instruction, effective—To alter a presumptive or unmodified instruction when using a stored program computer, such alteration produces a complete instruction and when it is actually executed it is called an effective instruction or an actual instruction. The modification process uses words or parts of words specifically called modifiers or index words. These are added to or combined with the presumptive or unmodified instruction by means of arithmetical or logical operations.

instruction, input-output—Computer instructions which operate input-output devices like card readers, printers, and terminals.

instruction, macro—1. A particular kind of source-language statement that can produce a variable number of machine instructions. 2. Usually symbolic mnemonic type instructions that programmers can write in a source program to call for special or library routines that perform wanted functions as open, seek, close, etc. Macro instructions result in one-for-many instructions and are extensively used.

instruction set—1. Set of instructions that a computing or data-processing system is capable of performing. 2. The set of instructions that an automatic coding system assembles.

instruction time—1. The portion of an instruction cycle when the control unit is analyzing the instruction and setting up to perform the indicated operation. 2. The portion of an instruction cycle when the actual work is performed or operation executed; i.e., the time required to decode and perform an instruction.

integer—A complete entity, a whole, fractional, or mixed number.

integer programming—Relates to a class of optimization problems in which the values of all of the variables are restricted to be integers. Normally, the optimization problem without this integer restriction is a linear program; additional adjectives indicate variations — for example, integer quadratic programming.

integer variables (FORTRAN)—An integer variable consists of a series of not more than six alphameric characters (except special characters), of which the first is I, J, K, L, M, or N.

integrated management information and control system—A management oriented system conceived and designed by management as a singular entity to control an entire organization. Some of the commonly integrated systems are accounting, inventory control, quality control, purchasing, receiving, and financial control. The integrated management information and control system is the prevailing application type of third generation computers and it blends both the administrative and operational applications into a single information system which provides management with timely and meaningful business information.

integrated system—The combination of processes which results in the introduction of data which need not be repeated as further allied or related data is also entered. For example: shipment data may also be the basis for inventory inquiries, invoicing, marketing reports, etc.

intellectronics—The use of electronics to extend man's intellect. For example, the use of a computer to recall facts and formulas, and by applying logic to a situation, to arrive at the logical conclusion.

interface—1. One common boundary between automatic data-processing systems or parts of a single system. In communications and data systems, it may involve code, format, speed, or other changes as required.

interleaving—A process designed for the purpose of splitting the memory into two sections with two paths to the central processor to speed processing. Core memory access takes longer than logic or arithmetic operations but a second word can be read during the half-cycle when the previously read word is being written back into the memory.

intermediate pass (sorting)—That part of a merging operation which, because of the number of strings or otherwise, does not reduce the file to a single sequenced string.

intermediate storage—One particular kind of an electronic scratch pad. As input is turned into output, it usually goes through a series of changes. An intermediate memory storage holds each of the successive changes just as long as it is needed. It can hold data picked up or developed in one program cycle for use in succeeding program cycles. It can

87

accumulate data from cycle to cycle.

internal control systems—Built in programmed controls of the system to govern the flow of computer operations.

internal sort—The process of sequencing two or more records within the central computer memory; the first phase of a multipass sort program.

internal storage—The major memory of the computer from which instructions can be directly executed and data accessed by the central processor. Memory is assumed to be core unless otherwise stated.

interpret—1. The process of printing on a punched card the graphic symbols of the information punched in that card. 2. To translate non-machine language into machine language. 3. To decode. 4. The translation of coded characters into standard letters, numbers, and symbols.

interpreter—1. A particular machine that will take a punch card with no printing on it, read the information in the punched holes, and print a translation in characters in specified rows and columns on the card. 2. An executive routine that, as the computation progresses, translates a stored program expressed in some machine like pseudocode into machine code and performs the indicated operations, by means of subroutines, as they are translated. An interpreter is essentially a closed subroutine that operates successively on an indefinitely long sequence of program parameters, the pseudoinstructions, and operands. It may usually be entered as a closed subroutine and left by a pseudocode exit instruction.

interpreter (program)—A subroutine, essentially closed, (executive) which translates a stored pseudocode program into machine language and performs the desired and specified operations. Such an interpreter program usually consists of sequences of pseudoinstructions and operands (program parameters) which are introduced as a closed subroutine and left by a pseudocode exit instruction.

interpreter/reader—A specialized service routine designed to read an input stream, store programs and data on random-access storage for later processing, identify the control information contained in the input stream, and store this control information separately in the appropriate control list. A reader/interpreter may be considered very nearly as the opposite of an output writer.

interrupt—1. A break in the normal flow of a system or routine such that the flow can be resumed from that point at a later time. An interrupt is usually caused by a signal from an external source. 2. An interrupt is a special control signal that diverts the attention of the computer from the main program, because of a particular event or set of circumstances, to a specific address which is directly related to the type of interrupt that has occurred. 3. To stop current control sequence; i.e., to jump when affected by signals from on-line peripheral equipment or to skip as triggered by results of programming test techniques.

interstage punching—A procedure of card punching in which either odd-numbered or even-numbered columns are used to the exclusion of others.

I/O—Abbreviation for input/output.

iterative—To describe a procedure or process which repeatedly executes a series of operations until some condition is satisfied. An iterative procedure can be implemented by a loop in a routine.

ITS—Invitation To Send. A specific Western Union term used for a character sequence sent to an outlying teletypewriter terminal which polls its tape transmitter.

* _ * _ *

job—In computer usage it is a unit of work to be done by the computer. A job is a single entity from the standpoint of computer installation management, but may consist of one or more job steps.

jump instruction—1. A computer instruction causing a jump in the sequence of instructions to occur. 2. A more acceptable term for unconditional jump instruction, control transfer instruction or transfer instruction.

jump operation—One where the computer departs from the regular sequence of instruction executions and "jumps" to another routine or program, or even some preceding or forward instructions to thus alter control, repeat a process or loop, etc.

junk—A garbled or otherwise unintelligible sequence of signals or other data, especially as received from a communications channel, i.e., hash or garbage.

justify, left—The process of formating a left margin for the type on a printed page. Typewriters produce left justified copy.

justify, right—The process of formating a right margin for the type on a printed page. More difficult and expensive than left justification.

* _ * _ *

key—1. A character group usually forming a field, utilized in the identification or location of an item. A marked lever manually operated for copying a character; e.g., typewriter paper-tape perforater, card punch manual keyboard, digitizer or manual word generator. 2. That part of a word, record, file, etc., by which it is identified or controlled. 3. The field by which a file of records is sorted into order; e.g., the key for a file of employee records is a number, department, or letter.

keyboard entry—1. Relates to an element of information inserted manually, usually through a set of switches or marked punch levers, called keys, into an automatic data processing system. 2. A medium for achieving access to, or entrance into, an automatic data processing system.

keyboard printer—This special unit permits keyboard insertion of transaction data and printed page output of computer responses at speeds related to the common-carrier service available. Either telegraphic or voice grade lines can be utilized. The keyboard and printer can be used separately or in combination.

The keyboard contains a full four-bank set of keys, 10 numeric, 26 alphabetic, 10 special character keys, and a space bar. The printing unit prepares a copy of all transaction data as it is typed on the keyboard. Computer responses are also printed by the printing unit.

keypunch—1. A special machine to record information in cards or tape by punching holes in the cards or tape to represent letters, digits, and special characters. 2. To operate a device for punching holes in cards or tape.

key, sorting—The record fields which determine, or are used as a basis for determining, the sequence of records in a file.

keyword—A significant or informative word in a title, abstract, body, or part of the text that generally is utilized to describe a document. A keyword or set of keywords may describe the contents of a document, label the document, and/or assist in identifying and retrieving the document.

keyword-in-context index (KWIC)—This lists available programs arranged alphabetically by the keywords in the program titles. There is an index entry for each significant keyword in the title. Certain words are not accepted as indexing words but will be printed as part of the title.

A KWIC index is prepared by highlighting each keyword of the title in the context of words on either side of it and aligning the keywords of all titles alphabetically in a vertical column.

kilobauds—Relates to new and higher capacity data channels, i.e., for special applications, some channels capable of 20 kilobauds are available.

* _ * _ *

label—1. A device for identification used for introducing a record, groups of records, or an address; a number, symbol, tag, or slip. 2. A name (symbol) which indicates an instruction or data group. Usually this is a mnemonic label for easy recognition. 3. A set of symbols used to identify or describe an item, record, message, or file. Occasionally it may be the same as the address in storage. 4. A string of alphameric information placed at any location for informational and instructional purposes. 5. To assign a symbol, acronym, or word, as a means of identification, to a body of data, tape, card, deck, block; to create a specialized associated record or filing "handle."

laced card—A card which has been punched in a manner such that it has a lace-like appearance, but which usually contains no information or meaning.

language—1. A defined character set that is used to form symbols, words, etc., and the rules for combining these into meaningful communications; e.g., English, French, ALGOL, FORTRAN, COBOL, etc. 2. A combination of a vocabulary and rules of syntax. 3. Delineated or defined group of ordered characters to form words, and the specific rules for interpreting these formulations into meaning, e.g., as ALGOL, QUIKTRAN, PL/1. Types: command, common, FORTRAN, general-purpose, machine, problem-oriented, procedure-oriented, higher-order, source, symbolic, and target.

language, artificial—One specifically designed for ease of communication in a particular area of endeavor, but one that is not yet natural to that area. This is contrasted with a natural language which has evolved through long usage.

language, assembly—The standard machine-oriented programming language (e.g., EASY, ARGUS) belonging to an assembly system.

language, executive control—1. A set of control commands, carefully minimized, yet capable of performing all of the desirable or mandatory functions required in a modern executive system. This command language is open ended and easily expanded, so that features and functions may be added as the need arises. 2. The basic format of an executive control statement is quite simple, and is amenable to a large number of input devices. Statements are not restricted to card image format, and may be of variable lengths. Each statement consists of a heading character for recognition purposes, followed by a command (which categorizes the statement), followed by a variable number of expressions. The end of a statement is signified by the end of a card, a carriage return, or an equivalent signal, depending on the type of input device.

language, fabricated—A language specifically designed for ease of communication in a particular area of endeavor, but one that is not yet natural to that area. This is contrasted with a natural language which has evolved through long usage.

language, general purpose—Combined programming languages which use English words and statements where they are convenient and which serve as mathematical notation for procedures conveniently expressed mathematically. COBOL, FORTRAN, and ALGOL are widely used general purpose programming languages in both science and business.

language, intermediate—1. One that is a compromise between a machine or absolute language and a higher order or machine-independent language. Example would be a language for which translators exist to or from two or more other languages, i.e., it might be a composite language. 2. A language which acts as a bridge in translating from a source language to one of many target languages. 3. A distinct means of communication which can be translated by the equipment into machine usable language. Examples are magnetic tape codes.

language, machine-independent—One which is not written for application or use with any specific computer or system or class of computers. Such languages are usually problem-oriented and widely accepted, such as FORTRAN, COBOL, ALGOL, etc.

languages, list processing—Particular languages developed by symbol manipulation and used primarily as research tools rather than for production programming. Most have proved valuable in construction of compilers and in simulation of human problem solving. Other uses have been generalization and verification of mathematical proofs, pattern recognition, information retrieval, algebraic manipulation, heuristic programming and exploration of new programming languages.

language translator—1. A program which converts a language to equivalent statements in another computer language, usually for a different computer. 2. A routine which aids in the performance of natural language translations such as French to English. 3. Any assembler or compiling program which brings forth same or equivalent output from human-readable statements.

latency—1. In various serial storage devices, the time required to locate the first bit (or character) in a particular storage location. 2. Also the delay while waiting for information called from the storage to be delivered to the arithmetic unit, i.e., access time minus the word time.

leader—An unused or blank length of tape at the beginning of a reel of tape preceding the start of the recorded data.

leader record—A specific record designed to contain the description of information contained in a classification or group of records, which follow this initial document. Also known as header record. Contrasts with trailer record.

learning program—The particular program designed to alter itself by making changes based on the experience of the program and results unknown until portions of the program have been run. Such a program is designed to increase efficiency and provide instructions for program modification on a predestined basis concerning various analysis techniques built in to the program itself, resulting in corrective action or alterations of program instruction based on various criteria pre-established within the program.

least significant character—The one in the rightmost position in a number or a word.

level, addressing—Determining the number of steps of an indirect address which have been applied to a particular program. First level is direct addressing, i.e., the address part of the instruction word has the address of the operand in storage. In second level addressing (indirect), the address part of the instruction word gives the storage location where the address of the operand may be found.

library back-up system—Besides his own program complex file, the user has available to him a collection of elements in a library. This library is itself a complex and is built up at an installation as is any other complex. If, during the allocation process (or for that matter, in nearly any search of contents), a given element or entry point is not found, the library table of contents is searched and the appropriate element is taken from the library. Thus the elements in the library serve to "back up" the user's complex.

If, however, the user's complex contains an element whose name is the same as one in the library, or an element which has an externally defined symbol which appears in the library, the user's complex will override the library. Note that all problems of library maintenance are automatically solved by treating the library as "just another complex." All that is required is a simple utility routine (LIBRY) which copies a complex to the system drum area.

library, direct access—The "librarian" portion of the control programs keeps track of library programs of the operating system. The library may be stored on a single secondary storage unit, or it may be distributed over several different storage units for more efficient operation. The library is initially established by selection and editing of a complete set of programs to produce a specially tailored program library which fits the needs of the individual user. The librarian keeps this set of programs up to date by adding, deleting, and modifying as required. User written application programs can be incorporated into the library along with subroutines, the control program, compilers, sort-merge, and utility programs. Most efficient operation is possible when the program library is stored on a direct access device.

library facilities—Relates to a basic library of general-purpose software furnished by manufacturers to perform common jobs; to this the user can add his own often-used programs and routines. Programs in the library can be conveniently assembled into an object program by the use of macro instructions.

library, source (program)—Concerns a collection of computer programs in compiler language and/or assembler language for call when needed.

limited, computer (sorting)—A particular sort program in which the execution time of the internal instructions determine the elapsed time required to sort. Cf. tape limited.

limited, tape (sorting)—Sometimes called a sort program in which the effective transfer rate of tape units determines the elapsed time required to sort. Cf. process limited.

linear—1. Relating to order in an algebraic equation in which all of the variables are present in the first degree only, i.e., an equation in which none of the variables are raised to powers other than unity or multiplied together.

linearity—A constant ratio of incremental cause and effect. Proportionality is a special case of linearity in which the straight line passes through the origin. Zero-error reference of a linear transducer is a selected straight-line function of the input from which output errors are measured. Zero-based linearity is transducer linearity defined in terms of a zero-error reference where zero input coincides with zero output.

linear program—An algorithmic program used to develop a class of problems satisfied by a set of solutions, the requirements being to select the least costly (or the most profitable) solution belonging to the set.

linear programming—1. A method used in mathematics and operations research to find a best solution for a certain type of problem, e.g., to determine the ratio of quantities to mix, blend, select, etc., for an optimum mixture. Sometimes called optimum programming and mathematical programming. 2. The analysis of problems in which the linear function of a number of variables is to be maximized (or minimized) when those variables are subject to a number of constraints in the form of linear inequalities.

linear programming control language—The language used to prescribe the course of a linear programming run on a computer. The language consists mainly of verbs (agendum names) which call in a body of code (program or subroutine) embodying the desired algorithm for execution.

line, code—One instruction, usually written on one line in a code for a specific computer, to solve a problem. This instruction is usually stored as a whole in the program register of the computer while it is executed, and it may contain one or more addresses of registers or storage locations in the computer where numbers or machine words are to be obtained or sent, and one or more operations to be executed (synonymous with program line).

line control—The randomly timed or cycle timed control by programming and hardware that tells each terminal when to start transmitting. A method of communication line and terminal control.

line coordination—The procedure of insuring that equipment at both ends of a circuit are set up for a specific transmission.

line discipline—Relates to distinct procedures which act to adjust the operating parameters of transmission systems to achieve correct or desired values.

line-feed code—A function code that causes page teleprinters or similar devices to rotate the platen up one line.

line printer—One where an entire line of characters is composed and determined within the device prior to printing.

link, library—A special set of data usually

partitioned according to some criteria and is accessible by execute statements and other macrostatements such as: attach, link, load, transfer control, etc.

list—1. A string of items written in a meaningful format that designates quantities to be transmitted for input/output. 2. An individual series of similar items, as the names of cities and the current population of each; i.e., a one-dimensional array of numbers. 3. To print every relevant item of input data.

list, push-down—A list of items designed so that the last item entered is the first item of the list, and the relative position of the other items is pushed back one.

list, push-up—Refers to a list of items where each item is entered at the end of the list, and the other items maintain their same relative position in the list.

load—1. The process of filling internal storage of a computer with information from auxiliary or external storage. 2. To enter or add to the internal storage of a computer, various information from auxiliary, intermediate, or external storage.

loading, scatter—A procedure or process of loading a program into main memory such that each section or segment of the program occupies a single, connected memory area but the several sections of the program need not be adjacent to each other.

location—1. A position of unit storage in the main internal storage that stores one computer word; a storage register. 2. A place in main memory or auxiliary storage where a unit of data may be stored or retrieved.

logarithm—The logarithm of a number is defined as the exponent indicating the power to which it is necessary to raise a given number, called the base, to produce the original number.

logic—1. That science dealing with the canons and criteria of validity in thought and demonstration; the science of the formal principles of reasoning. 2. The basic principles and applications of truth tables, the relationships of propositions, the interconnection of on-off circuit elements, etc., for mathematical computation in a computer.

logical expressions—A logic expression consists of logical constants, variable array elements, function references, and combinations of those operands, separated by logical operators, and parentheses. A logical expression may contain arithmetic expressions, separated by relational operators, and separated from other elements specified by logical operators and parentheses. Logic expressions are most often used in logical IF statements but can also be used in logical assignment statements and as arguments of functions. The logical expression may take on only two values, true or false. When a logical expression appears in a FORTRAN statement it is evaluated according to the given rules. It will always yield one of the two values, TRUE or FALSE.

logical record—One where the scope, direction, or length is governed by the specific nature of the information which it contains instead of by some feature of limitations at the storage device that holds it. Such records differ in size from the physical records in which they are contained. Physical records might be limited to 400-character physical record size, (example, an airline standard) but many logical records might require fewer or more than the limit.

logical symbol—1. A sign used as an operator to denote the particular operation to be performed on the associated variables. 2. A symbol used to graphically represent a logical element.

logical variable—A variable which may have only the value "true" or "false". (FORTRAN IV)

logic analysis—The determination or delineation of the specific steps required to produce the desired computer output or derive the intelligence information from the given or ascertained input data or model. Such logic studies are completed for many computer processes, programs or runs.

logic decision—A specific decision made in a computing system or environment as a direct result of the internal organization of the system, but one of the binary or yes or no type, and basically relating to questions of equality, inequality or relative magnitude, i.e., is the result of some computation less than, equal to, or greater than some reference point or number.

logic function—A specific expression representing an operation which includes one or a combination of logic operators.

logic symbol—1. A symbol used to represent a logic element graphically. 2. A symbol used to represent a logic connective. 3. A specific symbol or group of symbols designed to represent various logic representation, and thus the nature or specific type of logic operation, which that element can or will perform, such as, the symbol which represents the AND gate also represents and consummates the AND operation.

longitudinal redundancy check—An error control device or system based on the arrangement of data in blocks according to some preset rule, the correctness of each character within the block being determined on the basis of the specific rule or set.

look-up, table—A process or procedure for searching identifying labels in a table so as to find the location of a desired item. By extension, a digital computer instruction which directs that the above operation be performed.

loop—The repetitious execution of a series of instructions caused by having the last instruction in the series return the machine to the first instruction in the same series.

loop operation—An operation which has an associated set of instructions which restore modified instructions or data to their original or initial values at each entry to the loop, or sequence of instructions which may be obeyed repetitively.

loop termination—Loops can be terminated when reading data from cards, the cards can simply be let to run out, causing a "hang up" or stop. More commonly, however, in reading data, the last card contains some particular code number which may be tested and thus used to terminate the loop. Most often, the first card contains the number of data sets to be read, and this number is put into some counter "location," which is later tested for zero to end the loop.

low order—That which pertains to the weight or significance assigned to the digits of a number; e.g., in the number 123456, the low order digit is six. One may refer to the three low-order bits of a binary word as another example.

* – * – *

machine address—The direct, absolute, unindexed address expressed as such, or resulting after indexing and other processing has been completed.

machine code—1. Composed of the absolute numbers, names, or symbols assigned by the machine designer to any part of the machine. 2. Same as operation code.

machine, electrical accounting (EAM)—The set of conventional punch-card equipment including sorters, collectors, and tabulators (clarified by tabulating equipment).

machine-independent—This term is used to indicate that a procedure or a program is conceived, organized, or oriented without specific reference to the operating characteristics of any one data-processing system. Use of this adjective usually implies that the procedure or program is oriented or organized in terms of the logical nature of the problem, rather than in terms of the characteristics of the machine used in solving it.

machine instruction—1. Upon machine recognition, a code element causes a predefined sequence of operations. 2. An instruction that the particular machine can recognize and execute.

machine language—1. The particular set of symbols, characters, or signs, and the rules for combining them, that conveys instructions or information to a computer. 2. Information or data is expressed in code that can be read directly, used or written by the computer or peripheral machines without further processing (same as machine-oriented language and related to object language).

machine operators—This is a relatively elementary job. They load and unload, set up, and control the equipment in the data processing installation, which may include one or more computers and perhaps a variety of punched card equipment, such as keypunches, sorters, and perhaps some data communications equipment.

machine-oriented language (MOL)—Instructions of communication or a language which does not require translation before it is acceptable to the computer equipment, but is instead coded for immediate acceptance without re-translation.

machine-oriented programming system—A specific system that uses a language that is oriented to the internal language of a specific computer. Systems that are considered to be machine oriented are assembly systems and macro systems.

machine readable—That which has the capability of being able to be sensed or read by a specific device, i.e., one that has been designed to perform the reading and sensing function, i.e., tapes, cards, drums, disks, etc., are capable of being machine readable.

machines, accounting—A machine that reads information from one medium (e.g., cards, paper tape, and magnetic tape) and produces lists, tables, and totals on separate forms or continuous paper. Clarified by tabulating equipment.

machine translation—Transmitting automatically from one representation to another representation. The translation may involve codes, languages, or other systems of representation (related to automatic dictionary).

machine word—An information unit of a standard number of characters which a machine regularly handles in each transfer, e.g., a machine may regularly handle numbers or instructions in units of 36 binary digits; this is then the machine word. Related to word information.

macroelement—A particular group or ordered set of data elements which are handled as a unit and provided with a single data use identifier.

macro-assembly program—A processor of language that accepts words, statements, and phrases to produce machine instructions. It is more than an assembly program because it has compiler powers. The macro-assembler permits segmentation of a large program so that portions may be tested separately. It also provides extensive program analysis to aid in debugging.

macroprogramming—Relates to a process of writing machine-procedure statements in terms of macro instructions.

macro trace—Designed as an error detection aid as are core and file dumps, loggings and simulators. A macro-trace records pertinent information when macro-instructions are being executed. The macro-trace can print out the record of macros or it can record them and also dump working storage and the needed registers.

MADCAP—Language for mathematical problems and set operations.

magic paper—An on-line system for manipulation of symbolic mathematics.

magnetic core—1. A magnetic material which is pulsed or polarized by electric currents carried in a wire or wires wound around it. This device is capable of assuming and remaining at one of two conditions of magnetization, thus providing storage, gating, or switching functions. See: core memory. 2. A miniaturized ring of ferromagnetic substance that may be instantaneously magnetized to a negative or positive flux and remains so until changed by further computer operations.

magnetic disc (disk)—A circular plate which is flat with a magnetic surface on which data can be stored by selective magnetization of portions of the flat surface.

magnetic ink—Ink made up with magnetic particles which can be detected or read by automatic devices; e.g., the ink used for printing on some bank checks for magnetic ink character recognition (MICR).

magnetic ink character recognition—The sensing of characters as printed in magnetic ink as by codes developed and used by the American Bankers Association for bank checks with standardized characters, inks, etc. developed by the USA Standards Institute.

magnetic memory—Usually any portion of the memory that uses the magnetic properties of a material to store information.

magnetic storage—Relates to a device (or devices) that utilizes the magnetic properties of materials to store information.

magnetic tape—A storage device externally located in the form of a ferrous oxide coating on a reel of metallic or plastic tape upon which bits may be recorded magnetically as a means of retaining data.

magnitude, relative—The relationship or comparison of the magnitude of one quantity to another, most often related to base magnitude and expressed as a difference from or a percentage of the base or reference.

mag tape—The informal or slang expression for magnetic tape.

main memory—Basically, the fastest storage device of a computer and the one from which instructions are executed (contrasted to auxiliary storage).

maintenance—1. The procedures of testing, measuring, replacing, adjusting, and repairing to keep equipment or programs in satisfactory working order. 2. Updating of object program master files, selection of programs to be run, and control of checkout and production operation.

maintenance, file—Periodically modifying a file to incorporate changes that occured during a given period.

maintenance, file (graphic)—Relates to the process designed to update physical representation such as microfilm, film prints, CRT output copies, etc.

major cycle—1. Relates to the maximum access time of a recirculating serial storage element. 2. The time for one rotation of a magnetic drum or of pulses in an acoustic delay line. 3. A number of minor cycles.

majority decision element—Same as: majority decision gate.

majority decision gate—A binary input unit which has the capability of implementing the majority logic operator, i.e., if A is a statement, B is a statement and C is a statement, the result is true if more than half of the statements are true and false if half or more of the input statements are false, i.e., the majority cause the threshold decision.

major-minor sorting—The punched card sorting technique that starts with the right (least significant) digit of the minor column and progresses to the left with all records used in each pass.

malfunction routine—A specific routine designed to locate a malfunction in a computer, or to aid in locating mistakes in a computer program. In general, any routine specifically designed to aid in debugging or troubleshooting. (Related to debugging.)

management, data—A term referring collectively to all OS/360 routines that give access to data, enforce storage conventions, and regulate the use of each individual I/O device.

management, data base—A systematic approach to storing, updating and retrieval of information stored as data items, usually in the form of records in a file, where many users, or even many remote installations, will use common data banks.

management, data processing—This includes many of the same management functions of any operating organization: supervision and administration, reporting, long-range planning, project control, maintenance of standards, liaison, etc. In data processing, however, these functions have some unusual aspects. Supervision of a data processing function is not an easy task without a thorough knowledge of the technical details and skills. A combination of rigid, detailed operations and creative development must often be supervised simultaneously.

management-information system—1. A communications process in which data are recorded and processed for operational purposes. The problems are isolated for higher-level decision making, and information is fed back to top management to reflect the progress or lack of progress made in achieving major objectives. 2. The availability of data a man needs to run his business, and the capability of producing that information. An MIS gives the executive the capability of controlling the operation of a firm on a real time basis.

management science (EDP)—The field of management science is extending the computer far beyond the automation of routine accounting operations and into the complex decision-making process of management. Through revolutionary computer programming techniques such as simulation, the objective, scientific approach of management science is providing increased management capability and control.

In addition to the physical or operational process like inventory management, product planning and control, resource allocation or market forecasting, this also includes the fiscal processes such as bond management, capital investment, risk, analysis, profit planning and product pricing.

Manufacturer's broad resources are prepared to meet management's growing demand for this expanded capability and to extend the tradition of "total systems" capability into revolutionary data-processing techniques and applications.

management services—Pertains to that specific category of consulting or other assistance made available from accounting or management consulting firms related to data processing service, systems, or specific problems.

management, storage—Relates to the problems in the time-shared management of storage — the protection of user files and the reduction of constraints on the size of user programs due to limited core space — which are common to all time-shared systems and have received considerable attention in software development. Related to Security of User Files and Core Memory, reentrant routines.

manager, operations—The human who is hired directs the computer installation, plans the scheduling of computer time, allocates personnel, maintains the program library and controls operations within the computer center.

manager, programming—This human is responsible for planning, scheduling, and supervising program development and maintenance work.

manipulated variable—In a process that is desired to regulate some condition, a quantity is altered by the computer in order to initiate a change in the value of the regulated condition.

manipulative indexing—An indexing technique where the interrelations of terms are shown by coupling individual words. An indexing scheme by which descriptors may be correlated or combined to show any interrelationships desired for purposes of more precise information retrieval.

man-machine simulation—The scope of simulation clearly includes models of systems in which human beings participate (operational or behavioral models). However, the possibility also exists of incorporating people within the model. In other words, the model is no longer completely computer-based but requires the active participation of a man.

manual control—Relates to the direction of a computer by means of manually operated switches.

manual input—Many devices available will cause input to occur strictly by manual operations, i.e., from the console, from terminal devices, and other various operations.

map—1. The process of transforming information from one form to another. 2. To establish a correspondence between the elements of one set and the elements of another set.

map, memory—A hardware-implemented print-out provided for dynamically relocating, protecting, and executing programs in scattered fragments of memory.

marginal check—A procedure for preventive maintenance in which certain operating conditions (e.g., supply voltage or frequency) are varied about their nominal values in order to detect and locate incipient defective parts.

margin guide—A paper tape device which measures the distance across the tape from the guide edge to the center of the nearest track.

margin, justified—A data arrangement or type printed on pages in a manner such that the left or right end characters of each horizontal line lie in the same right or left column, i.e., under one another without protruding in an uneven manner, and thus the words at ends are in-line and even.

mark—1. In communications, that particular impulse which, in a neutral circuit, causes the loop to be closed; or in a polar circuit, causes the loop current to flow in a direction opposite to that for a space impulse. 2. A sign or symbol used to signify or indicate an event in time or space; e.g., end of word or message mark, a file mark, a drum mark, an end-of-tape mark.

mark, drum—A character used in signifying the end of a record on a drum.

marker, end-of-tape—That special mark, character, long blank or other coding which indicates the end of a tape or recording, i.e., often times this is a reflective strip and easy-to-see, or a transparent section, or, in paper tape, a special bit pattern.

Markov chain—A model often used for determining the sequence of events in which the probability of a given event is dependent only on the preceding event.

mark scan—To read a document for a specific mark in a particular location; the mark may be a pen or pencil mark since the operation is usually based on optical scanning and light reflectance, i.e., mark scanning differs from mark sensing because mark sensing requires an electrographic pencil with conductive or ink.

marks, control (CM)—1. A one-slab block written on magnetic tape to indicate the type of data that follows, or to indicate the end of useful information. 2. The control mark (any one-slab block) supplies special control features which can be utilized by the programmer. However, several specified CM configurations have been reserved for particular features on data tapes, as FF for end of file.

mark, storage—A particular point location that defines the character space immediately to the left of the most significant character in accumulator storage. An example would be:

a 7 4 6 7 4 8 9

in which the letter "a" would be the storage mark.

masking—1. This involves replacing characters in the accumulator with characters from a specified storage location or register. 2. The process of extracting a non-word group or field of characters from a word or a string of words. 3. The process of setting internal program controls to prevent transfers which otherwise would occur upon setting of internal machine latches.

mass-data multiprocessing—Multiprocessor systems handle vast masses of general-purpose data. Handling scientific, engineering, and business data with equal ease, such a system tied into a coast-to-coast communications network gives a consolidated data processing operation. Two or more processors, each with direct access to banks of common memory, continuously process a conventional work load, and provide answers to special projects, such as product analysis, market research, site analysis, and operations research. The total system is under executive control of one processor. This important concept is the basis for time sharing, i.e., the use of up to 100 remote-inquiry stations, each with near-simultaneous access to a single processor which has on-line mass-data retrieval capability.

mass (executive) storage—In most systems the executive system is designed to provide installations with an effective and efficient utilization of the mass storage devices available. The result is an ability to relieve operators and programmers of responsibilities in maintaining and physically handling cards, magnetic tapes, etc., thus, eliminating many of the errors that heretofore inherently accompanied the use of large-scale software systems. At the same time, the overall efficiency of operating is considerably improved. Provisions are made for the maintenance of permanent data files and program files on the mass storage devices, with full facilities for modification and manipulation of these files. Security measures are invoked by the executive system to insure that files are not subject to unauthorized use. Provisions are also made within the executive system for automatic relocation of files of low usage-frequency to magnetic tape, as unused mass storage space approaches exhaustion. When the use of files related in such a manner is requested, they are retrieved and re-stored, under control of the executive system, with no inconvenience to the user.

mass storage file—A secondary storage type, usually slower, designed to supply the computer with the required information and data for an immediate up-to-date report on a given account or program supports.

mass storage systems—These systems are made up of a mass storage device such as a magnetic-tape unit. Other mass storage devices may be used, such as a CRAM unit, disk unit, or cartridge tape unit. The operating system is basically the same with minor exceptions. The magnetic tape unit is used as the system unit, which contains the master file of operating system routines, input-output drivers, utility routines, and library sub-routines.

master card—One which contains fixed or indicative information for a group of cards. It is usually the first card of that group.

master clock—The electronic or electric source of standard tuning signals, often called "clock pulses" required for sequencing computer operation. This source usually consists of a timing-pulse generator, a cycling unit, and sets of special pulses that occur at given intervals of time. In synchronous computers the basic time frequency employed is usually the frequency of the clock pulses.

master control—1. An application-oriented routine usually identified with the highest level of a subroutine hierarchy. 2. Computer program to control operation of the system, designed to reduce the amount of intervention required for the operator. Master control schedules programs to be processed, initiates segments of programs, controls input/output traffic, informs operator and verifies his actions, and performs corrective action on program errors or system malfunctions.

master file—1. A file which contains relatively more permanent information, and is usually updated periodically. 2. A main reference file of information.

master/slave system—That computer configuration for business or scientific use (as production automation) in which one computer, usually of substantial size or capability, rules with complete control over all input-output and schedules and transmits tasks to a slave computer. The latter computer often has a great capacity, and it performs the computations as directed and controlled by the master unit.

master unit—That specific unit which takes care that a variety of jobs is executed simultaneously and which has the capability of regrouping several units together to thus control independently a complete automatic data processing system or job.

matching—A comparing technique generally used to verify coding. Individual codes are machine-compared against a group of master codes to select any that are invalid.

match-merge—A process of comparison of two files, usually based on key words designed to place them in a pre-arranged sequential order of those records which match to the arbitrarily selected key words. The resulting segregation of those records which do not match, merge to combine or join two different units of equipment.

mathematical model—Relates to the general characterization of a process, object, or concept, in terms of mathematics, thus enabling the relatively simple manipulation of variables to be accomplished in order to determine how the process, object, or concept would behave in different situations.

mathematical programming—See linear programming as an example.

mathematics, fixed-point—A method of determining the assumed location of the radix point by placing a symbol at the point or by other rules and or conventions as predetermined.

mathematics, floating-point—An automatic method of determining the location of the radix point in values, such math is usually performed by using a signed mantissa times the radix raised to an integral number, such as the decimal number 62.4 being equivalent to .624 times 10^2.

matrix—1. An array of numbers that is rectangular—subject to mathematical operations, such as addition, multiplication, and inversion, according to specified rules. Any table in a matrix of circuit elements such as diodes, wires, magnetic cores, and relays, arranged and designed to perform a specified function.

maximum operating frequency—The highest clock rate or repetition at which the modules will perform reliably in continuous operations, under worst-case conditions, without special trigger-pulse (clock) requirements.

MAYBE compiler—This is used to provide the instructions, commands and orders for operation of the data channel and various devices. In addition, MAYBE automatically produces the necessary system linkages to process the data channel interrupts and central computer traps. The MAYBE compiler is a macro-generator which feeds symbolic input to the standard assembly program. MAYBE was coded in NOMAD and utilizes standard system I/O routines. The MAYBE language includes approximately 75 declarations and statements divided into the following classes: (1) storage allocation declarations; (2) replacement statements; (3) iteration statements; (4) control and linking statements; and (5) device manipulating statements. MAYBE is essentially a compiler for use of system programmers.

MCUG—Abbreviation for Military Computer Users Group.

mechanical dictionary—The language-translating machine component which will provide a word for word substitution from one language to another. In automatic-searching systems, the automatic dictionary is the component which substitutes codes for words or phrases during the encoding operation. (Related to machine translation.)

mechanical digital calculator—A mechanical adding machine.

mechanical translation—Now accepted as a generic term for language translation by computers or similar equipment.

mechanized data—The data or material which is used on a sensing device or unit, i.e., punched cards, tapes.

media conversion—Small, tightly coded subroutines operating under control of the executive system perform on-line conversion of data between card, printer, punch, and tape equipment concurrently with other programs. Low-speed devices use magnetic drum as a large buffer area between themselves and operating pro-grams. Use of the magnetic drum as a buffer provides increased throughput capability as programs using these drum buffers effectively "read" or "print" information at drum transfer speeds.

medium, data—A specific material, in, on, or by which data can be stored, repre-sented, or communicated by static use or by variation of one or more of its physical characteristics or parameters.

megabit—One million binary bits.

megacycle—A million cycles per second; 10^6 cycles per second.

memory—1. The same as storage. The term memory carries "magic brain" connota-tions which are considered undesirable; hence, storage is preferred. 2. Any device into which a unit of information can be copied, which will hold this information, and from which the information can be obtained at a later time. (The terms memory and storage are interchange-able.) 3. An organization of storage units, primarily for the retrieval of information and data. Memory types include disk, core, drum, or relay memories. Ex-tremely rapid access-storage elements from which instructions are executed and data operated on are referred to as main memory as contrasted to auxiliary-mem-ory modules. Types: addressed, associa-tive, bootstrap, circulating, core, dynam-ic, external, high speed, internal, main, nonvolatile, permanent, quick-access, random-access, read-only, regenerative, scratch-pad, single-level, static, volatile, and working.

memory, associative—The storage loca-tions are identified by their contents rather than their addresses. Enables faster interrogation to retrieve a particular data element.

memory buffer register—1. A register

designed so that a word is stored as it comes from memory (reading) or just prior to its entering memory (writing). See register. 2. The memory buffer serves as a buffer register for all information passing between the processor and the core memory, and serves as a buffer directly between core memory and peripheral equipment during data-break information transfers. The memory buffer is also used as a distributor shift register for the analog-to-digital converter.

memory core—Concerns those storage devices composed of ferromagnetic cores, or apertured ferrite plates, through which select lines and sense windings are threaded. See memory.

memory, dynamic—To store data on a device or in a manner that permits the data to move or vary with time, and thus the data is not always available instantly for recovery; e.g., acoustic delay line, magnetic drum, or circulating or recirculating of information in a medium.

memory exchange—1. The switching of the total contents of two storage devices or locations, such as, two registers. 2. A switching device capable of controlling and handling the flow or exchange of data between storage units or other elements of a system.

memory, external—A facility or device, not an integral part of a computer, on which data usable by a computer is stored, such as off-line magnetic-tape units or punch-card devices (contrasted with internal storage).

memory hierarchy—A combination of memories with different sizes and speeds and usually having different cost-performance ratios. A hierarchy might consist of a very-high-speed, small semi-conductor memory, a medium-speed core memory and a large, slow-speed core.

memory, high-speed—The new devices recently introduced to the market have speeds (input and access) in microseconds and are considered high or ultra high-speed devices.

memory, internal—The storage facilities forming an integral physical part of the computer and directly controlled by the computer. In such facilities all data are automatically accessible to the computer; e.g., magnetic core, and magnetic tape on-line (contrasted with external storage).

memory location—A specific position in a computer storage device.

memory map—1. A hardware-implementation which provides for dynamically relocating, protecting, and executing programs in scattered fragments of memory. 2. A procedure which produces a listing of all variables, constants, and statement identifiers in a FORTRAN program and the storage location assigned to each. The memory map allows the programmer to examine values in his program from a memory drum. The memory map is listed during compilation. A memory map is normally given with each program unless control character is specified in the job definition or a sense switch is on.

memory mapping—A particular mode of computer operation wherein the eight high-order bits of any virtual address greater than 15 are replaced by an alternative value, thus providing for dynamic relocatability of programs (some computers).

memory, normal—A standard set of main memory locations which are contiguous and specifically located for storage of programs, data, data sets, and most often organized in a logical or subject order or sequence. If some programs are larger than main memory, overlays to auxiliary memory may be used.

memory protection—A method specifically designed to insure that the contents of main memory within certain designated but variable bounds will not be destroyed or altered. Special programming devices or hardware thus guard against the effects of equipment malfunction and program bugs in real-time systems.

memory register—One in computer storage as in contrast with a register in one of the other units of the computer.

memory storage—The filing system of the computer. It holds standards or current facts such as rate tables, current inventories, balances, etc., and sometimes programming instructions. The memory storage can be internal, that is, a part of the computer itself, such as drums, cores, or thin-film; or, it can be external, such as paper tape, magnetic tape, or punched cards.

memory, virtual (pointer)—For storage efficiency some computers are designed so that parts of programs and data may be scattered through main memory and auxiliary storage. Various pointers or sets of pointers automatically keep track of the location of these program portions. The user of computers so designed may be unaware of this scattering procedure and most often operates computing procedures as though he were using normal memory.

mercury memory—Delay lines which use mercury as the medium for storage of a circulating train of waves or pulses. Also called mercury storage.

merge—1. The process which produces a single sequence of items, ordered according to some rule (that is, arranged in some orderly sequence), from two or more sequences previously ordered according to the same rule, without changing the items in size, structure, or total number. Merging is a special kind of collating. 2. To combine two or more files into one, usually in specified order.

message, book—A message to be sent to two or more destinations.

message (communications)—A transmitted series of words or symbols intended to convey information.

message switching—There exists a need for message switching communication systems among large corporations spread out over a large number of widely separated locations. Where communications traffic is high, a computer-controlled switching system is needed. In this type of application, the data flow pattern involves message traffic between a number of terminals and a central switching center. The sending terminal transmits each message to the center, which stores it temporarily, performs any processing or code conversion functions that may be required, and then transmits the message to one or more designated receiving terminals. Large networks may utilize two or more switching centers which are interconnected by high-speed communications links.

metal-oxide semiconductor memory (MOS)—A memory whose storage medium is a semiconductor circuit, often MOS, metal oxide semiconductor. Often used for high-speed buffer memories and for read-only memories. Most of today's memories are magnetic cores.

metron—A unit which expresses a quantity

of metrical information.

MICR (Magnetic Ink Character Recognition)—A check-encoding system employed by banks for the purpose of automating check handling. Checks are imprinted (using magnetic ink) with characters of a type face and dimensions specified by the American Banking Association. There are fourteen characters—ten numbers (0-9) and four special symbols—which are used to provide amount, identifying, and control information.

microcircuits—1. Miniaturized circuitry components common to the so-called third generation of computer equipment. Microcircuits frequently reduce cost, increase reliability, and operate faster than tubes and many transistors. 2. A specialized electronic circuit composed of elements which are fabricated and interconnected to make them inseparable and miniaturized.

microcode—1. A coding system using sub-operations not ordinarily accessible in programming; e.g., coding that makes use of parts of multiplication or division operations. 2. A list of small program steps. Combinations of these steps, performed automatically in a prescribed sequence, from a macro operation like multiply, divide, and square root.

microprogram—1. Refers to a program of analytic instructions which the programmer intends to construct from the basic subcommands of a digital computer. 2. A sequence of pseudocommands which will be translated by hardware into machine subcommands. 3. A means of building various analytic instructions as needed for the subcommand structure of a computer. 4. A plan for obtaining maximum utilization of the abilities of a digital computer by efficient use of the sub-commands of the machine.

microprogrammable instruction—All instructions which do not reference core memory (do not contain a memory address) can be micro programmed, allowing the programmer to specify several shift, skip, or input/output transfer commands to be performed within one instruction.

microprogramming simulation—This procedure has emulation as its chief function since a microprogram can imitate the basic instruction set of the machine being emulated. Word lengths, arithmetic, and logic details, as well as other functions of another machine, are simulated. Each fundamental instruction or operation of the imitated machine is made up of a sequence of microcoded steps allowing registers to be loaded, data to be moved, etc. Quite often the microcoded sequences which make up each basic machine operation are hardwired into a control store. Such control store, in many new machines, are either being made from Read-Only Memory (ROM), which may be easily removed for substitution, or from semiconductor Reloadable Control Store (RCS), such as the IBM 370/135 and 145. Microprogramming offers user programmers opportunities to tailor their own machines to their own jobs; i.e., powerful instructions can be developed which would require only a single line of program code to complete a number of complex but repetitive jobs called for specific installation requirements.

microsecond—One millionth of a second. One second = 1,000,000 microseconds.

middle punch—Same as eleven punch. Also known as the "X" punch located as a row next to the top row on an 80 column card; used for the J through F of the alphabet and for special characters.

minimal latency coding—A procedure or method for programming for those computers in which the waiting time for a word depends on its location, i.e., locations for instructions and data are so Chosen that access time is reduced or minimized. Same as minimum delay coding or optimum coding.

minimum-access programming—Programming such that minimum waiting time is required to obtain information out of storage. (Synonymous with minimum-latency programming, and contrasted with random-access programming.)

minor cycle—The interval of time between the appearance of corresponding parts of successive words in a storage device that provides serial access to storage positions.

minus-zone—The "bit" position which indicates that an associated quantity has a minus value. Opposite of plus zone.

(MIS) management-information system—A communications process in which data are recorded and processed for operational purposes. The problems are isolated for higher-level decision-making, and information is fed back to top management to reflect the progress or lack of progress made in achieving major objectives. An MIS gives the executive the capability of controlling the operation of a firm on a real-time basis.

mixed-base number—Relates to a number consisting of two or more characters representing a sum, in which the quantity represented by each character is based on a different radix.

mixed-radix number—Relates to a number consisting of two or more characters representing a sum, in which the quantity represented by each characater is based on a different radix. (Synonymous with mixed-base number.)

ML programmer—That computer programmer who is responsible for writing computer programs in machine language.

mnemonic—Pertaining or intending to assist the human memory. A mnemonic term, then, is an abbreviation or acronym that is easy to remember.

mnemonic instruction codes—1. Concerns computer instructions written in a meaningful notation, e.g., add, mpy, sto. 2. Relates to codes devised and written in symbolic notation for easier human recognition and retention. Such codes must be converted into operation codes by some translating device or routine before the computer can execute them. 3. The writing of operation codes in a symbolic notation which is easier to remember than the actual operation codes of the machine. Must be converted to actual operation codes before execution, which is done as part of an assembly, interpretive, or compiling routine.

MOBIDIC—Stands for mobil digital computer, developed by Sylvania Electric Products Company.

mod—An abbreviation for modifications made in programs after they are written; each modification is thus properly identified to indicate it is the latest by using a mod number. For example: mass storage operating system, mod Z, version 3.

mode—1. A particular operation method, e.g., the binary mode, the interpretive mode, the alphameric code, etc. 2. The most frequent value in the statistical sense. Types: access, analysis, binary, byte, card, compute, freeze, hold job-program, manual, and recording.

mode, access—In COBOL, the technique that is used to obtain a specific logic record from, or place a specific logic record into, a file assigned to a mass-storage device.

mode, job program—In this mode, both read/write and jump-storage protection is in effect. Therefore, job programs are limited entirely to those areas assigned by the executive. If the job program reads, writes, or jumps to an out-of-limits address, an interrupt will return control to the executive for remedial action.

model—1. Representation in mathematical terms of a process, device, or concept. 2. A general, often pictorial, representation of a system being studied.

mode, real-time—Real-time in many systems is a mode of operation in which data that are necessary to the control and/or execution of a transaction can be processed in time for the transaction to be affected by the results of the processing. Real-time processing is most usually identified with great speed, but speed is relative. The essence of real time is concurrency—simultaneity. Real-time is refinement in the integration of data processing with communications. Real-time eliminates slow information-gathering procedures, dated reporting techniques and lax communications; insures that facts within the system are as timely as a prevailing situation, as current as the decisions which they must support. Real-time provides answers when answers are needed, delivers data instantly whenever the need for that data arises. Incoming information is edited, updated and made available on demand at every level of responsibility. Imminent departures from established standards are automatically detected, and management is notified in time for action.

mode, real-time guard—In many systems the guard mode is activated only by the instruction "Load Internal Function," which establishes certain operational parameters. When operative, any attempt to perform a restricted operation will result in an interrupt to an address in central store. Guard mode is terminated by the occurrence of any interrupt.

It is possible for any program to use the "Prevent-All Interrupts and Jump Instruction," thereby allowing real-time programs to operate effectively when guard mode is established. However, when in guard mode, interrupts cannot be disabled for over 100 microseconds. (UNIVAC)

modes of priority—The organization of the flow of work through a computer. The mode depends upon the sophistication of the system and the machine and will vary from a normal-non-interrupt mode to a system in which there are several depths of interrupt. There also may be different modes for different functions such as the I/O mode.

modification, address—1. Relates to the specific procedure designed for changing the address part of an instruction which can be accomplished by using computer instructions developed from the results obtained in continuing the operation of a program, i.e., automatically by indirect addressing or by programming address modifications. 2. The changing or modification in which only the address part of the presumptive instruction (to be modified) is modified. 3. A process used to obtain the address of the effective memory location, starting from a given reference address value in an instruction word.

modularity—1. A particular state in the determination of the design of the equipment and programming systems such that the hardware and software components can be readily identified, altered, or augmented without replacements of particular units or sections. 2. Operating system programs conform to specific standards, so that control programs will have an identical interface with all processing programs. These standards are well documented so that user-written programs can follow the same conventions. The user is free to supplement supplied programs to meet special situations. By following the rules indicated in the standards, portions of control or processing programs can be changed or replaced in modular fashion.

modulo—A mathematical operation that yields the remainder function of division. Thus 39 modulo 6 = 3.

(MOL) machine-oriented language—The process of communicating instructions or language which does not require translation before it is acceptable to the computer equipment, but is instead coded for immediate acceptance without retranslation.

monadic operation—An operation performed on one operand, e.g., negation. (Synonymous with unary operation.)

monitor—A CRT receiver usually found in the control room of a transmitter station.

monitor program—One that was developed to indicate the progress and other characteristics of work in various computer systems.

monitor, time-sharing—As a general rule, a time-sharing monitor provides all I/O service to user programs; selective communications service for interactive message processing (selective "end-of-message" processing control characteristics); error processing and recovery; multiprocessing "forks"; multilevel, nested, intervention ("break") capability; memory allocation and control; interstation communication; and scheduling of user program operations. The monitor permits the user to create "control" programs and "dependent" programs. A dependent program may also be a control program for a lower level dependent program. This hierarchy of dependency may be extended to various depths. The highest level control program is usually the Time-Sharing Executive.

monte-carlo method—1. Those procedures that involve statistical sampling techniques in order to obtain a probabilistic approximation to the solution of a mathematical or physical problem. 2. The branch of linguistic study which deals with the history and functions of derivational forms and inflections. 3. A statistical trial and error calculating technique used when a great number of variables exist, and successive repeated calculations are required to establish probabilities.

most significant character—That character which is in the left-most position in a number or word.

most significant digit (MSD)—The leftmost non-zero digit, or the one which contributes the largest quantity to the value of a number.

movable random access—A particular feature of a storage device like disk packs, tape strips, or card strips which can be physically removed and replaced by another, thereby allowing for a theoretically unlimited storage capacity. Contrasted with both sequential storage and fixed media random access storage.

move—In communications applications, to transmit.

MQ register—A register which is treated as an extension of the accumulator register in multiply and divide operations. Same as the extension register.

MSD, most significant digit—See most significant digit.

msec—Millisecond (1/1000 sec).

MTBF—An abbreviation for Mean Time Between Failures.

multifont optical arena—Refers to basic character reading equipment having the ability to discern many fonts or character formats.

multipass sort—A particular sort program designed to sort more data than can be contained within the internal memory of a central computer. Intermediate storage, such as disk, tape, drum, is required.

multiple access—A system where output or input can be received or dispatched from more than one location.

multiple address—Concerns a specific type of instruction that specifies the addresses of two or more items which may be the addresses of locations of inputs or outputs of the calculating unit, or the addresses of locations and instructions for the control unit. The term multiaddress is also used in characterizing computers; e.g., two, three, or four address machines. (Synonymous with multiaddress.)

multiple module access (MMA)—An MMA unit is positioned between each storage module and the several processors which may reference it to resolve potential storage-access conflicts. This unit furnishes five priority-ordered processor connection paths. Should an access conflict occur between processors, the MMA will grant storage access to the processor having the relative highest priority attachment to the MMA, then to the next, and so on. Communications between processors and a single storage module can therefore be conducted on an asychronous basis—if the storage module is "busy" servicing one process, a passive wait cycle is induced in others of lower priority that may be referencing it.

multiple-precision arithmetic—1. Almost the same as double-precision arithmetic except that each number is represented by more than two words. 2. A computer system feature which allows more than one word to be used to accommodate a quality expressed in more than one word length; this avoids the truncation or cutoff of a lesser significant digit.

multiple programming—The programming of a computer which allows two or more arithmetical or logical operations to be executed simultaneously. (Contrasted with serial programming.)

multiple punch—Two or more holes in a single column of a card which permits the representation of a larger number of different characters, one character in each column.

multiple regression—A special analysis program for determining the mathematical relationships and relative significances of manufacturing parameters associated with a given problem.

multiplexed operation—A simultaneous operation sharing the use of a common unit of a system in such a way that it can be considered an independent operation.

multiplexer—A machine which will interleave (time-division) or simultaneously transmit (frequency-division) two or more messages on the same communications channel.

multiply, logical—1. Concerns a logical operator which has the property that if P is a statement and Q is a statement, then P AND Q is true if both statements are true, false if either is false or both are false. Truth is normally expressed by the value 1, falsity by 0. The AND operator is often represented by a centered dot (P·Q), by no sign (PQ), by an inverted "u" or logical product symbol (P ∩ Q), or by the letter "x" or multiplication symbol (P×Q). Note that the letters AND are capitalized to differentiate between the logical operator AND, and the word "and" in common usage. 2. The logical operator that makes use of the AND operator or logical product. (Synonymous with logical multiply AND, and clarified by conjunction.)

multiprocessing—1. The use of several computers to logically or functionally divide jobs or processes, and to execute various programs or segments asynchronously and simultaneously. 2. Two or more processors in a system configuration; one processor to control the system, with the others subordinate to it. All processors have direct access to all memory; each can perform computations and request input/output on individual programs stored in system core memory. Devices request memory access and wait until memory is available. They start immediately upon receipt of a memory access, and need not wait for the next clock cycle.

multiprogramming—A particular method for handling numerous routines or programs simultaneously by overlapping or interleaving their execution; i.e., permitting more than one program to time-share machine components.

multisequential system—A particular computing system which works much like a multiprocessor, i.e., one computer controlling several satellite computers and one which is capable of interleaving the execution of instructions which can also execute more than one instruction at a time, i.e., one capable of concurrent working of several computers.

multi-thread processing—An ordered sequence of events or programs required for the complete processing of a message is known as a thread. In single-thread processing all work is completed before work is begun on a new message. In multi-thread processing message threads are handled in parallel.

mylar tape—A particular data processing tape manufactured by E. I. Dupont de Nemours Co., made of polyester film with a magnetic oxide coat used to store data as magnetized spots on the surface and a substitute tape for punched paper tape in many systems.

* – * – *

name, file—Alpha-numeric characters assigned to identify a related set of records which constitute a particular file.

NAND—A logical operator which has the property that if P is a statement, Q is a statement . . . then the NAND of PQR . . . is true if at least one statement is false, false if all statements are true.

nanosecond—One billionth second. Nanosecond speeds were first introduced to the data processing industry with a thin-film memory computer.

Napier's bones—A method used in aiding multiplication through the use of data tables or rods. It was introduced by John Napier.

NDRO—Stands for Non-Destructive Read Out and relates to the interrogation or printout of a nondestructive type of storage, i.e., read, nondestructive.

NEAT system (National's Electronic Autocoding Technique)—An automatic system for programming that is used in creating an object program in machine language from a source program written by a programmer. One instruction in the object program is created from one instruction in the source program. Mnemonics and references are used in the source program, as well as macro instructions that generate subroutines in the object program. It will translate and compile source programs that are written in the COBOL vocabulary.

negation element—A device or modem with capability of reversing a signal, condition, state, or an event into its alternate or opposite.

negative acknowledge character—A specific communications character designed for control or for accuracy checking which is transmitted by a receiver back to a sender as a negative response.

nest—1. A subroutine or block of data embedded into a larger routine or block of data.

network, active—A electronic network which contains any sources of power other than signal inputs.

network load analysis—The flow listing of messages between stations to organize and create station characteristics by volumes of documents, frequency of processing, and special time requirements.

Neumann, John Von (1903-1957)—A great pioneer of the modern computer. In 1947 he devised a procedure for converting the ENIAC externally programmed computer to a stored-program computer. He used numerals as instruction codes which could be stored electronically just as data numerals were stored, to thus eliminate instruction wiring. His projects toward developing computers capable of reproducing themselves is yet unfinished. He is most often recognized as the true father of modern computing.

neural net—A unique function of memory and information processing necessary for a biological type of computer memory. It includes random organization; the distribution of memory traces through the entire system; the simultaneous participation of any element in many memory traces; no catastrophic failure; implicit or response reinforcement memory, and automatic response (no search and comparison would be needed).

neutral transmission—The technique which transmits teletypewriter signals, whereby a mark is represented by current on the line and a space is represented by the absence of current. By extension to tone signaling, neutral transmission is a method of signaling employing two signaling states, one of the states representing both a space condition and also the absence of any signaling.

new sync—Permits rapid transition from one transmitter to another on multipoint private-line data networks.

nine edge—The lower or bottom edge of a card. This edge is most commonly used for entering the equipment first because of the external equipment requirements.

nine's complement—1. Found by subtracting an original negative number from a counter having the 9 value in each position. A zero value represented by the digit 9 in each position of the counter.

2. Given a digit, say x, the nines complement is defined as y, such that $y = 9-x$. A radix-minus-one complement with the radix equal to ten.

ninety (90)-column card—A 90 vertical column punched card, representing 90 characters. The columns are divided in half horizontally, such that the vertical columns in the upper half of the card are numbered 1 through 45, and those in the lower half are numbered 46 through 90. Six punching positions may be used in each column; these positions are designated, from top to bottom, to represent the digits 0, 1, 3, 5, 7, and 9 by a single punch. The digits 2, 4, 6, and 8 and other characters may be represented by a combination of two or more punches. (Related to punch card and eighty-column card.)

NMAA—Abbreviation for National Machine Accountants Association.

no-address instruction—One which specifies an operation that the computer can perform without having to refer to its storage unit.

no-charge machine fault time—Refers to the unproductive time due to computer fault such as the following: nonduplication, transcribing error, input-output malfunction, and machine malfunction resulting in an incomplete run.

noise—1. Those extra bits or words that must be ignored or removed from the data at the time the data is used. 2. Errors introduced into data in a system, espcially in communication channels. 3. Random variations of one or more characteristics of any entity such as voltage, current, and data. 4. Loosely, any disturbance tending to interfere with the normal operation of a device or system.

noise, gaussian—Noise which designates that the particular voltage distribution is specified in terms of probabilities.

no-job definition error—A condition in which the job did not contain a job definition control card and could not be processed.

NOMA—National Office Management Association.

NOMAD language—NOMAD is an algebraic compiler adapted from the MAD (Michigan Algorithmic Decoder) language to meet the special needs of the installation. It is a high speed compiler which permits a wide latitude of generality in expressions.

nominal (rated) speed—The maximum speed or data rate of a unit or facility which makes no allowance for necessary delaying functions such as checking, tabbing, etc.

nondestructive read—1. A particular storage area that cannot be erased and reused, e.g., punched cards or perforated paper tape. 2. A reading process that does not destroy the data in the source. 3. A reading of the information in a register without changing that information.

nonerasable storage—One where information cannot be erased during the course of computation, e.g., punched paper tape, and punched cards, magnetic slug, missing core, and silvered or aluminized paper.

nonlinearity—A relationship between the output and input which is not representable by a straight line. The output signal does not vary directly as the input signal but is also related to other operating parameters such as hysteresis or friction.

nonlinear programming—A term covering all types of constrained optimization problems except those where the objective function and the constraints are all linear. Special types of nonlinear programming for which some theory has been developed are convex programming, concave programming, and quadratic programming.

nonlinear system—Most often considered any system whose operation cannot be represented by a first order mathematical equation.

nonnumeric character—Any allowable character except a numeric digit.

nonprogrammed halt—A machine stoppage not due to the results of a programmed instruction, such as an automatic interrupt, manual intervention, machine malfunction, power failure, or other cause.

nonvolatile memory—When power is removed from the system, this storage medium retains its information.

NO OP—An instruction commanding the computer to do nothing, except to proceed to the next instruction in sequence.

no operation—An absent or omitted instruction left blank deliberately, often to permit insertion later of data or information without any rewriting, or for the program itself to develop one or more instructions. Often times, a specific instruction which merely advances the instruction content and to perform no other function.

Normal Form, Backus (BNF)—A formal language structure for syntax parsing used in design of ALGOL-60.

normalization routine—Concerns a floating-point arithmetic operation which is related to normalization of numerals in which digits other than zero are developed in the low order; i.e., less significant

positions during the left shift.

normal-stage punching—1. A system where only even-numbered rows of the card are used. (Contrasted with interstage punching.) 2. For punched cards with 24 rows, each column is treated as though it were two separate columns; one digit being represented by holes in the even numbered rows, i.e., normal stage punching, and the other by those in the odd-numbered rows, i.e., the interstage punching. A punched card with 80 columns of 24 rows is thus used as though it were a punched card with 160 columns of 12 rows.

NOT-AND element—A logic element having at least two binary input signals and a single output signal. The variable represented by the output signal is the non-conjunction of the variables represented by the input signals, i.e., an element whose output signal represents 1 when any one or more of its input signals represent 0.

notation—A representational system that utilizes characters and symbols in positional relationships to express information. Types: basic, decimal, octal, Polish, polyvalent, positional, prefix, radix, scientific, symbolic, and ternary.

notation, Iverson—Those symbols developed by Dr. Kenneth Iverson to describe the formal structure of computer languages. Used in APL.

notation, scientific—Quantities are expressed as a fractional part (mantissa) and a power of ten (characteristic).

NOT-BOTH operation—Sheffer stroke operation.

not-busy interrupt—When an external device recognizes its address and is not busy, it sends a response on the not-busy line to the computer. If no such response

114

is received, the processor will assume that the addressed device is busy. The processor will send a start signal only if a not-busy response is received. If a device is disconnected, it will appear as busy to the computer (some computers).

NOT operation—A Boolean operation on one operand in which the result has the alternative value of the operand, i.e., if the two possible states of the operand are represented by a zero and a one, the corresponding results are one and zero. Same as negation, Boolean complemention or inversion.

noughts complement—SEE radix notation.

nsec—Nanosecond, one billionth of a second.

null—1. An absence of information, as contrasted with zero or blank for the presence of no information. 2. Zero.

number, binary notation—A number, usually consisting of more than one figure, representing a sum, in which the individual quantity represented by each figure is based on a radix of two. The figures used are 0 and 1.

number, complex—The combination of real number and an imaginary number in the form of (a + bi) is called a complex number as (5 + 2i) which is the same as $(5 + 3\sqrt{-1})$. The number on the left part of the pair is the "real part" of the complex number, while the right part is the pure imaginary part of the complex number.

number generator, manual—A basic device designed so that data may be manually inserted and held, and whose contents may be sensed by a computer, process controller, or other device. The manual input unit is used to manually insert a word into computer storage or to hold a manually inserted word until it is read during the execution of a program.

number representation—Any system designed to represent the numbers by an agreed set of rules.

number sequence—A number assigned to an item to indicate the relative position in a series of related items.

numbers, floating point—In many cases, the solution of a problem requires values of numbers that are either too large or too small to be expressed by the computer. The physical size of the number can be reduced by "scaling" or shifting the number to the right or left a predetermined number of places so that the most significant bits of the number may be used. For instance, the decimal number 6,510,000 may be expressed as 0.651×10^7, 0.0651×10^8, 0.00651×10^9, etc. The exponent of the number-system base is the scale factor or the number of places the number is shifted.

number system—1. Generally considered, a defined set of numbers, not to be confused with systems of numeration. 2. Integer—An integer is a whole number as differentiated from a fraction or a decimal. A decimal may be used but it cannot have digits other than zeros to the right of the decimal point and still be classified as an integer. In some cases a noninteger may be a solution but only the integer portion of the number has meaning.

numerical analysis—The particular study of techniques of obtaining useful quantitative solutions to problems that have been expressed mathematically, including the study of the errors.

numerical code—A restrictive type of code which has a character set consisting of digits only.

numerical control—Relates to systems in

which digital computers are used for the control of operations, particularly of automatic machines; e.g., drilling or boring machines, wherein the operation control is applied at discrete points in the operation or process. (Contrasted with process control, in which control is applied continuously.)

numeric atomic symbol—For list processing languages these symbols can be decimal integers, octal intergers or floating-point numbers.

numeric key punch—A key punch that processes only numeric data.

* — * — *

O and M analysts—Analysts concerned in the broad field of an organization's financial dealings.

object code—One which is produced by a compiler or special assembler which can be executed on the target computer.

object computer—One which uses the object program to thus execute the instructions, as contrasted to a computer that might be used to merely compile the object program from the source program.

object language—1. One developed by the compiler from the source language; this machine language is directly comprehensible to the computer without further refinement or definition by interpreters, assemblers, or compilers. 2. A result of transforming or translating a source language by any of the many devices or procedures.

object-language program—Same as object routine.

object routine—1. The routine in machine language that is the output after translation from the source language. 2. The running routine.

OCAL—On-line Cryptanalytic Aid Language.

octal notation—A number system with a radix of 8 and which uses positional notation with the eight digits, 0 through 7.

octal number—A number containing one or more figures, representing a sum in which the quantity represented by each figure is based on a radix of eight. The figures used are 0, 1, 2, 3, 4, 5, 6, and 7.

odd-even check—1. In an odd check, a digit (1) is carried along as a check if the total number of ones in the machine word is even, and 0 if the total number of ones in the machine word is odd. In an even check, the digit values are 0 for even and 1 for odd. Words are considered to be even parity or odd parity with check bit depending on the number of numeric ones which are permitted by the computer conventions. 2. Same as parity check.

OEM—Frequently used abbreviation for Original Equipment Manufacturer.

off-line—A system and peripheral equipment or device in a system in which the operation of peripheral equipment is not under the control of the central processing unit.

off-line equipment—Those devices not in direct communication with the central processing unit of a computer (synonymous with auxiliary equipment).

off-line processing—The operations executed by auxiliary computer equipment independent of the computer main frame, such as a card to magnetic tape conversion. In an off-line mode, human intervention and control is required between data entry and ultimate processing.

116

off-line system—In teleprocessing, a system where human operations are required between the original recording functions and the ultimate data processing function. This includes conversion operations as well as the necessary loading and unloading operations incident to the use of point-to-point or data gathering systems.

off-punch—A punch not correctly positioned in a column of a card.

off-time—Refers to a computer that is not scheduled for use, maintenance, repair, or engineering modifications.

on-demand system—One where information or service is available at time of request.

one-plus-one address instruction—Concerns a standard instruction which has an operation part, exactly two address parts, and one of these explicitly specifies the location of the next instruction to be executed—and any other parts, including tags, special characters, etc. Used with computers which have serial delay lines.

one-for-one translation—A phrase often associated with an assembly routine where one source-language instruction is converted to one machine-language instruction.

ones complement—A radix minus-one complement with the radix equal to two.

on-line—A system and peripheral equipment or device in a system where the operation of such equipment is under control of the central processing unit. Information reflecting current activity is introduced into the data processing system as soon as it occurs. It is directly in-line with the main flow of the transaction processing (clarified by on-line equipment, and synonymous with in-line processing and on-line processing).

on-line access banking—A specific procedure of real-time computing services for banks that includes deposits, withdrawals, credit, loans, bill payments, income tax statements, insurance, and stock transactions. A complete financial-on-line-real-time-world-wide computer utility.

on-line equipment—The processing equipment of compatible computer speed that is directly connected to the main processing unit.

on-line system—A system where the input data enters the computer directly from the point of origin and/or in which output data is transmitted directly to where it is used.

on-line input—When the input device transmits data directly to (and under the control of) the central processing unit.

on-line processing—1. The use of terminals, files, and other auxiliary equipment under direct and absolute control of the central processor to eliminate the need for human intervention at any stage between initial input and computer output. 2. Operations performed by auxiliary computer equipment while it is connected to and a part of the computer, such as magnetic tape units feeding data directly to the central processing unit.

on-line, real-time operation (OLRT)—A particular system operation in which the input data to the system are given directly from the measuring devices, and the computer results are thereby obtained during the progress of the event. For instance, the data that are received from measurements during a run, with real-time computation of dependent variables during the run, enables the computer to make changes in its output.

on-line storage—Storage under direct control of the central processing unit.

onomasticon—A specially designed vocabulary of proper or special names, e.g., a list of titles, chemical compounds, companies, executives, etc.

OP code—A command usually given in machine language.

open-ended system—A term for optical character recognition which denotes a system in which the input data are taken from sources other than the computer with which the character reader is associated or data which is not part of the system.

open loop—Referring to a control system in which there is no self-correcting action for misses of the desired operational condition, as there is in a closed loop system.

open subroutine—1. A separately and specifically coded sequence of instructions that is inserted in another instruction sequence directly in low order of the line. 2. A directly inserted subroutine to the main line program specifically where it is required. 3. A subroutine that must be relocated and inserted into the main routine at each place it is used.

operand—1. Any quantity entering into or arising from an operation. An operand may be an argument, a result, a parameter, or an indication of the location of the next instruction. 2. A piece of data upon which an operation is performed. 3. The address or name portion of an operation, e.g., x is the operand of the operation (and x).

operate mode—Considered to be the same as the compute mode when the input signals are connected to the computing unit, including integrators, for the generation of the solution as contrasted to the HOLD, FREEZE OR INTERRUPT modes.

operating programs—These programs direct the loading, segmentation, library search, space- and time-sharing of memory for a group of programs running both sequentially and concurrently.

operating system—A collection, usually integrated, of service routines for supervising the sequencing of programs by a computer. Operating systems may perform debugging, input-output, accounting, compilation, and storage-assignment tasks (synonymous with monitor system and executive system).

operating system, compatible—A series of programs which allow programs in the emulation mode to be operational along with programs of BOS and DOS.

operating system overhead—Concerns the distribution of operating time of the system over all jobs or tasks related to the total cost of the complete system and developed by percentages and ratios.

operating system 360 (OS/360)—One from IBM which spans a range from computers with sequential scheduling to large multi-programming computers which can perform task multijobbing. For the very small computers in the 360 series, other types of operating systems are available.

operating time—Relates to that calculated part of any available time during which the hardware is operating and yielding results for which there is a high confidence level of correctness. Most often includes: development time, production time, and makeup time.

operation—1. An action specified by a single computer instruction or pseudoinstruction; an arithmetical, logical, or transferral unit of a problem, usually executed under the direction of a subroutine. 2. A combination of at least one operator and one operand, e.g., add x. 3. The process of executing a defined action.

operation, asynchronous—That type of processing in which one operation is completed before the next operation is initiated, i.e., initiation and execution are independent on a portion of the equipment while the remaining equipment is free.

operation, auxiliary—One which is performed by equipment not under continuous control of the central processor unit.

operation code—1. Those symbols that state a basic computer operation to be performed. 2. A combination of bits specifying an absolute machine-language operator, or the symbolic representation of the machine-language operator. 3. That part of an instruction that designates the operation of arithmetic, logic, or transfer to be performed.

operation cycle—That part of a machine cycle where the actual execution of the instruction takes place. Some operations (e.g., divide, multiply) may need a large number of these operation cycles to complete the operation, and the normal instruction/operation alternation will be held up during this time. Also called execution cycle.

operation, dyadic—An operation performed on two operands.

operation, illegal—Relates to a condition which results when a computer either cannot perform the instruction or will perform the invalid and undesired results. The limitation is often due to built-in computer constraints.

operation, independent—Operations which do not inhibit the operation of any unit which is not directly connected or involved in the operation concerned.

operation, input-output—1. Each channel is capable of operating in three different transfer modes, input, output, or function. The input and output modes are employed when transferring data to or from the central computer. The function mode is the means by which the central computer establishes initial communication paths with a peripheral subsystem. During this mode of transmission, the central computer sends one or more function words to a peripheral subsystem directing the specified units to perform the desired operation. 2. The input/output section acts as an autonomous processor which runs independently of the instruction-execution cycle, scanning the input channels for the presence of input or output word transfer requests and transferring data between the channels and central storage, controlled by the input/output access-control location associated with the channels.

operation, logical—1. One where a decision affecting the future sequence of instructions is automatically made by the computer. The decision is based upon comparisons between all or some of the characters in an arithmetic register, and their counterparts in any other register on a less than, equal to, or greater than basis; or, between certain characters on arithmetic registers and built-in standards. Also, a shifting operation in which the digits dropped off one end of a word are returned to the other in circular fashion. 2. Operations on a word on a character-by-character basis without regard for other characters, as in logical OR operations.

operation, machine—A predetermined operation set which a computer is designed, built and operated to perform directly, i.e., a jump, etc.

operation mode, conversation—In this mode the system is used exclusively for servicing remote terminals. Real-time man-machine communications are maintained.

operation part—In an instruction, the section that usually specifies the kind of operation to be performed, but not the location of the operands.

operations flow chart—A graphic representation of the inter-communicated inter-connected logical steps necessary to solve a particular problem.

operations research—Using analytical methods adopted from mathematics for solving operational problems. The objective is to provide management with a more logical basis for making sound predictions and decisions. Among the common scientific techniques used in operations research are the following: linear programming, probability theory, information theory, game theory, monte-carlo method, and queuing theory.

operation time—The elapsed time required by the equipment in order to execute a specific operation.

operator—1. Designates what operation to perform, e.g., add is the operator of the operation (add x). 2. In the description of a process, that which indicates the action to be performed on operands. 3. The person who actually manipulates the computer controls, places information media into the input devices, removes the output, presses the start button, etc.

operator command—Any one of various instructions which are issued to the control program through a console unit which causes requested information to be developed, new operations to be begun, regular operations to be altered, or existing operations to be terminated.

operator, exclusive OR—A logical operator that has the property that if P and Q are two statements, then the statement P*Q, where the * is the exclusive OR operator, is true if either P or Q, but not both, are true, and false if P and Q are both false or both true, according to the following table, wherein the figure 1 signifies a binary digit or truth.

P	Q	P*Q	
0	0	0	(even)
0	1	1	(odd)
1	0	1	(odd)
1	1	0	(even)

Note that the exclusive OR is the same as the inclusive OR, except that the case with both inputs true yields no output; i.e., P*Q is true if P or Q are true, but not both. Primarily used in compare operations.

operator, keypunch—This human converts source documents into machine-acceptable form by keypunching from handwritten or typed forms.

OPM—Abbreviation for operations per minute, which is equivalent to characters per minute when control functions are omitted.

OP register—Relates to that specific register in which the operation code of the instruction set is stored.

optical character recognition (OCR)—Using photosensitive devices to identify graphic characters.

optical scanning—A technique for machine recognition of characters by their images.

optical-sensing device, film—An equipment

120

piece capable of reading the contents of a film by optical methods; i.e., a system consisting of a light source, sensors, photocells and a film-moving mechanism. The output of the device is digitized and transferred directly to an electronic computer. An example of such a device is the FOSDIC system developed jointly by the Bureau of Census and the National Bureau of Standards.

optical type font—A medium that can be read by both people and machines—a major advance in simplifying the creation of input for data processing systems. As the sales person or machine operator records the original entry on an adding machine, accounting machine, or cash register, the information is printed on the journal tape in the stylized font that can be read by the optical reader. The optical reader can operate on-line with the computer for immediate processing of reports. Or, the reader can operate off-line, converting the journal-tape information into punched paper tape.

optimize—A designed procedure to cause a system, process, or operation to take on its most desirable configuration or procedures in the best or most efficient way, i.e., to arrange instructions, data, etc., in storage so that a minimum of space or machine time is expended in storing or accessing them.

optimum merging patterns—The way to determine the sequence in which specific sorted tapes in a file should be processed so as to minimize the total number of merge passes required to create a single file of sequenced records.

optimum programming—1. A particular method of programming such that only the minimum waiting time is required to obtain information from the memory. Also called minimum-latency programming, forced coding, and minimum-access programming. 2. A term with several ambiguous connotations all of which are more explicitly indicated by other terms, such as linear programming or minimum-access programming. 3. Programming in order to maximize efficiency with respect to some criterion, e.g., least storage usage, least time share of peripheral equipment, or least use of time between operations.

OPUS—Octal Program Updating System. A system used to update EASY I program tapes, designed by Honeywell.

OR—1. A logical operator having the property that if P is a statement and Q is a statement, then the OR of P.Q. is true if and only if at least one is true; false if all are false. P or Q is often represented by P+Q, PUQ. Related to inclusive OR and exclusive OR.

order code—The rather extensive variety of instructions which can be executed by a unit of equipment. Also, instruction repertoire.

ordering bias—1. A particular and unique characteristic of a sequence which keeps it away from or toward a needed order or desired order. In consequence, some degree of effort is required to achieve the desired order than would normally be expected, say, from a random distribution. 2. A check on the exactness of the order of alphabetic words or numerals.

Ordinary Life Operations, System for (SOLO)—A dynamic, total system approach—tailored to the general needs of all life insurance companies, yet effectively adaptable to the individual company. SOLO organizes the required information for new policy issue—usually

121

one of the most expensive processes of the life insurance operation—into an economical operation. And it also solves the problems involved in a life insurance company's everyday record keeping. SOLO, with its wide range of capabilities, can process automatic internal changes—including premium billing, loan interest, coupon/dividend funds, policy face amount changes—as well as changes due to conditions outside the computer system, such as benefits to be added or deleted, inquiry as to policy status, loan payment, or loan request. (Honeywell)

organizational syndrome, geometric—The geometric organizational syndrome arises from the fact that joint decisions are needed to reach compromises related to the central file concept. Because the interaction pathways of four people are more than double the number of two people, the progression is geometric in nature and not arithmetic. To illustrate, there is one communication path with two people, three with three people, six with four people, ten with five people, fifteen with six people, and so on.

original language—Prior to processing by the machine, the original form in which a program is prepared.

ORSA—Operations Research Society of America.

oscilloscope tube—A cathode-ray tube (CRT) used to display waveshapes and forms, most often as part of research or laboratory instrument measuring and checking.

OS 360 operating system—An operating system from IBM which spans a range from computers with sequential scheduling to large multiprogramming computers which can perform task multijobbing. For the very small computers in the 360 series, other types of operating systems are available.

output—1. Results from the computer such as answers to mathematical problems, statistical, analytical or accounting figures, production schedules, etc. 2. Information transferred from the internal storage of a computer to secondary or external storage; information transferred to any device exterior to the computer. 3. The state or a sequence of states occurring on a specified output channel. 4. The device or collective set of devices used for taking data out of a device. 5. A channel for expressing a state on a device or logic element.

output buffer—1. A buffer designed to receive and store data being transmitted into a computer, and which usually includes instructions. 2. The buffering or transfer device or technique which receives data from internal storage and transfers it to an output media such as magnetic tape.

output device (paper tape)—Output data comes to this device from the computer. Paper tape is placed in the device, which punches the data into the tape. Some computer paper-tape units combine the input and output functions.

output stacker—A device that collects the cards after they have passed through a machine.

overflow—1. With respect to an arithmetic operation, the generation of a quantity beyond the capacity of the register or location which is to receive the result; over capacity; the information contained in an item of information which is in excess of a given amount. 2. The portion of data that exceeds the capacity of the allocated unit of storage. 3. Overflow develops when attempts are made to write longer fields into a field location of a specific length; a 12-digit product will overflow a 10-digit accumulator.

overflow check—The overflow check is a specific feature associated with arithmetic operations, and is a means of immediately recognizing results that exceed the capacity of the counter or accumulator in which they are developed. In order to recognize an overflow and associate it with the proper calculation, the check should be performed immediately after the arithmetic operation. A machine or system which employs this feature can be programmed to detect and signal the condition.

overflow error—Refers to a floating-point arithmetic operation which results in an overflow condition.

overflow indicator—1. Refers to a specific bistable trigger that changes state when overflow occurs in the register with which it is associated. It may be interrogated and/or restored to the original state. 2. A special internal computer-indicator component that is indicated to be "on" if an overflow condition exists due to an arithmetic miscalculation in programming designs.

overflow operation—Concerns a part of the result of an operation which has exceeded the capacity of the intended unit of storage, and actions which relate to the generation of overflow.

overflow position—Refers to an extra position in the register in which the overflow digit is developed.

overhead (accounting)—Relates to specific costs which are not directly attributable to productive work but which are instead allocated, amortized, or spread over the entire production costs to develop accuracy of detail for total cost projections.

overhead (operating system)—Relates to the distribution of operating time of the system over all jobs or tasks related to the total cost of the complete system. It is usually developed by percentages and ratios.

overhead operation—Relates to operations which are designed as organization types, i.e., the recording of the locations to be used by different parts of a program to insure that data are not overwritten unless they are no longer required. Same as housekeeping and red-tape operations.

overlapped channels—Although processors have been improved in internal speed and performance, the added speed and power are not always utilized to full advantage. For example, in processing, many computing operations must be suspended during I/O operations because the circuits in the processor are being used to handle the input/output data. To solve this problem, overlapped channels have been developed.

Overlapped channels (several channels can be serviced simultaneously) in many ways act like a small computer that can take over I/O operations and free the processor for other jobs. This development represented a major step in the utilization of system capabilities.

overlapped-operations buffer—In many systems magnetic core buffers outside the main processor memory compensate for speed differences between slower electromechanical input/output devices and processor speeds. A procedure is used in which operations are overlapped, with all units operating simultaneously at rated speeds. Buffering eliminates the need for more expensive, multi-I/O channels, and eliminates complex I/O timing considerations from the programming job.

overlap, read-punch—Read-punch overlap operations permit the computer to process simultaneously two separate, related files, Thus, the read-punch can be extremely useful in applications that do not require punching. The overall time required to perform these applications is reduced because collating can be eliminated and faster card throughput results.

overlays—Procedures are now designed so that programs or runs too large for memory can be divided into logical segments or overlays. One overlay overlays another, or several segments may be in memory at one time. Overlays are also used when various operations occur infrequently, such as deductions for community chest, union dues, etc. The overlays are called in only when the functions they perform are required. An overlay subroutine is provided to call in these overlays. This subroutine functions in a manner similar to the system supervisor.

overlay segments—Overlay segments relate to an overlay program structure that is not resident in main memory simultaneously with other parts. Very large programs are often segmented into overlays, and such segments are called into memory from auxiliary storage and thus main memory capacity is not overstrained. Overlay segments are ordered as first-level, second-level, etc.

overlays, memory-allocation—In many larger systems the monitor remains resident in lower memory at all times. Object programs are loaded into memory starting at the end of the monitor. The program loader resides in upper memory. Object programs cannot be loaded into the loader area. This area can be overlayed by common storage. Part of the loader can also be overlayed by library subroutines.

overlays, segmentation—A segment of a program is defined as that portion of memory which is committed by a single reference to the loader. Usually a segment overlays some other segment and may have within itself other portions which in turn overlay one another, i.e., subsegments. That part of a segment which is actually brought into memory when the loader is referenced is called the fixed part of a segment. Segments are built up from separate relocatable elements, common blocks, or other segments.

overlay supervisor—A specific subroutine which controls the location and execution sequence of parts of computer programs during conditions of restricted storage space availability.

overload—Refers to an analog computer and relates to a condition existing within or at the output of a computing element that causes a substantial computing error because of the saturation of one or more of the parts of the computing element.

overload level—Refers to the operating limit of a system, component, etc.; it is that point at which operation ceases to be satisfactory as a result of signal distortion, overheating, damage, etc.

overload module testing—Refers to the destructive read off or use caused by overloading or underloading the computer components. This causes failure of substandard units. The test is designed to minimize nonschedule down time.

* _ * _ *

packed decimals—A system technique of data representation. Two digits per character can be used to increase speed and capacity in fields where alphabetics and special characters are not being used.

packing factor—The number of information pulses or bits that can be written on a given length of magnetic surface.

pad character—One which is used to use up time while a function (usually mechanical) is being accomplished, e.g., carriage return, form eject, etc.

paging—The breakdown of a program and data into fixed blocks, often 1,000 words so that transfers between disk and core can take place in page units rather than as entire programs.

paper tape—A paper strip capable of storing or recording information. Storage may be in the form of punched holes, partially punched holes, carbonization or chemical change of impregnated material, or by imprinting. Some paper tapes, such as punched paper tapes, are capable of being read by the input device of a computer or a transmitting device by sensing the pattern of holes that represent coded information.

paper tape, chadless—A paper tape with the holes partially punched. It is commonly used in teletype operations.

paper tape channels—Those positions across the tape used to represent a character, including parity if any.

paper tape reader-punch—This specific reader/punch is a useful, multipurpose unit that can be used for inputting source documents, programs, and data captured from paper input tapes created by a wide variety of office machines, for inter-mediate storage with communications systems, and for special production operations such as newspaper type justifi-cation or numeric machine tool control.

paper throw—When paper in a printer moves through a distance greater than the normal line spacing without printing, it is called a paper throw or a paper slew, i.e., the speed for throw is usually greater than for single-line feed.

parallel—Having the same direction.

parallel access—1. Pertains to simultaneous access to all bits in a storage location comprising a character or word. Equal access time for any bit, character, or word in a storage device. 2. The process of obtaining information from or placing information into storage where the time required for such access is dependent on the simultaneous transfer of all elements of a word from a given storage location (synonymous with simultaneous access).

parallel addition—A procedure developed so that all the corresponding pairs of digits of two numbers being added are processed simultaneously during one cycle of execution with one or more cycles being used to propagate and adjust for any carries which may have been generated. Contrasted with serial addition.

parallel computer—One where the digits or data lines are handled concurrently by separate units of the computer. The units may be interconnected in different ways as determined by the computation to operate in parallel or serially. Mixed serial and parallel machines are frequent-ly called serial or parallel according to the way arithmetic processes are per-formed. An example of a parallel com-puter is one which handles decimal digits in parallel, although it might handle the bits which comprise a digit either serially or in parallel (contrasted with serial computer).

parallel data medium—A medium for recording or entering data and as an input-output media for computers such as cards, tapes, paper, and disks. Usually the data carrier is easily transportable.

parallel operation—1. Using two or more lines simultaneously for the flow of information through the computer. 2. Information, arithmetic, or data transmission or operations that are performed simultaneously. 3. Flow of data through a single processor using two or more channels simultaneously.

parallel processing—The procedure of a computer so that programs for more than one run are stored simultaneously in its storage, and executed concurrently.

parallel programming—The particular feature of programming which provides for two or more results when concurrent operations are to be performed simultaneously. Contrast with serial programming.

parallel storage—1. One where characters, words, or digits are dealt with simultaneously. 2. Storage in which all bits, characters, or (especially) words are essentially equally available in space, without time being one of the coordinates.

parallel transfer—All bits stored in one string of flip-flops are transferred simultaneously to another string, using one wire (or a pair of wires) for each flip-flop.

parameter—1. Referring to a subroutine, it is a quantity which may be given different values when the subroutine is used in different main routines or in different parts of one main routine, but which usually remains unchanged throughout any one such use. 2. A quantity, in a mathematical calculation, that may be assigned any arbitrary value. 3. In generators, the quantity used to designate input-output devices, to specify subroutines to be included, or to define the routine to be generated. 4. A constant or a variable in mathematics that remains constant during some calculation. 5. A definable characteristic of an item, device, or system.

parameter statement—A type of statement used to give specified integer values to specified variables at compile time, e.g., parameter I = 2 causes the integer 2 to replace I whenever it occurs in the source program. This facilitates the assignment of different values to frequently referenced parameters in different compilations of the same program.

parameter testing—A test of an individual subprogram to check and insure that input produces the required output. It is not an integrated testing procedure.

parametric programming—A particular technique for investigating the effect on an optimal linear-programming solution of a sequence of proportionate changes in the elements of a single row or column of the matrix. Most commonly, the method is applied to either the objective-function row or the right-side column.

parametron—A very unique device composed of two stable states of oscillation; the one is twice the frequency of the other and thus having a capability of storing one binary digit.

parenthesis-free notation—A linear or one-dimensional notation system using strings of symbols to indicate various logic, arithmetic or algebraic expressions but which avoids the use of parentheses, i.e., each string of operands may contain operators and operands. See Polish notation as an example.

parity—In reference to computer operations, parity relates to the maintenance of a sameness of level or count, i.e., keeping the same number of binary ones in a computer word to thus be able to perform a check based on an even or odd number for all words under examination.

parity check—A check by summation in which the binary digits, in a character or word, are added, and the sum checked against a single, previously computed parity digit; i.e., a check tests whether the number of ones in a word is odd or even (synonymous with odd-even check, and related to redundant check and forbidden-combination check).

parity error—Used to indicate if, during the course of the previous block transfer, a data parity error was detected or one or more bits have been picked up or dropped out from either the timing track or the mark track.

parity, even—Counts the number of binary ones which is always maintained as an even number. If the ones in the data part of the word or character are even, the parity bit is a zero, if odd, the parity bit is a one.

parity, odd—See: odd-even check.

parity-line circuit—A many-station net in which all stations are on a single circuit. The stations must share the circuit since only one station may transmit at a time.

parsing, language theory—To break down the components of a sentence into structural forms.

partial arithmetic—A procedure used to perform arithmetic on a digital computer in which several parts of one or more numbers are used in arithmetic operations which yield several results.

partial carry—1. When a carry resulting from the addition of carries is not allowed to propagate, it is called a partial carry. When it is allowed to propagate, it is called a complete carry. 2. A computer word which is composed of carries developed at each position when many binary digits are added in parallel, i.e., a carry can be shifted left one place and added back in, and a new partial carry can be developed by the add-back.

partial program—A specific program incomplete by itself and generally a specification of a process to be performed on data. It may be used at more than one point in any particular program, or it might be made available for inclusion in other programs, i.e., a subroutine, and which is often called subprogram, incomplete program, etc.

partitioning—The process of subdividing one large block into smaller subunits that can be handled more conveniently, e.g., partitioning a matrix.

parts programmer—A person who translates the physical explanation for machining a part into a series of mathematical steps, and then codes the computer instructions for these steps.

Pascal, Blaise (1623-1662)—A French mathematician and essay writer who in 1642 built a successful digital calculating machine. It was the first adding machine to resemble the modern desk calculator.

password—The unique set of digits or characters assigned to a user as part of his identification number in communicating with the computer.

patchboard—A removable board consisting of hundreds of terminals into which patch cords (short wires) are connected, which determine the different programs for the machine. To change the program, the wiring pattern on the patchboard or the patchboard itself must be changed.

patch plugboard program—A small type of plugboard which contains a program change in the form of pin or patchcord design and which can be mounted on main program plugboards.

patch routine—Enables octal changes (or corrections) to be made to specified programs at object program execution time. Changes occur in core memory only and do not affect the object program stored on the run tape.

path, sneak—An electrical path unplanned and undesired within a circuit.

pattern recognition—The recognition of shapes or other patterns by a machine system. The patterns may be either a physical shape or a speech pattern.

PCM—1. Punched card machine—The conventional punch card equipment set including sorters, collators, and tabulators (synonymous with EAM and clarified by tabulating equipment). 2. Pulse code modulation: Modulation of a pulse train in accordance with a code.

PCMI—An abbreviation for Photo-Chromic MicroImage, a trademark of the National Cash Register Company (NCR) which describes a microimage process developed by NCR that can develop reductions of 1:40,000 in area, i.e., 1.6 billion words or 7.5 billion characters can be stored on less than 2 square inches of the surface of a film.

PDM (pulse-duration modulation)—Using a series of pulses to convey the information contained in the modulating function. The characteristics of a train of pulses may be modified in one of several ways to convey information, including amplitude, (PAM), position (PPM), and duration (PDM).

peek-a-boo system—A system of information-retrieval that uses peek-a-book cards; i.e., cards into which small holes are drilled at the intersections of coordinates (column and row designations) to represent document numbers (synonymous with batten system).

peephole masks—A set of characters in a character recognition unit residing at a set of strategically placed points and which would theoretically show all input characters as being unique regardless of their style, i.e., for any one character there is only one set of points.

pencil—System for storing, retrieving, and manipulating line drawings.

penumbral—The specific headings that are partially relevant to the data being sought.

perforated tape—A tape, usually paper, upon which data may be stored in the form of punched holes. Hole locations are arranged in columns across the width of the tape. There are usually 5 to 8 positions (channels) per column, with data represented by a binary-coded decimal system. All holes in a column are sensed simultaneously in a manner similar to that for punch cards.

perforation rate—The character rate at which rows, or words are punched in a paper tape.

peripheral—Operation of input/output and other devices not under direct computer control; most commonly used to designate the transfer of information between magnetic tapes and other media.

peripheral equipment—1. Those various units or machines used in combination or conjunction with the computer but not part of the computer itself, such as typewriters, sorters, tape readers, and others. 2. Operations not considered a part of processing, computing or logic, but instead mainly input and output operations, such as magnetic tape conversion, card punching, printing, reading. See: auxiliary equipment.

peripheral operation—The operation, not under direct computer control, of input/output and other devices; most commonly used to designate the transfer of information between magnetic tapes and other media.

peripheral transfer—A procedure or process for transferring data between two units of peripheral or auxiliary equipment.

permanent dynamic storage—A distinct type or form of dynamic storage. Examples are a magnetic disc or drum, i.e., in which the maintenance of the data stored does not depend on a flow of energy.

permanent memory—Information in storage that remains intact when the power is turned off. Also called nonvolatile storage.

permutation—Any of the total number possible of changes in position or form in a group.

permuted index—A form of document indexing developed by producing an entry in the index for each word of specific interest and by including the context in which it occurs, most often restricted to title words.

PERT/COST system—One designed to facilitate planning, scheduling, control, and monitoring of both large- and small-scale research and development projects.

PERT (Program Evaluation and Review Technique) network—Requires an extensive analysis of an overall project in order to list all the individual activities, or jobs which must be performed in order to meet the total objective. These activities are then arranged in a network that displays the sequential relationship among them. PERT provides a means of reporting and analysis for project administrators. Information required can be developed and areas which impose the greatest time restrictions on the completion of a product can be highlighted. Areas with an excess of time for completion, called slack areas, are also highlighted.

PGEC—Abbreviation for Professional Group on Electronic Computers, a technical group devoted to the advancement of computer-related sciences, i.e., programming, engineering, storage devices, etc., a part of the Institute of Electrical and Electronics Engineers (IEEE).

phase—Variation of frequency modulation. A varying of the carrier frequency by a signal, with the maximum deviation being at the point of maximum phase angle. A constant amplitude.

phoneme—A primitive unit of auditory speech in a given language.

photocomposition—A procedure for typesetting which uses a computer and a film recording system and develops a photograph on the face of a cathode-ray tube display. The characters, words, etc., to be used for a printed plate are produced by the computer on the face of the tube for copying and usually in full-page format.

photoelectric reader—A peripheral equipment unit which has the capability of converting data in the form of patterns of holes in storage media, as tapes or cards, into electric pulse patterns by means of photosensitive diodes and transistors, i.e., a reader used for rapid input to a computer and one which usually can also drive a printer, plotter, etc.

photomicrography—The process of making a larger photograph of a much smaller original.

physical record—A punched card is a physical record. Magnetic tapes and disks have physical records as bounded by beginnings and ended by interrecord gaps (IRGs), i.e., physical records on these media are simply the start/stop boundaries while punched paper tape and drums have other special boundaries.

physical simulation—The system's components and processes which are essentially physical (hardware) and hence generally subject to precise definition. Example: an item of electronic equipment such as a radar detector.

PI codes—Program indicator codes. Used when two or more programs are in the same program tape, the use of PI codes permits automatic selection of programs and permits switching from one program to the other.

picosecond—One thousandth nanosecond, or 10^{-12} seconds; abbreviated psec.

piece work programming—The technique of programming using an outside service organization to prepare programs for which payment is arranged by accomplishment, rather than on a time—cost basis. Software companies are usually consulted for the above.

pilot—1. An original or test program, project or device. 2. In transmission, a signal usually of a single frequency, transmitted over the system to test, indicate or control its characteristics or to establish conventions or rules.

ping-pong—The programming technique of using two magnetic-tape units for multiple-reel files and switching automatically between the two units until the complete file is processed.

PL/1—An abbreviation for Programming Language 1, developed by and used often in IBM equipment.

PL/1 (programming language)—Compilers used in compiling object programs from source programs written in a new programming language. This language has some features that are characteristic of FORTRAN and incorporates some of the best features of other languages, such as string manipulation, data structures, and extensive editing capabilities. Further, it has features not currently available in any language. The language is designed to take advantage of recent developments in computer technology and to provide the programmer with a flexible problem-oriented language for programming problems that can best be solved using a combination of scientific and commercial computing techniques. It is designed to be particularly useful for the increasing number of semicommerical, semi-scientific applications such as information retrieval and command and control applications.

plane—A screen of magnetic cores. Planes are combined to form stacks.

plot—To map or diagram. To connect the point-by-point coordinate values.

plotter—1. A visual display or board in which a dependent variable is graphed by an automatically controlled pen or pencil as a function of one or more variables. 2. A device that inscribes a visual display of a dependent variable.

plotter, XY—A device used in conjunction with a computer to plot coordinate points in the form of a graph.

plug board—1. A removable panel consisting of an array of terminals that may be interconnected by short electrical leads according to a prescribed pattern and hence designating a specific program. An entire prewired panel may be inserted for different programs. 2. A control panel or wiring panel.

plus zone—A set of characters in a particular code which is associated with the adjacent bit which represents a plus sign.

point—In positional notation, the character or implied character that separates the integral part of a numerical expression from the fractional part, e.g., a decimal point or binary point.

point, re-entry—The point at which an instruction or a program is reentered from a subroutine or main program is called the re-entry point.

point, rerun—1. That stage of a computer run at which all information pertinent to the running of the routine is available either to the routine itself or to a rerun in order that a new run may be reconstituted. 2. One of a set of planned-for points in a program used so that if an error is detected between two such points, it is only necessary to go back to the last rerun point to rerun the problem.

point, restart—1. One of a set of preselected points located in a program such that if an error is detected between two points, the problem may be rerun by returning to the last such point instead of returning to the start of the problem. 2. To return to a previous point in a program and resume operation from that point.

point-to-point circuits—Private communication lines for the exclusive use of the purchaser, and which join together one or more points.

polish notation—1. A distinct technique or device credited to the Polish logician J. Lukasieqicz for treating algebraic statements as manipulatory strings of symbols followed by manipulatory strings of operations. 2. A specific form of prefix notation.

polyester—As related to magnetic tape, an abbreviation for polyethylene glycol terephthalate, the material most commonly used as a base film for precision magnetic tape. The chief advantages of polyester over other base film materials lie in its humidity and time stability, its solvent resistance and its mechanical strength.

polymorphic system—A specific or particular system which can take on various forms ideally suited to the problems at hand, usually by altering, under its own control, its interconnections and the functions of its component parts, i.e., it may occur with respect to logic construction or organization and a master unit controls a variety of jobs being executed simultaneously and automatically.

polyphase merging—A technique used in a sort program to merge strings of sequenced data. Given T work tapes, merging is performed at the power of T − 1. The effective power of the merge varies between T − 1 and T/2, depending on the amount of input data and the number of strings.

polyvalent notation—A method for describing salient characteristics, in condensed form, using two or more characters, where each character or group of characters represents one of the characteristics.

positional notation—1. The procedure used in conventional number systems wherein the value assigned to a particular digit is determined by the symbol used (for example, 3) and by the position of the symbol relative to the radix point (for example, 300.0). 2. A number representation by means of an ordered set of digits, such that the value contributed by each digit depends on its position as well as on the digit value. 3. A method of representing numbers in which the digits are arranged sequentially, each succeeding digit is interpreted as the coefficient of successive powers of an integer referred to as the base of the number system. For example, in the decimal number system each succeeding digit is interpreted as successive coefficient powers of the integer or base 10.

position, bit—A specific location in memory, space, or time at which a binary digit occurs or is located.

position, overflow—An extra position in the register in which the overflow digit is developed.

position, sign—The left-hand digit position in a numeric field, or the left-hand character position in an alpha-numeric field, in which is stored the sign (minus symbol if negative) of the quantity stored in that field.

post billing system—A system by which the customer invoices are prepared after items have been shipped to the customers.

post editing—An editing procedure or process on the output of a prior operation, especially those related to accounting, or programs which might have syntax or construction errors.

post mortem—A special check routine which prints out information either automatically, or when called for, concerning the contents of all or a specified part of storage after a problem has "died" on the computer. Its purpose is to assist in the location of a program error or a machine malfunction.

postmultiply—To multiply a matrix "A" by some conforming matrix "B," that is, by a matrix "B" that has as many rows as the given matrix "A" has columns (A×B).

postnormalize—Normalizing the arithmetic operation result.

postulate—To assume without specific proof; to accept a proposition without immediate empirical evidence; to accept as evident from general life experience or general acceptance. For example, to postulate by an analogy, projection, or extrapolation; to petition that such knowledge has already been developed.

potentiometer—A voltage divider which has a variable contact arm that permits the selection of any portion of the potential applied across its total resistance.

power failure interrupt—A signal that occurs on many machines for the purpose of informing the machine that the external power is failing. Usually a power failure interrupt will not destroy the operating status of the machine because most machines store enough power internally to go through a predetermined number of instructions.

pragmatics—A particular study of the range or extent to which practical use may be used in constructions of a language, i.e., opposite from theoretical or ideal.

prebilling system—A system in which customer invoices are prepared before the shipping department prepares and ships the goods to customers.

precision, multiple—Using computer words of two or more to represent a single

132

numeric quantity or numeral, i.e., with twice as many or more digits as are normally carried in a fixed-length word used to keep track of several parts of each numeral. Precision is enhanced especially in matrix manipulation which often requires the use of multiple precision arithmetic.

precision, single—The number of words or storage positions used to denote a number in a computer. Single-precision arithmetic is the use of one word per number; double precision, two words per number, and so on. For variable word-length computers, precision is the number of digits used to denote a number. The higher the precision, the greater the number of decimal places that can be carried.

pre-compiler program—A uniquely designed program which detects errors and provides source program correction before the computation of the object deck or program.

pre-edit programs, checking—A pre-edit checking of the application or operational program before the test run — a pre-edit run can remove such things as disobedience to established supervisory care, program segmentation rules, and so on.

prefix notation—A technique of forming one dimensional expressions without need for brackets by preceding with a string or vector of operators, an operand string or vector that may itself contain operators upon operands.

premultiply—To multiply a matrix "B" by some conforming matrix "A"—that is, by a matrix "A" that has as many columns as the given matrix "B" has rows ($A \times B$).

prenormalize—Normalizing the operands of an arithmetic operation before the operation is performed.

presort—The first part of a sort, in which records are arranged into strings that equal or exceed some minimum length.

presumptive address—A number that appears as an address in a computer instruction, but which serves as the base, index, initial or starting point for subsequent addresses to be modified. (Synonymous with reference address.)

prewired options—Optional equipment that is closely related to the processor device, such as the extended arithmetic element, memory extension control, and one of the analog-to-digital converter options, is prewired so that the time, effort, and cost involved in adding this option at the factory or in the field is a minimum.

primary storage—Most often the fastest storage device of a computer and the one from which instructions are executed (contrasted with auxiliary storage).

print control character—A specific control character which is used to affect printing operations such as feeding, spacing, font selection.

printer—1. A device that expresses coded characters as hard copy. 2. An output device for spelling-out computer results as numbers, words, or symbols. Printers range from electric typewriters to high-speed printers which prepare invoices, checks, statements or documents at a 10 lines-per-second clip, and faster.

printer, high-speed (HSP)—A printer which operates at a speed more compatible with the speed of computation and data processing so that it may operate on-line. At the present time a printer operating at a speed of 1500 lines per minutes and 100 characters per line, is considered high-speed.

print line—The normal set of printed characters and spaces arranged in a horizontal row and considered as a unit.

print restore (PR) code—The function which causes a printer to resume printing when it has been in a nonprint case. The PR code triggers this function.

priority—1. The sequence in which various entries and tasks will be processed by the analysis of action codes and other priority-real-time systems, as controlled by program level indicators. 2. The positioning of various routines as input/output ahead or taking precedence over the normal control sequence of the basic routine. (Example: priority circuits.)

priority interrupt—Priority interrupt levels must be assigned using the interaction of functions with each other as a primary basis. The on-line systems designer must ensure all possible interrupts are operating compatibly when worst-case conditions occur. Debugging can become a "horrendous" task; consequently these problems must be solved during the design of the system, not during program and hardware checkout. It may be necessary to reassign the priority levels of key interrupts dynamically under program control. Hardware solutions to this have ranged from large banks of flip-flops to core switching matrices. At least two advances are required in the priority interrupt area to make effective use of the higher performance hardware being developed for on-line systems use. They are time-related priority assignments and externally weighted priority. Adequate solutions have not been found to meet all foreseen requirements, although designers are learning to make use of what is available to make the computer react to the on-line environment.

priority ordered interrupts—Some time-sharing computers can have over 200 priority ordered interrupts for external lines. This extensive interrupt capability allows a terminal to be attached to more than one interrupt line. If the attached interrupts cover a range of priorities, by selectively arming and disarming the external interrupt lines, the executive program can change the relative priority of a terminal's attention requests allowing different classes of service or response to be given to the terminal.

priority scheduling system—A unique type of job scheduler, in larger systems, so designed that a resultant improved system performance is achieved by means of input/output queues.

private memory—The high-speed integrated-circuit memory of a CPU or an IOP.

probability—This can generally be described as the long-range or historical record of experience as measured and scaled for order and inspection. It can be more specifically stated as a ratio of elements in a class (a subset) to a total of a population or random sample drawn from a population—which ratio is a result of experience and calculation.

probability, conditional—The probability that event B will take place provided that A has taken place is called the conditional probability of B relative to A, and it will be written symbolically as $P_A(B)$.

probability distributions—These are tables that show the relative frequencies of each subset into which the total population is divided or segmented. Such tables can be read to show the probability of occurrence of each value so listed.

probability theory—A particular branch of

theory which pertains to measured likelihood of occurrence of chance or random events, and used to predict, analyze, or anticipate behaviors of groups, samples, and events.

probable error—The standard deviation of a distribution of means or any other statistical measure computed from samples is termed the standard error of the mean (σx) or the standard errer of any other statistical measure. The error which will not be exceeded by 50% of the cases is known as the probable error. It is equal to .6745 times the standard error.

problem, benchmark—A routine used to determine the speed performance of a computer. One method is to use one-tenth of the time required to perform nine complete additions and one complete multiplication. A complete addition or a complete multiplication time includes the time required to procure two operands from storage, perform the operation and store the result, and the time required to select and execute the required number of instructions.

problem, check—A problem chosen to determine whether the computer or a program is operating correctly.

problem-oriented language—1. One of the source languages oriented to the description of a particular class of problems. 2. A specific language designed for solutions of a particular class of problems. COBOL AND FORTRAN programs are designed for various classes of problems whether scientific or commercial types, and although they require elaborate and extensive translation and compilation, they are relatively simply developed and quite easily understood even by the novice computer personnel.

procedure analysis—The business activity analysis used to determine precisely what must be accomplished and how.

procedure division—A COBOL routine that describes the procedures to be used in processing the data described in the data division; it contains all the necessary steps to solve a given problem. Procedures are written as sentences which are combined to form named paragraphs. Likewise, paragraphs may be combined to form sections. Paragraph and section names are assigned by the programmer so that control may be transferred from one section or paragraph to another.

procedure-oriented language—One of the source languages oriented to the description of procedural steps in machine computing.

process control—Descriptive of systems in which computers, most frequently analog computers, are used for the automatic regulation of operations or processes. Typical are operations in the production of chemicals wherein the operation control is applied continuously, and adjustments to regulate the operation are directed by the computer to keep the value of a controlled variable constant. (Contrasted with numerical control.)

process control system—A remote system in which the user is not a human being but is instead a mechanical, electronic, or thermal sensing device for input or a mechanical, electronic or thermal controlling device for output.

processing, automatic data (ADP)—Data processing performed by a system of electronic or electrical machines so interconnected and interacting as to reduce to a minimum the need for human assistance or intervention.

processing capacity—Often the maximum

135

limitation of places of a number which can be processed at any one time. Example: A 12 place number.

process-limited (sorting)—A sort program in which the execution time of the internal instructions determine the elapsed time required to sort. Cf. tape limited.

product area—Some computers have an area in main storage to store results of multiplication operations specifically.

production run—A run that fulfills the program objective. It occurs after the projected program has been successfully checked out.

product reference record, manual—One page of the master product file.

program—1. A plan to automatically determine the solution of a problem. A complete program includes plans for the transcription of data, coding for the computer, and plans for the absorption of the result into the system. The list of coded instructions is called a routine. 2. A set of instructions or steps that tells the computer exactly how to handle a complete problem—payroll, production scheduling, or other applications. 3. Programming consists of planning and coding, including numerical analysis, specification of printing formats, and any other functions necessary to the integration of a computer into a system. Types: assembly, automatic recovery, background, bootleg, checking, coded, compiling, computer control, dynamic, editor, general heuristic, hybrid, interpreter, library, line, main, master, monitor, pre-compiler, service, source, support, systems, star, stored, subject, supervisory, target, trace, and translating.

program-address counter—The address of the current instruction is recorded in the register (synonymous with instruction counter).

programatics—A specific branch of study or discipline which deals and relates to the study of the techniques of programming and programming languages.

program card—A card, prepunched, that serves to instruct the machine in the steps or operations it is to perform.

program check—1. A system which determines the correct program and machine function either by running a sample problem with similar programming and a known answer, or by using mathematical or logic checks such as comparing A times B with B times A. 2. A check system built into the program for computers that do not have automatic checking. This check system is normally concerned with programs run on computers that are not internally self-checking (synonymous with routine check, and related to automatic check).

program compatibility—A distinctive feature of most programming aids and the objective programs that they produce is operational compatibility. This property enables the operating system to integrate all elements.

program debugging—This process is mainly the process of making corrections to the program. It is followed by documentation, (which is really a continuing process). The programmer must keep precise records of the entire programming procedure; documentation includes a brief description of the problem, the program, its results, and the process which was used to obtain them.

program drum—The program card is mounted on this revolving cylinder.

Program Evaluation and Review Technique (PERT)—Use of PERT requires an extensive analysis of an overall project, in order to list all the individual activities or jobs which must be performed in order to meet the total objective. These activities are then arranged in a network that displays the sequential relationships among them. This analysis must be extremely thorough and detailed if it is to be realistic. PERT provides a means of reporting and analysis for project administrators. Information required can be developed and areas that impose the greatest time restrictions on the completion of a product can be highlighted. Areas with an excess of time for completion, called slack areas, are also highlighted.

program file—A system which is flexible, easily updated, and used for the maintenance of the entire software library.

program flowchart—A visual representation of a computer problem in which machine instructions or groups of instructions are designated by symbols.

program generator—A program permitting a computer to write other programs, automatically. Generators are of two types; (a) The character-controlled generator, that operates like a compiler in that it takes entries from a library tape (but unlike a simple compiler in that it examines control characters associated with each entry) and alters instructions found in the library according to the directions contained in the control characters. (b) The pure generator is a program that writes another program.

program language—One that is used by programmers to write computer routines.

program library—An assembled set or organized set of computer programs, routines, or common or specifically designed software, i.e., catalog of program titles, abstracts, reels of magnetic tapes or cabinets of punched cards, tapes containing various programs or routines, source or object programs classified for intelligence or retrieval, etc.

program linking—In some computers, if a program is too large to be stored in memory, the programmer can divide it into "links" by means of a FORTRAN link statement. At run time, routines in the monitor system automatically handle the execution of the segments of the linked program.

program loading—During the execution of the processing program, and as a result of many different actions of the control programs, additional programs or program segments may be brought into main storage. The loader alters all necessary addresses in the object program to allow loading at an address of main storage assigned by the control program. The loader has the capability to load separately assembled program segments as if they were a single program, to call in segments from the system program library and combine them with other programs, to link one program segement with another through the use of symbolic references, and to enable different program segments to refer to common data areas. The loader can also perform program overlays, and enable patching of object programs.

programmed dump—A library subroutine called by object programs at run time. The dump may return control to the calling program or to the monitor upon completion. This allows the programmer to take selective dumps during program execution for debugging purposes. The dump returns to the calling program upon completion, if it is called with the name P dump. If it is called with the name dump, the dump is taken and control is returned to the monitor to process the next job (some computers).

programmed halt—A stoppage or interruption of machine operations caused deliberately by a programmer with his program instruction. The halt is automatic with this instruction in the program.

programmed instructions—Using special subroutines, as if they were single commands, by employing one of the program instructions of the system repertoire. This capability allows the programmer to define his own special commands through the use of subroutines which may be changed by the operating routine if desired. The number of instructions required in a typical program is reduced because each subroutine may be called by a single instruction instead of 2 or 3. Programmed instructions also provide, with standard recommended subroutines, complete instruction compatibility.

programmer—A person who prepares problem solving procedures and flow charts and who may also write and debug routines.

programmer analyst—A computer center specialist who has capability in programming as well as analysis of problems, systems, and specific specialties as desired.

programmer-defined macros—Those coding segements, which are used frequently throughout a program, can be defined at the beginning and referenced by a mnemonic code with parameters. This increases coding efficiency and readability of the program.

programmer, senior—Under general supervision, develops and prepares machine-logic flowcharts for the solution of business, engineering and/or scientific problems through the use of electronic data-processing equipment.

programmer, systems—This individual is primarily concerned with writing either "operating systems" (computer internal control programs) or languages for computers. Systems programmers produce these control programs and/or monitors that operate central processor and peripheral equipment. They write test programs that detect errors and malfunctions. They design utility programs to control formats of output and do sorting and merging of files. It is they who are primarily responsible for efficiency of many computer systems.

program, micro—1. Refers to a program of analytic instructions which the programmer intends to construct from the basic subcommands of a digital computer. 2. A sequence of pseudocommands which will be translated by hardware into machine subcommands. 3. A means of building various analytic instructions as needed from the subcommand structure of a computer. 4. A plan for obtaining maximum utilization of the abilities of a digital computer by efficient use of the subcommands of the machine.

programming—The art of reducing the plan for the solution of a problem to machine-sensible instructions.

programming audit—A program which enables use of the computer as an auditing tool.

programming control panel—A panel made up of indicator lights and switches by which a programmer can enter or change routines in the computer.

programming, hybrid—Routines in the hybrid programming library are designed to help the engineer decide which parts of a problem should be solved in digital domain. They also deal with timing, function-generation integration, and general simulation problems, provide diagnosis of hardware operation, and check whether the analog device is scaled and wired correctly.

programming language—A specific language used to prepare computer programs.

programming, minimum latency—Programming in such a way that minimum waiting time is required to obtain information out of storage. (Contrasted with random-access programming.)

programming module—A set of programming instructions which is treated as a unit by an assembler, compiler, loader, or translator.

programming system—An inventory of programs, programming languages, routines and subroutines for use in specific computing systems, i.e., such are the bases for operating systems or total systems of data processing and computing.

program package—A particular group or collection of logically related operational program segments, i.e., all those having to do with the processing of a certain type of inquiry.

program register—1. Located in the control unit, it stores the current instruction of the program and controls computer operation during the execution of the program. 2. A temporary storage device or area which retains the instruction code of the instruction currently being executed. Also known as instruction counter or instruction register.

program, relocatable—A special routine whose instructions are written in a special manner so that it can be located and executed in many areas of the memory. Some modification before execution may be involved to the instructions originally coded relative to a fixed starting place in the memory. Relocatable programs allow for the highly flexible real-time use of the main memory.

program segment—Various computer instructions set in groups of an artificially fixed size to fit into standard-sized areas of main storage in order to facilitate memory allocation and program read-in.

program-sensitive error—An error coming from the unforeseen behavior of some circuits when a comparatively unusual combination of program steps occurs during a run.

program simulator—A program used when an interpretative program allowing programs written for one type of a computer is to be run on a different type of computer.

program step—1. One instruction or command phase in a sequence of instructions; thus, a single operation. 2. An increment, usually one instruction, of a program.

program storage—The internal storage portion reserved for the storage of programs, routines, and subroutines. In many systems, protection devices are used to prevent inadvertent alteration of the contents of the program storage (contrasted with working storage).

program tape—A tape that contains the sequence of instructions required for solving a problem.

program test—A checking system used before running any problem, in which a sample problem of the same type with a known answer is run.

program translation, interpretive—A specialized program relating and handling the execution of a program by translating each instruction of the source language into a sequence of computer instructions and allowing these to be executed before translating the next instruction, i.e., the translation of an instruction is performed each time the instruction is to be obeyed. If the interpretive program allows for programs written for one type of a computer to be run on a different type, it is often called a simulator program.

PROMOCOM—A project which monitors and uses control programming to employ the G-E critical path method; it allows reporting of projected progress and project status for efficient management control.

PRONTO—Used for point-to-point work only. Built-in macros for such operations as drilling, boring, tapping, and counterboring; flexibility in calling for a variety of operations on individual holes; and a smaller hardware requirement make PRONTO a possible alternative approach where requirements and facilities are smaller. (General Electric) .

protected location—A reserved storage location used for special purposes in which data cannot be stored without undergoing a screening procedure to establish suitability for storage therein.

protection, memory—A method specifically designed to insure that the contents of main memory within certain designated but variable bounds will not be destroyed or altered. Special programming devices or hardware thus guard against the effects of equipment malfunction and program bugs in real-time systems.

PRT (program reference table)—Consists of the locations reserved for program variables, data descriptions that give information about data arrays, and other program information. When a program references a word in its PRT, the relative address of the word is used, never the absolute address. The relative address of any particular location is based on its position relative to the beginning of the PRT. The first PRT word is word zero. This method of addressing is used because it does not rely on actual addresses that exist at run time. At run time, a relative address is related to an absolute address through the use of rR. When a program is executing, rR is set to the absoluted address of the base of that program's PRT, according to wherever it was read into core. (Burroughs).

psec—Abbreviation for picosecond or one-trillionth of a second.

pseudoinstruction—1. A particular symbolic representation in a compiler or interpreter. 2. A group of characters having the same general form as a computer instruction, but never executed by the computer as an actual instruction (synonymous with quasi-instruction).

pseudolanguage—One which is artificial and uniquely constructed to perform a distinct task, i.e., a special set of rules is devised with particular meanings assigned to chosen expressions. Some types of programs are quite easily written in pseudo-language, especially various problem or procedure-oriented types, and most of these have some English-type statements in either semantics, syntax, logic, or mnemonics.

pseudo-operation—An operation that is not part of the computer's operation repertoire as realized by hardware; hence an extension of the set of machine operations.

PTT (Program Test Tape)—A Honeywell tape that contains programs and test data to be tested during a checkout run.

pull operation—An operation in which an operand (or operands) is taken from the top of a pushdown stack in memory and placed in a general register (or registers). The operand remains in the stack unaltered; only a pointer value indicating the current top-of-stack is changed.

pulse—1. A change in the intensity or level of some medium, usually over a relatively short period of time; e.g., a shift in electrical potential of a point for a short period of time compared to the time period, i.e., if the voltage level of a point shifts from −10 to +20 volts with respect to ground for a period of two microseconds, one says that the point received a 30-volt, 2-microsecond pulse. 2. A change in the intensity or level of some medium over a relatively short period of time.

pulse-amplitude modulation (PAM)—The coding of a continuous or analog signal onto a uniformly-spaced sequence of constant-width pulses by amplitude-modulating the intensity of each pulse, i.e., similar to AM radio broadcasts except that the carrier is a pulse and not a sine wave.

pulse-code modulation (PCM)—The sampling and quantization of signals in the transmission of analog data and the value of the quantized sample is transmitted as a distinct pattern of pulses, i.e., the value can be expressed as a binary number and transmitted as a sequence of pulses representing 1s and spaces representing zeros.

pulse duration modulation—Pulse-time modulation in which the value of each instantaneous sample of the modulating wave is caused to modulate the duration of a pulse. Note: In pulse modulation, the modulating wave may vary the time of occurrence of the leading edge, the trailing edge, or both edges of the pulse.

punch—1. To shear a hole by pressing sharp edged tool through a material into a die. 2. The hole resulting from the action.

punch-card control units—These units contain all logic, control and power electronics to make compatible card formats.

punched card—A card capable of being punched with holes to represent letters, digits or characters.

punched card field—A column set fixed as to number and position into which the same item or items of data are regularly entered.

punched card format—The most common card is 7-3/8 inches by 3-1/4 inches and consists of 80 vertical columns, numbered from left to right. The rows reading from top down are numbered 12, 11, 0, 1, through 9. Usually only the 0 through 9 rows are actually printed on the cards, it being understood that the 12 row is the first row on the top of the card and the 11 row is the second row just above the 0 row. For a numeric code, a single punch for any particular column in a given row indicates the numerical value, i.e., if row 4 in column 5 is punched, it indicates the number 4 in column 5. Alphabetic characters consist of combinations of 12 and some single digit, 11 and some single digit or 0 and some single digit 2 through 9.

punched paper tape—1. Paper or plastic material from 300 to 1,000 feet long into which data is recorded in the form of small round holes punched into prescribed positions. 2. Another input and/or output medium, used primarily in systems where information is received

141

over wire communication circuits.

punch-EL—A punch of a special type to indicate end of line or the end of a paper tape record.

punch, eleven (11)—A punch in position 11 of a column. This is the X punch often used to control or select, or to indicate a negative number as if it were a minus sign.

push-down queue—A last in, first out, method of queuing in which the last item attached to the queue is the first to be withdrawn.

* _ * _ * _ *

Q test—A test of comparison of two or more units of quantitative data for their equality or non-equality.

quadratic programming—Maximization of an objective function that is quadratic, subject to linear constraints. This is one of the few convex programming problems, aside from linear programming, that have solution algorithms that terminate in a finite number of steps.

quadripuntal—This pertains to four punches, specifically having four random punches on a punch card. This term is used in determinative documentation.

quadruplex system—A Morse telegraphy system arranged for the simultaneous independent transmission of two messages in each direction over a single circuit.

quantization error—Same as quantization uncertainty.

quantization uncertainty—A specific gauge or measure of the uncertainty, particularly that of the irretrievable information loss, which occurs as a result of the quantization of a function in an interval where it is continuous.

quantize—To subdivide the range of values of a variable into a finite number of non-overlapping subranges or intervals, each of which is represented by an assigned value within the subrange; e.g., to represent a person's age as a number of whole years.

quantum—One of the intervals of a set or group used to quantize a function. A unit of time in a queue.

quantum clock—A device which allocates an interval or quantum of processing time to each program as set in priorities used in computing systems with developed time-sharing procedures.

quasi-instruction—1. A symbolic representation in a compiler or interpreter. 2. A character group with the same general form as a computer instruction, but never executed by the computer as an actual instruction. Same as pseudo-instruction.

queue—A line or group of items waiting for the attention of the processor, usually in core, that are chained together by address words in consecutive order and then acted on by the processor.

queuing—A special study of the patterns involved and the time required for discrete units to move through channels; e.g., the elapsed time for auto traffic at a toll booth or employees in a cafeteria line.

quibinary code—A binary-coded decimal code used to represent decimal numbers in which each decimal digit is represented by seven binary digits that are coefficients of 8, 6, 4, 2, 0, 1, 0, respectively.

quick-access memory—A part of memory that has relatively short access time, as compared to the main memory of the CPU, i.e., at least significantly faster than other devices in the same computer sys-

142

tem, such as disc-tape storage wherein, the disc is much faster and is considered high-speed relative to the tape and in respect to the CPU (Central Processing Unit).

QUIKTRAN—A subset of FORTRAN including built-in functions augmented by powerful and versatile operating statements for complete control maintenance. Special codes for easy parameter insertion and changes, such as assigning new values to variables, and for deletion and replacement plus cross-referencing and selective output, make this an outstanding innovation to computer science (IBM).

quinary—A system of number representation in which each decimal digit N is represented by the digit pair AB, where $N = 5A + B$, and where $A = 0$ or 1 and $B = 0, 1, 2, 3,$ or 4, e.g., decimal 7 is represented by biquinary 12. This system is sometimes called a mixed-radix system having the radices 2 and 5.

quotient-multiplier register—A temporary storage device in which the multiplier is placed, or in which the quotient for division is developed.

* — * — * — *

radial stackers—This refers to the many receptacles which hold supplies of cards which have been processed.

radial transfer—A process or procedure used for transferring data between peripheral equipment and the internal memory of the machine.

radix—The number system base; that is, a quantity that defines a system of representing numbers by positional notation; the number of digit symbols required by a number system. Examples: decimal, 10;

octal, 8; quinary, 5; binary 2.

radix complement—A complement on N, obtained by subtracting each digit of the given quantity from N-1, adding one to the least significant digit, and performing all resultant carrys; e.g., the twos' complement of binary 11010 is 00110; the tens' complement of decimal 456 is 544.

radix notation—1. An annotation which consists of a decimal number in parentheses, written as a subscript to a number, its decimal value indicating the radix of the number; e.g., $11_{(2)}$ indicates the number 11 is in the radix of two; $11_{(8)}$ indicates the number 11 is in the radix of eight. 2. A number written without its radix notation is assumed to be in the radix of ten (synonymous with base notation).

radix number—The number of characters for use in each of the digital positions of a numbering system. In the more common numbering systems the characters are some or all of the Arabic numerals as follows:

System Name	Characters	Radix
binary	(0,1)	2
octal	(0,1,2,3,4,5,6,7)	8
decimal	(0,1,2,3,4,5,6,7,8,9)	10
quinary	(0,1,2,3,4)	5

Unless otherwise indicated, the radix of any number is assumed to be 10. For positive identification of a radix 10 number, the radix is written in parentheses as a subscript to the expressed number, i.e., $12_{(10)}$. The radix of any nondecimal number is expressed in similar fashion, e.g., $11_{(2)}$ and $5_{(8)}$ (synonymous with base and base number).

radix sort—This particular method uses a technique similar to sorting on tabulation machines (e.g., IBM sorter). The elapsed time is directly proportional to the number of characters in the sequencing key and the volume of data.

RAM (random-access memory)—A particular storage method in which the time required to obtain information is independent of the location of the information most recently obtained. This strict definition must be qualified by the observation that we usually mean relatively random. Thus, magnetic drums are relatively nonrandom access when compared to magnetic cores for main storage, but are relatively random access when compared to magnetic tapes for file storage. (Contrasted with sequential-access storage.)

RAMAC—Random-access method of accounting and control, a data file that consists of a number of rotating disks stacked one on top of another. (IBM).

random-access—A quality of a memory device that allows data to be written in, or read from, the memory through direct locating rather than locating through reference to other data in the memory. No search is required; the machine can proceed directly to the desired memory location.

random-access device—Relates to a storage device in which the access time is effectively independent of the location of the data.

random-access memory (RAM) (bank)—Used to provide storage of on-line account records containing all information—account balance, available balance, unposted dividends and previous no-book transactions, account holds, etc., required for complete processing of transactions and inquiries, as well as for updating of passbooks.

random-access programming—Programming without regard to the time required for access to the storage positions called for in the program. (Contrasted with minimum-access programming.)

random-access storage—1. A storage medium in which the time required to obtain information is statistically independent of the location of the information most recently obtained. 2. A type of storage in which access can be made directly to any storage regardless of its position, either absolute or relative to the previously referenced information.

randomizing scheme—Plans for the distribution of file records among several file storage modules designed so that the accesses to these records will be distributed equally and the waiting times for file information will be set evenly.

random number—1. A digit set constructed in such a sequence that each successive digit is equally likely to be any of n digits to the base n of the number. 2. A number formed by a set of digits selected from a random table or sequence of digits. 3. A number formed by a set of digits selected from an orderless sequence of digits.

random-number generator—Either a special machine routine or hardware unit designed to produce a random number or a series of random numbers according to specified limitations.

random numbers—A grouping or unbiased succession of digits or numbers developed entirely as a result of a random or chance process. A particular satisfaction of various statistical criteria is considered an adequate test of randomness, principally the tests which show total absence of bias in any form in the selection process.

random number table—A table of random numbers is a set of numbers such that each of the digits from 0 to N has the same chance of appearing in any position in the table.

random sample—A sample is random if every item in the population has an equal chance of being included in the sample. This definition implies that the selection of the sample should be left to chance.

random sequential access—A random-sequential-access storage device is one in which the information storage medium is grouped in strips. The computer can gain random access to any one strip as easily as any other, but it is then necessary to scan sequentially along the strip to find the desired word. An example of a random-sequential-access storage device is a magnetic drum. This device is a cylinder that is coated with a magnetic film similar to that used on magnetic tape. It rotates at high speed. There are a large number of magnetic heads along the cylinder, each having access to a circular strip, or "track", of the magnetic coating. There are many storage locations around each track. Any magnetic head can be selected instantaneously, at random, but the words in a track pass by sequentially.

range—1. All the values that a function or word may have. 2. The difference between the highest and lowest of these values.

range check—A procedure for controlling the accuracy of data by verifying that the value of a piece of data falls between certain pre-established maximum and minimum values.

range of a DO statement—All FORTRAN statements included in the repetitive execution of a DO loop operation.

rapid access—Most often synonymous with random access and is contrasted with sequential access, i.e., dependency upon access of preceding data.

rate, bit—The rate at which binary digits, or pulses representing them, pass a given point on a communications line or channel. (Clarified by baud and channel capacity.)

rate, information (through a channel, per second)—The product of the average transformation per symbol and the average number of symbols per second.

raw data—Non processed data; it may or may not be in machine-sensible form.

reader—Any device, among hundreds, capable of sensing, detecting, or converting data, i.e., transforming to another form or medium. Types: card, high speed, optical, and photo-electric.

reader/interpreter—A service routine that reads an input stream, stores programs and data on random-access storage for later processing, identifies the control information contained in the input stream, and stores this control information separately in the appropriate control list. A reader/interpreter may be considered very nearly as the opposite of an Output Writer.

reader-sorter—A punch card equipment unit which senses and transmits input while sorting documents.

read in—read out—An optical feature which can be added to certain off-line office machinery permitting on-line operation.

read/jump protection—This permits the executive to stop the program at the point of error, terminate it, and provide diagnostic information to the programmer, thereby minimizing wasted time and smoothing the checkout process. A particular advantage of read/jump protection is that programs of a classified nature can be confidently run together; they are fully protected from audit (inadvertent or otherwise) by other programs.

read-only memory—A special memory that cannot be altered in normal use of the computer. Usually a small memory that contains often-used instructions such as microprograms or system software as firmwave.

read reverse—The unit can read tape under program control in either direction.

read screen—An optical character recognition (OCR) term representing that transparent component part of most character readers through which appears the input document to be recognized.

read time—1. The time to locate data or an instruction word in a storage section and transfer it to an arithmetic unit where the required computations are performed. 2. The time it takes to transfer information that has been operated on by the arithmetic unit to a location in storage; related to write time and word time.

read-write check—Checking specifically the accuracy of reading, writing, sensing, punching, recording, etc., completed by comparing or sensing what has been written and comparing and/or sensing what was expected to be read and/or written, i.e., running punched cards through key-verifiers or a comparator.

ready—The status or condition of being ready to run. A program, task, or hardware device that is in a ready condition needs only a start signal in order to begin operation.

ready condition—A specification or circumstance of a job or task signified when

all of its requirements for execution other than control of the central processor have been satisfied.

real constants—Those constants written with a decimal point, using the decimal digits 0, 1, ..., 9. A preceding + or − sign is optional. An unsigned real constant is assumed to be positive. An integer exponent preceded by an E may follow a real constant. The exponent may have a preceding + or − sign. An unsigned exponent is assumed to be positive.

real number—One of the set of all positive and negative numbers, including all types: integers, zeros, mixed, rational, irrational, etc., but not imaginary or complex.

real time—1. This pertains to the actual time during which a physical process transpires. 2. Pertaining to the performance of a computation during a related physical process to obtain results needed to guide that process. 3. A method of processing data so fast that there is virtually no passage of time between inquiry and result. Each inquiry may be communicated to the system separately, and the result received immediately.

real time data reduction—The processing of information as rapidly as the information is received by the computing system, or as rapidly as it is generated by the source.

real time executive system—The real-time executive system controls, sequences, and provides for the efficient allocation of facilities for operating the real-time system. Normally, the real-time executive system controls a real-time program operating concurrently with one or more batch programs. The real-time executive system eliminates the need for the programmer to plan for concurrency. It maintains and restores the operational environment of each program so that as far as the programmer is concerned, his program operates as if it were the only one being run in the system. The real-time executive system also provides a number of basic subroutines that assist in matters of console control, rerun, the loading of segments or overlays, and input/output control for the various subsystems. (UNIVAC).

real-time output—Specific data or information which is output, i.e., received from, or removed from a system in the time needed or designed, for interpretation or alteration of the program being computed.

real-time satellite computer—A satellite computer in the real-time system relieving the larger computer system of time consuming input and output functions, as well as performing preprocessing and postprocessing functions such as validity editing and formating for print.

real-time simulation—A simulator or simulation program operation, such that the instants of occurrence of many basic events in the simulator occur at the same times as they would in the system being simulated, i.e., one that is sufficiently fast or reduced in scope to insure that the instants at which output occur are indistinguishable from those that the system being simulated would produce.

real-time system—To process information or data in a sufficiently rapid manner so that the results of the processing are available in time to influence the process being monitored or controlled.

real variables (FORTRAN)—One that consists of a series of not more than six alphanumeric characters (except special characters) of which the first is alphabetic but can not be one of the integer indicators, i.e., I, J, K, L, M, or N.

reasonableness tests—Those that provide a means of detecting a gross error in calculation or, while posting to an account, a balance that exceeds a predetermined limit. Typical examples include payroll calculations and credit-limit checks in accounts receivable.

receive-only service—Service in which the data-communication channel is capable of receiving signals, but is not equipped to transmit signals.

reciprocal—The mathematical expression establishing the relationship of a number which exists when that number is divided into a single unit or one, i.e., the process of multiplying by the reciprocal of the number equivalent to dividing by that number.

recirculating loop—In reference to drum computers, a small section of memory that has much faster access than the remainder of memory.

recognition—The act or process of identifying (or associating) an input with one of a set of known possible alternatives.

recomplementation—An internal procedure performing nines or tens complementation, as required, on the result of an arithmetic operation.

record—1. A set of one or more consecutive fields pertaining to a related subject, as an employee's payroll record. Although a record need not be a block in length, such an arrangement is often useful. 2. A listing of information, usually in printed or printable form; one output of a compiler consisting of a list of the operations and their positions in the final specific routine and containing information describing the segmentation and storage allocation of the routine. 3. To make a transcription of data by a systematic alteration of the condition, property, or configuration of a physical medium, e.g., placing information on magnetic tapes or a drum by means of magnetized spots. 4. To group related facts or fields of information treated as a unit. Types: data, label, logical, master, physical, trailer, transaction, unit.

record gap—1. On a tape, the space between records usually produced by tape acceleration during the writing stage of processing. 2. A gap used to indicate the end of a record.

recording density—The number of bits contained in a given unit length of a linear track in a recording medium.

recording mode—In reference to COBOL the representation of data associated with a data-processing system in external media.

record length—1. The number of characters necessary to contain all the information in a record. 2. An arbitrarily chosen number of characters that comprise the records in a given program. To secure this record length, it is sometimes necessary to pad the records (clarified by pad character).

record mark—Used in some computers, this special character either limits the number of characters in a data transfer, or separates blocked or grouped records in tape.

record name—In COBOL, used to give a name to a record within a file and assigned the level number 01. Data names for elements within a record have lower-level numbers, 02, 03, etc.

record separator—A specific character designed for the purpose of demarcation of the logical boundary between records.

records management—A specific program designed to provide economy and efficiency in the creation, organization, maintenance, use, and disposition of records. Thus, needless records will not be created or kept and only the valuable records will be preserved.

recovery from fallback—The restoration of a system to full operation from a fallback mode of operation after the cause of the fallback has been removed.

rectangular coordinates—A set of three lines, called axes, that intersect at a common point in space in a way that each line, or axis, is perpendicular to the plane containing the other two.

recursive—Pertaining to a process that is inherently repetitive. The result of each repetition is usually dependent upon the result of the previous repetition.

recursive procedure—Any procedure, A, which, while being executed, either calls itself or calls a procedure, B, which in turn calls procedure A.

redaction—A new or revised input data edition.

redundancy—1. In reference to information transmission, redundancy is the fraction of the gross-information content of a message that can be eliminated without the loss of the essential information. Numerically, it is one minus the ratio of the net information content to the gross information content, expressed in percent. 2. An extra piece of information used to assist in determining the accuracy of moved digits or words in a computer (clarified by redundancy check).

redundancy check—A method of checking based on the presence of extra (redundant) information which is used only for checking purposes. Parity checking, check digits, control totals, and hash totals are all examples of redundancy checks.

reel, take-up—A specific reel on which tape is wound or may be wound during processing.

reenterable—The attribute of a program that describes a routine which can be shared by several tasks concurrently.

reenterable load module—A type of load module which can be used repeatedly or concurrently by two or or more jobs or tasks.

reentrant program—A program so written that after interrupting a lower-priority program, will allow the latter to be restarted from the point of interruption.

reentry system—A character recognition term for a system in which the input data to be read are printed by the computer with which the reader is associated.

reference address—A number that appears as an address in a computer instruction, but which serves as the base, index, initial or starting point for subsequent addresses to be modified. (Synonymous with presumptive address.)

reference record—A computer output that lists the operations and their positions in the final specific routine. The output also contains information describing the segmentation and storage allocation of the final routine.

reflected-binary code—Any type of binary code in which sequential numbers are represented by binary expressions, each of which differs from the preceding expression in one place only. (Synonymous with reflected code and cyclic code.)

reflected code—1. Any type of binary code that changes by only one bit when going from one number to the number immediately following. Synonymous with reflected-binary code and cyclic code.) 2. See reflected-binary code.

regenerative memory—A memory device whose contents gradually vanish if not periodically refreshed.

register—1. A temporary storage device used for one or more words to facilitate arithmetical, logical or transferral operations. Examples are the accumulator, address, index, instruction, and M-Q registers. 2. The hardware for storing one or more computer words. Registers are usually zero-access storage devices. Types: address, bonds, buffer memory, circulating, control, current-instruction, memory, memory address, memory buffer, return code, shift, standby, storage, and switch.

register, accumulator—That arithmetic unit part in which the results of an operation remain, and into which numbers are brought from storage, and from which numbers may be taken for storage.

register address field—The portion of an instruction word that contains a register address.

register, mask—The mask register functions as a filter in determining which portions of words in masked operations or logical comparisons are to be tested. In repeated masked-search operations, both the mask register and the repeat counter must be loaded prior to executing the actual search command. (UNIVAC)

regression—This is the rate at which an output changes in relation to the changes in inputs; more specifically, it represents the slope of a line which graphs the comparable values of inputs (independent variables) and the output (dependent variables).

149

relative addresing, time-sharing—Relative addressing is a feature of great significance in multiprogramming, time-sharing, and real time operations. It allows storage assignments to be changed dynamically to provide contiguous storage for operation of another program, and permits programs to dynamically request additional main storage according to processing needs. An additional advantage is that systems programs stored on mass storage may be brought in for operation in any available area without complicated relocation algorithms. Relative addressing is provided for through basing registers contained within the processor. A separate register controls the basing of the program instruction and data bank, and a third register controls the selection of the appropriate basing register.

relative code—One specifying or writing all addresses with respect to an arbitrarily selected position, or in which all addresses are represented symbolically in machine language.

relative magnitude—The magnitude relationship or comparison of one quantity to another, most often related to base magnitude and expressed as a difference from or a percentage of the base or reference.

relativization—A particular technique by which the next written instruction address and operand address are given relative addresses. The relative address is translated automatically to an obsolete address during execution of the program.

reliability—1. The techniques used to measure the ability to function without failure. 2. The amount of credence placed in the result. 3. A word to indicate a measurement of trustworthiness and dependability, and frequently used to imply reliability factor or coefficient.

reliability testing—A series of tests to indicate the life expectancy under specified conditions. The results are often specified in terms of probabilities and standard conditions.

relocatability, program (time sharing)—It is desirable that program and data segments be allocatable dynamically in a time-shared system. This avoids the constraint of dedicating a fixed portion of core memory to a user program and allows flexibility in intermixing programs in a multi-user environment. However, when executed, a program must have the operand addresses of its instructions modified to reflect the current assigned locations of the program and the data segments referenced by it. Hardware features which minimize the effort required to relocate a program or data segmented by providing automatic address adjustment increase the efficiency of a time-shared system.

relocation, dynamic—The allocation of memory space in a multiprogrammed computer in order to most efficiently utilize the total memory capacity. This is accomplished automatically by the computer by its changing the area of storage occupied by given program or portion of a program.

remote-computing system completeness errors—Programs that are incomplete (e.g., transfers to nonexistent statement numbers, improper DO nesting, illegal transfer into the range of a DO loop, etc.). Errors of completeness are detected after the user has indicated that his program is complete. All such errors are then extracted and immediately displayed at the terminal in a sequential list. When all the errors have been listed, the user can then individually correct or disregard them before initiating the execution of his completed program. Any disregarded errors, when redetected during execution, are considered as execution errors. (FORTRAN)

remote control language—The remote-computing system language comprises two types of statements; program statements and operating statements. Program statements which are upwardly compatible with FORTRAN IV are used to and from the user's program. Operating statements allow the user to communicate with the remote-computing system. Operating statements include modification, test display and output statements (some computers).

remote data terminal—Used to provide the capability of sending 80 or 90 column cards, keyboard information, and paper tape from a remote location to a central processor, as well as the capability of punching 80 or 90 column cards, punching paper tape, and printing information received from a central processor.

remote terminal—A device or modem for communicating with computers from sites which are physically separated from the mainframe of the computer, and usually distant enough so that communications facilities rather than direct cables are used.

removable random access—Describes a feature of storage device like disk packs, tape strips or card strips which can be physically removed and replaced by another, thereby allowing for a theoretically unlimited storage capacity. Contrasted with both sequential storage and fixed media random access storage.

reperforator—1. A contraction of the words: receiving and perforator. 2. A tape punch that automatically converts coded electrical signals into perforations in tape.

repertory, instruction—1. The instruction set that a computing or data processing system is capable of performing. 2. The set of instructions that an automatic coding system assembles.

repetition instruction—This causes one or more instructions to be executed an indicated number of times.

report generator—1. A technique for producing complete data-processing reports giving only a description of the desired content and format of the output reports, and certain information concerning the input file. 2. A software program that can direct the production of output reports if the computer is provided with format and specifications, input file detail, sorted input data, input-output procedure rules and other information.

representation—A combination of one or more characters to represent a unit.

representation, fixed-point—A form of notation in which all number quantities are expressed by the same number of digits, the point being implicitly located at the same specified position.

representation, floating point—A system of numeration wherein each numeral is a number which consists of a pair of numerals, one being a coefficient for a fixed positive integer radix raised to a power by an exponent, which is the second number of the pair. An example is: 0.0260 is the same as 260 -4 or 260 X 10⁻⁴.

representative simulation—A system in which the components, processes, and interactions of the model bear a clear relationship to the system under study. This tends to rule out highly abstract, mathematical models.

reproducer—1. Used for duplicating cards and card data, or for punching cards in any format. Also called gang punch. 2. A device that will duplicate on one card, all or part of the information contained on another card.

request-repeat system—A system employing an error-detecting code and so arranged that a signal detected as being in error automatically initiates a request for retransmission of the signal that was detected as being in error.

requirement function—A document most often prepared by systems analysts or operations-research staff people explicitly detailing one of the functions to be performed by the system. Specifications concerning the manner in which the function will be completed often accompany the message. Function requirements provide a basis for: guiding and assisting people who prepare programs; preparing instruction manuals; obtaining management acceptance of management procedure or policy changes to further integrate a computer "total system."

rescue dump—To record on magnetic tape the entire contents of the memory, which includes the status of the computer system at the time the dump is made. R dumps are made so that in the event of power failure, etc., a run can be resumed from the last rescue point (R point) rather than rerunning the entire program (NCR).

rescue points—For many applications it is very desirable, indeed essential, to create rescue points (R points) from which it is known that the program can be resumed

in a proper manner. If a processing mishap does occur after creating a rescue point, the operator can restart his run at any rescue point by use of the restart routine. For long runs, the liberal use of rescue points will mean that the run is, in essence, segmented. A mishap will affect only one segment and all the valid processing that preceded the establishing of the latest point is saved and need not be reprocessed (NCR).

research analyst—He investigates and reviews operations and identifies those suitable for data processing.

reset—A procedure which returns a device to zero or to an initial or arbitrarily selected condition.

residual error—The difference between a supposedly exact result derived from theory and an optimum result derived from experience or experiment.

resolution—The process of separating the parts which compose a mixed body.

resolution error—An error resulting from the inability of a computing unit to demonstrate changes of a variable smaller than a given increment.

response—The explicit quantitative expression of the output as a function of the input. The response characteristic, often presented graphically, gives the response as a function of some independent variable, such as frequency.

response time—The elapsed time between generation of an inquiry at a terminal and the receipt of a response at the terminal. Response time would be transmission time to the computer, processing time at the computer, access time to obtain any file records needed to answer the inquiry, and transmission time back to the terminal.

restore—1. Returning a variable address or

other computer word to its initial or preselected value. 2. To return a register, trigger, error-condition signal, etc., to zero or to a specific initial condition.

retina—In optical character recognition, a major component of a scanning device.

retrieval—1. The recovery of research material. 2. The act of finding stored material.

retrofit—An adjustment of existing systems or programs for the purpose of fitting in or accommodating a new part and performing all other changes necessary in related systems of programs.

return code register—One used to store data which controls the execution of follow-on or subsequent programs.

return-to-zero (RZ)—A method of writing information on a magnetic surface in which the current through the write-head winding is returned to zero after the write pulse.

reverse-digit sorting method—Sorting which begins with the unit's position of a given field and proceeds one column at a time (from right to left) until the field is completely sorted. Digit sorting method, reverse.

rewind—The process of returning a film or magnetic tape to its initial data point.

right hand justified—Data are right justified when the right-hand digit or character occupies its allotted right-hand position.

ring shift—A shift in which the digits are dropped-off at one end of a word and returned at the other in a circular fashion; e.g., if a register holds eight digits, 23456789, the result of a cyclic shift two columns to the left would be to change the contents of the register to 45678923. (Synonymous with circular shift, end-around shift, logical shift, and nonarithmetic shift.)

ripple adder—A binary adding system similar to the system most people use to add decimal numbers; i.e., add the "units" column, get the carry, add it to the "10's" column, get the carry, add it to the "100's" column, and so on. Again it is necessary to wait for the signal to propagate through all columns even though all columns are present at once (parallel). Note that the carry is rippled.

robot—A particular device equipped with sensing instruments for detecting input signals or environmental conditions but with reacting or guidance mechanisms which can perform sensing, calculations, etc., and with stored programs for resultant actions, i.e., a machine running itself.

rope storage—A unique storage device invented by Olsen of the Lincoln Laboratory of the Massachusetts Institute of Technology. Information is stored in the form of an array of cores and wires, the wires being wound in one direction or the other through the core. The pattern which results resembles a rope and permits a selection of a single core for a given pattern of pulses. The information is stored in the wiring rather than in the core itself, the core acting much as a switch. Same as: core-rope storage, linear selection switch, rope memory and Olsen memory.

ROTR—A typing reperforator, which can receive only. A teletypewriter receiver which produces perforated tape with characters along the edge of the tape.

rounding—When it has been decided how many decimals or significant numbers should be used, one important question remains: How shall the numbers be reduced to the desired values? The rule is as follows: When the first of the digits to be dropped is less than 5, the digits are dropped with no change in the preceding digit. When the digit to be dropped is greater than 5, or is 5 followed by other digits greater than zero, the preceding digit should be increased by 1. If, on the other hand, the digit to be dropped is exactly 5, increase the preceding digit by 1 if it is odd, otherwise drop the remainder. This is known as the "even-digit rule."

rounding error—Results from dropping certain less significant digits with some adjustment applied to the more significant digits retained. Also called round-off error.

routine—1. A machine instruction sequence that carries out a well-defined function. 2. A set of coded instructions arranged in proper sequence to direct the computer to perform a desired operation or series of operations. Types: algorithmic, assembly, benchmark, compile, control, conversion, dating, executive, executive system, object and service.

routine, executive—1. A program that controls loading and relocation of routines and in some cases makes use of instructions which are unknown to the general programmer. Effectively, an executive routine is part of the machine itself (synonymous with monitor routine, supervisory routine, and supervisory program). 2. A set of coded instructions designed to process and control other sets of coded instructions. 3. A set of coded instructions used in realizing automatic coding. 4. A master set of coded instructions.

routine, library—A collection of standard, proven routines and subroutines used to solve problems or parts of problems.

routine storage—The section of storage allocated to receive and store the group of instructions to be executed.

row—The horizontal vector of a matrix.

row pitch—The distance between the centers of adjacent holes along a paper tape.

RPG—An abbreviation for Report Program Generator.

R-register—The register that holds the ten low-order digits.

RT (reperforator transmitter)—A receiver-transmitter of a reperforator and a tape distributor, where each unit is independent of the other unit. It is used as a relaying device and is especially suitable for transforming the incoming speed to a different outgoing speed.

run—1. To process a batch of transactions while under the control of one or more programs, and against all the files that are affected to produce the required output. 2. Performance of one routine, or several routines automatically linked so that they form an operating unit, during which manual manipulation are not required of the computer operator.

runaway—A condition which arises when one of the parameters of a physical system undergoes a large, sudden, undesirable and often destructive increase.

run chart—A flowchart of one or more computer runs in terms of input and output.

run diagram—Files, transactions, information and data in a graphic representation that is to be handled under program control to produce the newly updated files, list of changes, or specific reports.

running accumulator—One which works as though it comprised a number of registers arranged in a column, with only the register at the top of the column connected to the rest of the storage, each word in turn, enters the top register and is then "pushed down" the column from register to register to make room for the next words to arrive, and as the words are transferred out of the storage units, again only from the top register, other data in storage moves back up the column from register to register to fill the space vacated.

* _ * _ *

sample, statistical—A statistical sample usually relates to a small portion of the entire universe which is drawn in such a way that every value in the universe has an equal chance of being included. A sample must be representative of the universe, and the principle of the random sample is that representativeness will result from the operation of chance in the selection of the values.

sampling—1. To obtain values of a variable at regular or intermittent intervals. 2. A procedure of systems analysis in which traffice volumes, file activity, and other transfers are estimated on the basis of representative samples taken. 3. A method of communication line control in which messages on a circuit are sampled by a computer that selects only those for which computer processing is required. 4. Sampling provides a random method of checking and control. In using it, a transaction or item is selected and the processing that it undergoes is checked in detail. This provides an indication of accurate and complete processing. 5. The selection of part of an aggregate to be used as a basis for inference about the nature of the total population.

sampling, analog—The computer process which selects individual hybrid input signals from the processor, converts them to an equivalent binary form, and stores the data in memory.

sampling, discrete—Discrete samping is a sampling process in which the individual samples are sufficiently long in duration that the accuracy of information transmitted via the channel per unit time is not decreased by the sampling process.

sampling, random—A sample is designed most often to be a true miniature of the universe from which it is drawn; therefore, a sample must be truly representative of the universe from which it is drawn, and the universe itself must be homogeneous.

A representative sample is a random sample—that is, a sample which has been selected entirely upon the basis of a chance, in accordance with the theory of probability. If chance alone governs the selection of the various items which make up a sample, that sample will be a representative sample, provided it is large enough.

satellite processor—The processor designed especially and primarily for card-to-tape conversion, printing of tape contents, and other selected, high-volume operations; frequently used to support and add to the capacity of a large processor to further increase its productivity.

saturate—A procedure designed to bring about a state of saturation, e.g., oversupply or over capacity.

scale factor—1. A multiplier used by the programmer converting quantities occurring in a problem into a desired range. 2. A method of modifying the location of a decimal point.

scalar—A device that produces an output equal to the input multiplied by a constant, such as a linear amplifier, a set of pulleys or speed gears. Related to scale factor.

scan—1. The examination of stored information for a specific purpose, as for content or for arrangement. 2. To examine the status of communication lines or other input-output channels to determine whether data is being received or transmitted. 3. The process of finding those objects within a group of objects that may be generating a particular information mark.

scanning machine—A machine which facilitates the input of data by automatically reading printed data and converting it into machine language. The two types are optical scanners and magnetic ink scanners.

scatter/gather by record—It permits tighter packing of data on tape, and saves tape time. But the feature is not limited to tapes; it works with all subsystems. It enhances sorting and merging capabilities.

scatter loading—A procedure or process of loading a program into main memory such that each section or segment of the program occupies a single, connected memory area, but the several sections of the program need not be adjacent to each other.

scatter-read/gather-write—Gather-write is the ability to place the information from several nonadjacent locations in core storage (for example, several logical records) into a single physical record such as a tape block. Scatter-read is the ability to place the information from a physical record into several nonadjacent locations in core storage.

scatter read-write—An operation designed to be performed under program control that reads a block of data from tape and breaks it up into processable elements. After processing, data is recombined and written on tape as a block.

scheduler, job—The control program that examines the input work queue and selects the next job to be processed.

Schneider front-end—Relates to a front-end train of amplifiers to interface gas chromatograph instructions to a real-time computer (IBM).

scientific notation—Expression of quantities as a fractional part (mantissa) and a power of ten (characteristic).

scramble time—Computer time set aside for use by programmers who have programs ready to run which are short, urgent and one-shot types, i.e., particular system rules or conventions schedule scramble time, as at some universities, Saturday night after midnight.

scratchpad memory—A high-speed storage device used to store the location of an interrupted program, and to retrieve the latter after the interrupting program has been completed.

scratch tape (sorting)—Also scratch tapes. During a sort program, tape(s) used to store intermediate-pass data.

SDA, (source-data automation)—The various techniques of recording information in coded forms on paper tapes, punched cards, or tags that can be used over and over again to produce many other records without rewriting.

SDI—Abbreviation for Selective Dissemination of Information. It is related to a particular literature search notification and hard copy supply system which thus serves clients with internal or external documents, i.e., any system for selectively distributing information in accordance with given profiles (abstracts as coded).

search—An examination, systematically

156

conducted, of the available information in a specific field of interest.

search, dichotomizing—A search in which the series of items is divided into two parts, one of which is rejected. The process is repeated on the unrejected part until the item with the desired property is found. This process usually depends upon the presence of a known sequence in the series.

search, Fibonacci—A searching technique based on dichotomy and developed in such a way that, in each step, the original set or the remaining subset is subdivided in accordance with successive smaller numbers in the specific Fibonacci series. When the number of items in such a set is not equal to a Fibonacci number, the number of items in the set is assumed to equal the next higher Fibonacci number.

second generation computer—A computer belonging to the second era of technological development of computers when the transistor replaced vacuum tubes. Machines using transistors occupy much less space, operate faster, require less maintenance, and are more reliable. The second generation computer was prominent in the years 1959—1964 and included the IBM 1401, the Honeywell 800, the RCA 501, and the Remington Rand Solid State 80. The third generation of equipment featured microcircuits or integrated circuit miniaturization of components which reduced cost, increased reliability and were faster than transistors.

second-level address—The part of a computer instruction which indicates a location where the address of the referenced operand is to be found. In some computers the machine address indicated can itself be indirect. Such multiple levels of addressing are terminated either by prior control or by a termination symbol. Same as: indirect address.

section—In reference to the COBOL system, a sequence of one or more paragraphs designed in accordance with COBOL rules. Also defined as one of the portions of the program.

seek—1. Refers to the process of obtaining specific records from a random-access file. The number of seeks is the number of file items inspected before the desired item is found. 2. To look for data according to information given regarding that data; occasionally used interchangeably and erroneously for search, scan, and screen.

segmentation—A programmer-defined and monitor-implemented method of dividing a program into essentially self-contained segments so that only certain parts need be in memory at any instant.

segmenting—The act of dividing information into unique sections which can be handled as a unit.

segment mark—On tape, a special character used to separate each section of a tape file.

segregating unit—A unit which pulls or separates individual cards from a group. This machine is equipped with two feeding magazines and four receivers that interfile or segregate the cards in various sequences—at the rate of hundreds of cards per minute from each feeding magazine.

selecting—The function of pulling from a mass of data certain items that require special attention. Typical selections are items containing specific digits, items for a specific date, items higher than a specific number, items below a specific number, items below two specific numbers, etc.

selective dump, programmed—In many systems the selective programmed dump is a library subroutine that is called by object programs at run time. The dump may return control to the calling program or to the monitor upon completion. This allows the programmer to take selective dumps, during program execution, for debugging purposes. The dump returns to the calling program upon completion if it is called with the name P DUMP. If it is called with the name DUMP, the dump is taken and control is returned to the monitor to process the next job.

selective tracing—Relates to a specific tracing on particular data most often related to some highly specific instructions such as, transfer instructions only, or for specified locations, registers, storage units or areas, etc.

selector IOP—A particular input/output processing unit which performs bidirectional data transfer between core memory and high speed peripheral devices. Up to 32 devices can be attached to a selector IOP, but the high data transfer rates allow only one device to operate at a given time (some computers).

self-adapting—This pertains to the ability of a computer system to change its performance characteristics in response to its environment.

self-checking code—Designed so errors produce forbidden combinations. A single-error detecting code produces a forbidden combination if a digit gains or loses a single bit. A double-error detecting code produces a forbidden combination if a digit gains or loses either one or two bits and so forth (related to self-checking number and error-detecting code).

self-complementing code—A special machine language in which the code of the complement of a digit is the complement of the code of the digit.

self-demarking code—1. Designed so the symbols are arranged and selected in a manner to prevent generation of false combinations by interaction of segments from two successive codes. 2. Same as error-detecting code.

self-modification program—The program ability to modify itself or to set a switch so that a set of events occurring at one time can effect the action of the program at a later time.

self-organization—The machine capability to automatically organize a program into a logical sequence using efficient steps of execution.

selsyn—Same as synchro.

semanteme—A language element that expresses a definite image for an idea, e.g., the word tree. (Contrasted with morpheme, an element of language that conveys relations between nouns, verbs, etc.)

semantics—A particular study of the meanings of words, signs and symbols, and the relationships of the things they denote.

semi-conductor—Often this device is considered an electrical device which is composed of high conductive metals and low conductive insulators designed to change the nature or strength of electrical flows in various circuits. Latest semiconductors are metal-oxide or MOS.

Send Receive Keyboard Set (KSR)—A combination transmitter and receiver with transmission capability from keyboard only.

sense—1. Examination of data particularly relative to a set of criteria. 2. To determine the present arrangement of some element of hardware, especially a manually set switch. 3. To detect special signals. 4. To read holes in paper or cards and magnetic spots on tape, drum, etc.

sensing, mark—A technique used to detect special pencil marks entered in special places on a card, and automatically translating the marks into punched holes.

sensitivity analysis—Usually relates to a test or trial of a range or number of input values to determine the response, interdependence, or friction of the output values. Sensitivity analysis is often called parametric programming because, in such investigations, one or more parameters are permitted to vary in order to determine whether or not a solution should be modified. Managers are often much concerned with what happens to the optimal solution when fluctuations in the values of parameters or coefficients are permitted to change, i.e., size of budget, factory, package, price, etc.

separator, file—A specific device designed for the purpose of identifying logical boundaries between items or files. Abbreviated FS.

SEPOL—An acronym for Soil-Engineering Problem-Oriented Language.

septenary number—Usually composed of more than one figure, representing a sum, in which the quantity represented by each figure is based on a radix of seven. The figures used are: 0, 1, 2, 3, 4, 5, and 6.

sequence—1. The process which puts a set of symbols into an arbitrarily defined order; i.e., to select A if A is greater than or equal to B, or select B if A is less than B. 2. In sorting the planned ordering of items in a data element according to the processor-collation table. 3. An arbi-

trarily defined order of a set of symbols, i.e., an orderly progression of items of information or of operations in accordance with some rule.

sequence-checking routine—1. A specific routine designed to check every instruction executed, and print out certain data; e.g., to print out the coded instructions with addresses, and the contents of each of several registers, or it may be designed to print out only selected data, such as transfer instructions and the quantity actually transferred. 2. That specific set of instructions which results in a review of the order of the instructions to be performed. Often times, a set of instructions which reviews the order of data, such as employee table number sequence, etc.

sequence error—Generated when a card is out of sequence within an object program.

sequence packing—A procedure which loads the upper half of an accumulator with the first data word, shifting this into the lower half, loading the second datum, shift, etc., so that the three data words are thus packed in sequence.

sequence register—A unit which controls the sequence of the instructions.

sequential access—A process which consists of reading or writing of data serially, and by extension, a data recording medium that must be read serially, as a magnetic tape.

sequential collating—A process of sequencing a group of records by comparing the key of one record with another record until equality, greater than, or less than is determined.

sequential programming—Relates to programming of a special type in which only one logic or arithmetic operation is

159

performed at a time, i.e., all programming is sequential, one step after another, unless a specific modifier labels it otherwise, such as time-sharing, interleaving, etc.

sequential scheduling system—A first-come, first-served method of selecting jobs to be run.

serial—1. The handling internally of data in sequential fashion (contrasts with parallel). 2. To handle one after the other in a single facility, such as transfer or store in a digit-by-digit time sequence.

serial computer—One designed to handle digits or data lines sequentially by separate units of the computer. Mixed serial and parallel machines are frequently called serial or parallel according to the way arithmetic processes are performed. An example of a serial computer is one which handles decimal digits serially although it might handle the bits which comprise a digit either serially or in parallel (contrasted with parallel computer).

serial programming—The computer programming by which only one arithmetical or logical operation can be executed at one time, e.g., a sequential operation (contrasted with multiple programming).

serial storage—A method of storage in which time is given as one of the factors used to locate any given bit, character, word, or groups of words appearing one after the other in time sequence, and in which access time includes a variable latency or waiting time of from zero to many word times. A storage is said to be serial by word when the individual bits comprising a word appear serially in time; or a storage is serial by character when the characters representing coded

decimal or other nonbinary numbers appear serially in time; e.g., magnetic drums are usually serial by word but may be serial by bit, or parallel by bit, or serial by character and parallel by bit (related to sequential-access storage, and contrasted with random-access storage and parallel storage).

service program—A distinct program that is designed to indicate a process of work, i.e., one which provides a service to another program, an input program, a monitor program, an output program.

service routines—A routine set for performing on-line, concurrently with other programs, input and output operations such as tape to printer, card to tape, etc.

set, character—Relates to a set of representations, called characters, from which selections are made to denote and distinguish data. Each character differs from all others, and the total number of characters in a given set is fixed; e.g., a set may include the numerals 0 to 9, the letters A to Z, punctuation marks, and a blank or space.

set theory—In the mathematical sense, a study of the rules for combining groups, sets, and elements.

sexadecimal number—1. A number, usually consisting of more than one figure, representing a sum in which the quantity represented by each figure is based on a radix of sixteen. (Synonymous with hexadecimal number.) 1. A specific numeration system which uses the radix of 16, i.e., 16 symbols are used, 0 through 9 plus the characters K, S, N, J, F, and L for digits beyond 9, and each sexadecimal digit thus can be represented by a group of four binary digits which is called a tetrad.

shift—1. The movement of a character or

160

group of characters to the left or right of a given point of reference in a memory or arithmetic unit. Also, a portion of a 24-hour period during which ADP equipment is operated. 2. To move the characters of a unit of information columnwise right or left. For a number, this is equivalent to multiplying or dividing by a power of the base number.

shift, arithmetic—A process designed to multiply or divide a quantity by a power of the number base; e.g., if binary 1101, which represents decimal 13, is arithmetically shifted twice to the left, the result is 110100, which represents 52, which is also obtained by multiplying (13 by 2) twice; on the other hand, if the decimal 13 were to be shifted to the left twice, the result would be the same as multiplying by 10 twice, or 1300. (Related to shift and cyclic shift.)

shift, end arround carry—A specific carry sent directly from the high order position to the least significant place, i.e., using 9's complement addition to subtract numbers.

shifting register—That particular register which is designed to adapt to perform shifts, i.e., a delay line register whose circulation time may be increased or decreased so as to shift the content.

shift instructions—Instructions which usually include operations which will shift the number either to the left or to the right within an arithmetic register. A shift operation is principally equivalent to multiplying or dividing by the radix of the number base in use, depending upon the direction of the shift, i.e., in a decimal computer, a shift of one place to the right is equivalent to dividing by 10, a shift one place to the left is equivalent to multiplying by 10.

shift, logic—A shift which is similar to a cyclic shift and designed so that it can affect all positions, i.e., a nonarithmetic shift.

short instruction—Refers to the use of an index specification in a FORTRAN Read or Write statement.

SIAM—Abbreviation for the Society for Industrial and Applied Mathematics.

sideways sum—Relates to a specific sum which is developed and completed by adding digits without regard to position, i.e., sideways sums are brought forward by attaching various weights to the different digit positions and most often forms check digits through odd or even parity techniques.

sifting—An internal sorting technique where records are moved to permit the insertion of records.

signal—1. A basic term relating to the event, phenomenon, or electrical quantity, that conveys information from one point to another. 2. The actual physical embodiment of the information within a message. Operations can only be carried out on the physical phenomena carrying the message. 3. An significant increase or decrease in an electrical force which can cause a device or circuit to initiate another action.

signaling, data rate—Concerns data transmission, an expression in bits per second relating to data transmission capacity of a particular channel.

signaling, d-c—A transmission method which utilizes direct current.

signal space—1. The exact number of digit positions in which the corresponding digits of two binary numeric words of the same length are different, and/or 2. The number of digit positions in which the corresponding digits of two words of the same length in any radix notation are different.

sign bit—A binary digit designating the algebraic sign of a quantity, plus or minus.

signed-magnitude arithmetic—With reference to a signed-magnitude computer; all the arithmetic operations are accomplished by the process of addition and subtraction of magnitudes. Since multiplication and division can be broken down into a series of additions and subtractions, respectively, signed-magnitude computers will perform these operations as well. Operations with signed-magnitude numbers are identical with the algebraic addition using a pencil and paper.

sign off—The closing instruction to the computer system which terminates communication with the system. On a remote terminal, the user generally signs off by typing the command "off" or "sign off."

sign on—The instruction which commences communication with the computer system. On a remote terminal, the user can generally receive access to the system by typing in his identification number and an appropriate password.

simplex—The circuit which is capable of one-way operations only. The term is seldom used today because no such circuit is offered by the common carriers. Terminal equipment may limit transmission to one direction only, but the circuit used will be half-duplex.

simplex mode—A communication channel operation in one direction only, with no capability for reversing.

simplex system—A system configuration not including standby equipment.

SIMSCRIPT—Developed as a general-purpose digital simulation system which is based on the idea that the system can be described in terms of "entities", which are the specific objects or things of which a system is composed, and "attributes" which are those properties which are associated with the entities, and "sets" which are groups of entities. A complete list of explicit entities, their attributes, and the possible set memberships are major prerequisites in the development of a simulation model. The state of a system once described is changed by the occurrence of an event which is a user-defined subroutine written with either SIMSCRIPT or FORTRAN statements. Entities can be created or destroyed; set memberships of individual entities can be altered, and numeral values of attributes can be changed. Because entries and attributes must be individually located, much of the SIMSCRIPT language is devoted to providing convenience and flexible methods for performing storage and retrieval functions. Input to the SIMSCRIPT translator usually is developed on sets of cards containing definition, initialization, and subprograms.

simulation—1. An operating system exponential mode using mathematical or physical models that operate on real world or specifically devised problems in a time-sequential method similar to the system itself. 2. Many problems cannot be solved analytically, but adequate criteria for success can be deduced from trial-and-error processes in which the model of the system is dynamically studied. For example, to determine the best operating conditions for a pilot manufacturing plant, one could build a mathematical model of the plant to "try out" the multitude of variables, para-

162

meters, i.e., conditions and circumstances, by simulating dynamic operations—all this "before" deciding on size, structure, location and variation of the plant. 3. The representation of physical systems and phenomena by computers, models or other equipment; e.g., an imitative type of data processing in which an automatic computer is used as a model of some entity, e.g., a chemical process. When information enters the computer to represent the factors of process, the computer produces information that represents the results of the process, and the processing done by the computer represents the process itself. 4. In computer programming, the technique of setting up a routine for one computer to make it operative as nearly as possible like some other computer.

simulation, discrete—The major components of the system are individually identifiable (discrete). Example: queuing networks.

simulation education—Subjecting man to a complex environment similar to one in which he may wish to operate so that he may gain a feel of its dynamic behavior. Example: management games.

simulation manipulation—The activation of a representation achieved by accepting inputs and generating outputs analogous to those of the system. This tends to exclude pure optimization models from the definition, since their computing algorithms do not usually reproduce the behavior of the system.

simulator program—A program used when an interpretative program allowing programs written for one type of a computer is to be run on a different type of computer.

simultaneous access—To obtain information from or to place information into storage where the time required for such access is dependent on the simultaneous transfer of all elements of a word from a given storage location.

simultaneous operations—The input and output channels for the computer are designed for maximum performance and flexibility. Any channel may control any input or output device within its speed range. This universal ability to attach any device is a major achievement of combined computer and I/O design.

All I/O operations may be performed simultaneously with program processing by the computer data channels. An especially powerful feature of these channels is the ability of the system to execute a complete sequence of I/O instructions—a small program independent of the main program. This capability, together with special features in the I/O control units, permits the channel to perform such outstanding operations as the searching of a disk file independently from the main computer program. The processing program is not interrupted until the complete I/O sequence is finished or unless an error condition occurs (IBM).

single-address message—A message which is deliverable to only one address as contrasted with message, multiple-address.

single column punch—A specific coding procedure in which any of the values 0 through 11 is represented by a single punch in a card column.

single level memory—A memory organization technique using dynamic relocation to combine fast internal memory with lower external mass memory. The combination appears as single fast internal memory.

single precision—The total amount of words, or storage positions, used to denote a number in a computer. Single-precision arithmetic is the use of one word per number; double-precision arithmetic, two words per number, and so on. For variable word-length computers, precision is the number of digits used to denote a number. The higher the precision, the greater the number of decimal places that can be carried.

SI (superimpose)—The process which moves data from one location to another, superimposing bits or characters on the contents of specified locations.

skew—In reference to facsimile transmission, skew is the deviation from a rectangular picture (frame) caused by the lack of time coincidence between the scanner and the recorder.

skip—An instruction which proceeds to the next instruction; a "blank" instruction.

slab—The basic information subunit for processing on some NCR computers. A slab consists of 12 bits which may be treated as two groups of 6 (alphanumeric information called alpha), or as three groups of 4 (numeric information called digit).

The term slab is a contraction of "syllable." A set of one to eight slabs makes up a word.

slave computer—1. A "fail-safe" or backup system (application) whereby a slave or second computer performs the same steps of the same programs so that if the master computer fails or malfunctions, the slave computer continues without a deterioration of operations. Various space or urgent missile computations require back-up or duplicate systems. 2. A computer that is used in a slave application.

SLIP—Symmetric List Processor, a high-level list processing language.

slot—In reference to a magnetic drum, all the cells under a set of read-write heads at one instant in time.

slow storage—A storage modem or device designed with access time more lengthy in relation to the speeds of arithmetic operations of the central processing unit (CPU) of a computer and more lengthy when compared to other faster access peripheral units.

SLT—Abbreviation for Solid Logic Technology.

snapshot debugging—Concerns a type of diagnostics and debugging technique designed so that the programmer specifies the start and the end of program segments where he wishes to examine the contents of various registers and accumulators. The snap shot tracing may indicate the contents not only of the various accumulators and registers but also of specified memory locations.

software—1. The internal programs or routines prepared professionally to simplify programming and computer operations. Uses permit the programmer to use his own language (English) or mathematics (algebra) in communicating with the computer. 2. Various programming aids that are frequently supplied by the manufacturers to facilitate the purchaser's efficient operation of the equipment. Such software items include various assemblers, generators, subroutine libraries, compilers, operating systems, and industry-application programs.

solid state—Pertains to various types of electronic components that convey or control electrons within solid materials.

164

Transistors, germanium diodes, and magnetic cores are solid state components; vacuum and gas tubes are not.

solid-state elements—Usually relates to electronic components whose operation does not require current to pass through space or a vacuum. As a direct result, power needed to push current through the element is greatly reduced, and there's no need for special cooling because there is very little heat build-up.

solid-state computer—1. A computer consisting primarily of solid-state electronic circuit elements. 2. A computer using semiconductor devices.

SOM—Start of message.

sort, fine—Usually off-line detail sorting by the sorter especially used in banks; for example, fine sorting could be the function of arranging checks and deposits into customer account number order.

sorting—Concerns the process of arranging data into some designed order according to rules dependent upon a key or field contained by each item.

sorting, disk—A sort program that utilizes disk-type memory for auxiliary storage during sorting.

sorting, drum—A sort program which utilizes magnetic drums for auxiliary storage during sorting.

sorting, merging—The process for the forming of a single file of sequenced records from two or more files of sequenced records.

sort/merge program—A program designed to satisfy the sorting and merging requirements of tape or random storage-oriented installations. It is a generalized program that can produce many different sorting or merging programs in accordance with control information specified by the user.

source data—1. Data created by the individual or organization. 2. The data transmission equipment supplying the data.

source file—A CRAM (Card Random-Access Memory) deck, disk, drum, or magnetic tape which contains the information file used as input to a computer run.

source language—1. Used to specify computer processing; translated into object language by an assembler or compiler. 2. A compiler language such as FORTRAN from which machine-language instructions are developed by the use of translation routines or compilers. 3. The language in which the input to the FORTRAN processor is written.

source machine—The machine used to translate the source program into . the object program.

source program—A program that must be translated into machine language before use.

source (program) library—Concerns a collection of computer programs in compiler language and/or assembler language for call when needed.

SPA—Abbreviation for Systems and Procedures Association, an organization on management personnel.

space character—Relates to a special operating and graphic character designed to prevent a print.

spacing—The condition existing on a telegraph circuit during transmission when a bit of intelligence corresponding to a "no" is being sent.

special character—One other than a digit or letter, e.g., * + − $ =.

specific address—It indicates the exact storage location where the referenced operand is to be found or stored in the actual machine-code address-numbering system (related to absolute code).

specification—1. In reference to programming, a precise definition of the records and programs needed to carry out a particular processing function. 2. As an equipment concept, a technical or engineering description of the hardware.

split—Breaking up one regular file into two ordered files, as contrasted with merge.

spot carbon—To be carbonized on some areas so that only certain entries will be reproduced on the copy.

SPS—Abbreviation for Symbolic Programming Systems, which is a programming language in which terms may represent quantities and locations.

(SPS) string process system—A package consisting of subroutines that perform basic operations on strings of characters. SPS is used by the Executive and by many of the 940 subsystems. It performs string reading and writing, hash-code string look-up, and string comparisons (some computer).

SPT (symbolic program tape)—A Honeywell tape containing a file of programs, each of which is in the original assembly language and also the machine language. From this tape, programs can be selected for either checkout or production runs.

SPX circuit—Abbreviation for Simplex Circuit.

SSC—Station Selection Code.

stack—The part of computer memory and/or registers used to temporarily hold information.

standard deviation—A statistical term concerning the best and most widely used measure of dispersion is σ, and it enters into many other measures of statistical development. As a result of the squaring process, greater emphasis is given to extreme deviations than is the case in the mean deviation. The normal curve has been analyzed in terms of standard deviations so that this measure of dispersion can be used to facilitate comparison with the normal distribution.

standard interface—That interface form (matching) previously designed or agreed upon so that two or more units, systems, programs, etc., may be easily joined or associated.

Standard Language Symbols—Special graphic shapes used to represent special meanings or functions that can occur in any computer program.

standard procedures programs—Suggested programming methods set by the manufacturer.

standard subroutine—A subroutine that is applicable to a class of problems.

standby register—The register where accepted or verified information is stored so as to be available for a rerun in case the processing of the information is spoiled by a mistake in the program, or by a malfunction in the computer.

star program—Handwritten and independently designed by a programmer and so checked that no mistakes or bugs are therein contained; i.e., the star program should thus run correctly the first time, excepting machine malfunctions. Same as blue ribbon program.

start of heading character—A single or set of characters communicated by a polled terminal, indicating to other stations on the line that the data to follow specify the addresses of stations on the line which are to receive the answering message.

start of text character—A specific control character in communications designed to terminate and separate a heading and mark the beginning of the actual text.

start-stop system—A system where each element code group comparative to an alphabetical signal is preceded by a start signal which serves to prepare the receiving mechanism for the reception and registration of a character, and is followed by a stop signal which serves to bring the receiving mechanism to rest in preparation for the reception of the next character.

statement—1. In reference to computer programming, a meaningful expression or a generalized instruction in a source language. 2. An instruction (macro) to the computer to perform some sequence of operations.

statement, execute—Specific job control command which identifies a load module to be accessed and executed, plus the specification of job steps.

statements, imperative—Action statements of a symbolic program that are converted into machine-language instructions.

static dump—Printouts of memory performed at a particular point in time with respect to a machine run, frequently at the end of a run.

station—A device containing a tape drive, together with reading and writing heads and associated controls (synonymous with tape station).

statistic—A statistic is usually considered to be a numerical property of a sample in contrast to a parameter, which is defined as a numerical property of a distribution, i.e., a population, or universe.

statistical analysis—One of the four main techniques of operations research. Data gathering, arranging, sorting, sequencing, and evaluating are common to statistical analysis and the three other techniques:

linear programming, queuing theory and simulation. Statistical analysis combines mathematical techniques and computer technology to handle a wide range of business and scientific problems wherever large amounts of information or data must be evaluated and analyzed, like sales forecasting.

statistical method—Statistical method is designed as a technique used to obtain, analyze and present numerical data. The elements of statistical technique include: (1) the collection and asembling of data; (2) classification and condensation of data; (3) presentation of data in a textular, tabular, and graphic form; and (4) analysis of data.

When data are grouped according to magnitude, the resulting series is called a frequency distribution; when grouped as to time of occurrence, it is called a time series; when grouped by geographic location, it is called spatial distribution. In addition, there are a number of special types of distributions in which the data may be arranged by kind or by degree.

statistical mistakes—Various types of mistakes to be avoided are:

1. Concealed change in the statistical unit—For example, the value of the dollar changes over time.

2. Misuse of percentages—For example, if 12 drops to 3, this is not a 300% drop because nothing can drop more than 100%. It is a drop of 75%.

3. Spurious accuracy—When working with data which are themselves approximate figures, do not carry calculations based on those figures to an excessive number of decimal places, but confine the expression of the result to the significant figures, determined with reference to the

accuracy of the original data.

Other pitfalls to watch for are: (a) deductive inconsistencies; (b) emotional or dual terminology; (c) fallacy of composition; (d) bias, slants, unsystematic errors; (e) incomplete theory; (f) "missing" variables; (g) aggregation of dissimilar units; (h) improper sample.

statistics, analytical—The design and use of analytical statistics is to enable one to draw statistical inferences about the characteristics of the entire statistical "universe" of data from a small sample.

statistics, business—A concept which relates to the evaluation of risks of wrong decisions due to the partial rather than total data availability. The statistical techniques of inductive inference concern bodies of precisely stated and empirically tested rules and laws for (1) securing information (2) manipulating and formulating such data in mathematically or diagrammatically meaningful expressions, and (3) preparing the bases for effective action and control.

statistics descriptive and inductive—Descriptive statistics usually involve methods that, essentially, do not go beyond the data with which we start; inductive statistics involves generalizations, predictions, estimations, and decisions.

status maps—A status report of programs and I/O operations, usually in tabular form.

status word—That information which is necessary to resume processing, following the handling of an interruption of operations.

stencil bit—In a group of binary digits, a specific bit which is in the operation of the instruction word and usually desig-

nates a specific type of operation, i.e., perhaps transfers of full or half-words by multiplication of a stencil word.

stochastic—1. Relates to solutions (from the Greek, meaning aim or target) which are concerned with "close to the best" solutions—solutions based on uncertainty but through the best use of precise laws of probability with known and measured errors explicitly considered and confidence intervals precisely defined. 2. A term that refers to trial-and-error procedures as contrasted with the fixed step-by-step procedures of algorithms; results defined in probability terms.

stochastic programming—A linear programming generalization in which any of the unit costs, the coefficients in the constraint equations, and the right hand sides are random variables subject to known distributions. The aim of such programming is to choose levels for the variables which will minimize the expected (rather than the actual) cost.

stochastic simulation—Properties of the representation rather than of the system itself. The introduction of random variables as essential elements of the model provides the basis for the label "stochastic." Example: a model of an inventory system in which the timing or quantity of demands for items and/or the replenishment lead times are randomly distributed is stochastic. If these and other elements are taken as determined (not necessarily constant), the model is deterministic.

stochastic variable—A particular statistical variable which has a probability with which it may assume each of many possible values in a distinct set.

stop element—The last element of a character designed for asynchronous serial transmission, used to ensure recognition of the next start element. In Baudot teletypewriter operation it is 1.42 mark bits; in IBM 1050 it is 1.0 mark bit.

stop instruction—1. A particular instruction that can stop the computer either before or after the halt instruction is obeyed, depending on the governing criterion. 2. A machine operation or routine that requires manual action other than the use of the start key to continue processing.

stop time—Elapses of time between completion of reading or writing of a tape record and the time when the tape stops moving.

storage—1. Portions of electronic data processing equipment capable of retaining data for later use. 2. Any device into which units of information can be copied, and which will hold this information, and from which the information can be obtained at a later time. Devices such as plugboards, which hold information in the form of arrangements of physical elements, hardware, or equipment; the erasable storage in any given computer.

storage capacity—The maximum number of units or data that may be stored in a given storage device at one time. It is variously expressed in terms of bits, characters, or words.

storage cycle—1. A sequence of events periodically occurring when information is transferred to or from the storage device of a computer. 2. Storing, sensing, and regeneration form parts of the storage cycle.

storage, dedicated—The allocated, reserved or obligated, set aside, earmarked or assigned areas of storage which are committed to some specific purpose, user, or problem, i.e., exclusively reserved space on a disc storage unit for an accounting procedure, problem or data set.

storage, destructive—Some storage devices are designed so contents at a location need to be regenerated after being read, if they are to be retained after being read, i.e., CRT (cathod-ray tube) storage and some cores are of the destructive type, and regeneration is most often automatic when retention is desired.

storage device—A device to insert, retain and then retrieve data for later use.

storage device, mass—Refers to a storage unit designed with very large storage capacity, such as magnetic drum, magnetic disc, cells, etc.

storage, direct access—A type of storage device wherein access to the next position from which information is to be obtained is not dependent on the position from which information was previously obtained.

storage drum—A random-access medium-sized storage device which can hold four million alpha-numeric characters or up to eight million digits, which can be retrieved at a rate of 1.2 million characters a second. Many units, providing on-line storage for millions of alpha-numeric characters, can be linked to a processor.

storage dumping—A procedure or process designed to transfer data from one particular storage device to another or from one particular area to another.

storage, electrostatic—1. The storage of data on a dielectric surface, such as the screen of a cathode ray tube, in the form of the presence or absence of spots bearing electrostatic charges that can persist for a short time after the electrostatic charging force is removed. 2. A storage device which uses electric charges to represent data.

storage, external—1. Storage from which the data to be operated on are normally obtained. It may be under the control of the computer, but data to be operated on must be transferred to secondary or internal storage before operations commence, and are returned to external storage only after operations are completed. External storage devices usually have larger capacities and lower access speeds than internal and secondary storage. 2. A storage device outside the computer that can store information in a form acceptable to the computer, e.g., cards, tapes.

storage, high-speed—A specific storage device which has relatively short access time, as compared to main memory of the CPU, i.e., at least significantly faster than other devices in the same computer system, such as disc-tape storage wherein, the disc is much faster and is considered high-speed relative to the tape and in respect to the CPU (central processing unit).

storage key—A special set of bits designed to be associated with every word or character in some block of storage, which allows tasks having a matching set of protection key bits to use that block of storage.

storage location—1. A storage position of one machine word and usually having a specific address. 2. The character position used to address a data field in a character addressable machine.

storage map—A pictorial aid that the programmer uses to estimate the proportion of storage capacity to be allocated to data.

storage mark—A particular point location that defines the character space immediately to the left of the most significant character in accumulator storage. An example would be:

a 7 4 6 7 4 8 9

in which the letter "a" would be the storage mark.

storage parity—Codes or devices used when transferring data to or from storage devices such as disk, drum, auxiliary core, etc.

storage register—A register in computer storage in contrast with a register in one of the other units of the computer. (Synonymous with memory register.)

store—1. Transferring an element of information to a device from which the unaltered information can be obtained at a later time. 2. To retain data in a device from which it can be obtained at a later time. 3. The British term for storage.

store-and-forward—A type of message-switching system.

stored program—1. An instruction set in the memory section that can run the computer or cut in to take over from the regular program when the occasion arises. Often used for alternate routines. 2. A computer program which is already in storage and is accessible to the computer on an automatic basis.

straight binary—A binary numeral expression in a system of positional notation in which each successive digit position is weighted by a factor of two times the weight of the prior position, i.e., 1011 binary, represents: $1 \times 2^3 + 1 \times 2^1 + 1 \times 2^0$ = decimal eleven.

straight-line coding—Avoids loops by the repetition of parts of the coding when required.

string—1. A connected character sequence of words or other elements. 2. A set of records arranged in an ascending or a descending sequence according to the increasing or decreasing magnitude of their keys.

string, flip-flop—An important computer property is that the state of one flip-flop can be transferred to another by means of special triggering circuits. That is, a number stored in one strip of flip-flops can be transferred to another string. In this way, numbers can be transferred from place to place in a computer.

string process system (SPS)—Consisting of a package of subroutines that perform basic operations on strings of characters, SPS is used by the Executive and by many subsystems. It performs string reading and writing, hash-code string look-up, and string comparisons (some computers).

striping—A flowcharting procedure in which the placement of a line across the upper part of a symbol is an indication that the process it represents is described in greater detail elsewhere in the same flow chart set.

strip record—Refers to a recording method in which information is stored vertically with strips visible for information location.

stroke—Refers to a line segment, point, or other mark used in the formation of characters.

structure flow charts—Generalized flow charts showing input, processing, files and output without indicating the precise methods of processing.

stub card—A card which contains a detachable stub. The stub is detached and is used as a receipt for future reference.

stunt box—Used to control nonprinting functions of a teletype terminal.

stylus (light pen)—Same as light pen, a pointer-controller device associated with a Cathode Ray Tube.

stylus printer—Used to form characters by forcing a set of selected styli or wires against the ribbon or paper. The specific wires of a 5 x 7 array are selected to form a character. Very closely examined characters appear as patterns of dots. Same as wire printer.

subalphabet—An alphabet subset, i.e., any group of less than 26 letters.

suboptimization—1. The specific process designed for fulfilling or optimizing some chosen objective that is an integral part of a broader objective. Usually the broad-level objective and lower-level objective are different. 2. When using a multiple pricing algorithm, suboptimization enters the first variable into the basis which gives by itself the greatest improvement in objective; the next variable entered gives the greatest additional improvement, and so on. This technique tends to prevent the first entering variable from being removed by the second, etc.

subprogram—1. A section of a larger program that can be compiled independently. 2. Part of a program. See program and routine.

subject program—Same as source program.

subjob—A routine or machine run. A program may be broken into several subjobs or tasks to more effectively utilize computer CPU time.

subroutine—1. That system or machine instruction sequence that completes the carefully defined function or program. 2. The set of instructions in machine code to direct the computer to carry out a well-defined mathematical or logical operation; a part of a routine. A subroutine is often written with symbolic relative addresses even when the routine

171

to which it belongs is not written in symbolic addresses. 3. A single routine may simultaneously be both a subroutine with respect to another routine and a master routine with respect to a third. Usually control is transferred to single subroutine from more than one place in the master routine and the reason for using the subroutine is to avoid having to repeat the same sequence of instructions in different places in the master routine (clarified by routine).

subroutine, dating—A specific subroutine which computes and stores dates and times associated and as programmed for file updating relating to work associated with computer runs of various types, but usually time-sensitive.

subroutine, editing—This subroutine has parameters whose values are selected prior to execution and are used for performing various operations usually on input and output data, and before main program operations.

subroutine library—A standard proved subroutine set which is kept on file for use at any time.

subscript—1. A letter or symbol used in typography and written below a set name to identify a particular element or elements of that set. 2. An indexing notation.

subscripted variable—One that is followed by one or more subscripts enclosed in parentheses.

subset—1. A set contained within a set. 2. A particular subscriber apparatus in a communications network. 3. A contraction of the words "subscriber set" which has been used for many years to refer to the device which is installed on a subscriber's premises. 4. A modulation/demodulation device designed to make business-machine signals compatible with the communications facilities and vice versa. A data subset accepts digital information, converts it into a suitable form for transmission over the telephone circuits, and then reconverts the data to its original form at the receiving end.

substitute mode—Relates to one method of exchange buffering, in which segments of storage function alternately as buffer and as program work area.

subtracter—A device which is capable of forming the representation of the difference between two numbers represented by signals applied to its inputs. Types: full subtracters, parallel and serial.

sum check—A specific check developed when groups of digits are summed, usually without regard for overflow, and that sum checked against a previously computed sum to verify that no digits have been changed since the last summation.

summary punch—A card punching machine that may be attached by cable to another machine (for example, a tabulator), and that will punch out on a card the information produced, calculated, or summarized by the other machine.

supervisor—A supervisor routine is an executive routine.

supervisory instruction—This instruction is designed and used to control the operation or execution of other routines or programs.

supervisory program—Such programs control loading and relocation of routines and in some cases make use of instructions that are unknown to the general programmer. Effectively, an executive routine is part of the machine itself.

support programs—Those programs which

support or aid the supervisory programs and the application programs and include diagnostics, testing, data generators, etc.

support systems—Those used to develop or support the normal translation functions of any of the machine, procedural, or problem-oriented languages.

suppression—In either on-line or off-line printing devices, an optional function that permits them to ignore certain input characters or groups of characters. Related to nonprint.

suppression, zero—A process to cause the elimination of insignificant zeros (those to the left of a quantity in a field or word) during a printing operation.

switch—1. That particular point in a program from which a program may proceed to one of several possible courses of action, depending on conditions established by the programmer; conditional statements are often used to establish switches of this kind; a branch point. 2. A mechanical, electromechanical, or electronic device, built into a unit of equipment, that can be interrogated in order to select a course of action. 3. A symbol used to indicate a branchpoint, or a set of instructions to condition a branch.

switching algebra—Relates to Boolean algebra which is applied to switching circuits, digital systems and some communications switching.

switching theory—A particular branch of theory which relates to combinational logic, its operation, behavior and consequences, i.e., concerning such devices as computers, Turing machines, logic elements, and switch networks.

switch message—A term used for one of the routing points in a store and forward switching system.

switch register (SR)—Twelve toggle switches on the operator console which provide a means of manually establishing a word to be set into the computer. The content of the SR can be transferred into the machine as an address by pressing the load-address key, or can be stored in core memory at the address contained in the machine by pressing the deposit key. The content of the SR can also be loaded into the AC (accumulator) under program control to allow program modification by programmed evaluation of the word manually set into the SR.

switch storage—Different than most types, in that it is in the form of arrays of manually set switches, and in which data may be entered by manually placing the switch in certain positions which either represent data or control data flow.

symbionts—Small routines, which run concurrently with the series of main programs. These symbionts move information back and forth between the peripherals and magnetic drum. Main programs desiring communication with these peripherals reference input/output subroutines that transfer data images between the drum and peripherals (UNIVAC).

symbol—The term for a substitute or representation of characteristics, relationships, or transformations of ideas or things.

symbolic address—A special label assigned to a specific word in a routine for the convenience of the programmer. The symbol used is independent of the location of a word within a routine. It identifies the field of data to be operated on or the operation to be used, rather than its storage location.

symbolic assembler—Permits the program-

173

mer to code instructions in a symbolic language. The assembler allows mnemonic symbols to be used for instruction codes and addresses. Constant and variable storage registers can be automatically assigned. The assembler produces a binary object tape and lists a symbol table with memory allocations and useful diagnostic messages.

symbolic code—Expression of programs in source language; i.e., by referring to storage locations and machine operations by symbolic names and addresses (synonymous with pseudocode and contrasted with machine-language code).

symbolic coding—1. Used to write instruction in nonmachine language; i.e., coding using symbolic notation for operators and operands. 2. Writing programs in any language other than absolute machine language. 3. In digital computer programming, any coding system using symbolic code rather than the machine code.

symbolic deck—A deck of punched cards containing programs written in symbolic language rather than binary language.

symbolic instruction—1. An assembly language instruction directly translatable into a machine code. 2. An instruction using symbols to represent or express the operator part and the address parts.

symbolic language—Used to express formal logic by means of a formalized artificial language or symbolic calculus whose purpose is to avoid the ambiguities and logical inadequacies of natural languages. Advantages of the symbolic method are greater exactness of formulation, and power to deal with complex material.

symbolic notation—The technique of representing a storage location by one or more figures.

symbolic programming—Using arbitrary

symbols to represent addresses in order to facilitate programming.

symmetric linear programming—Mathematical technique which is fast and efficient for solving distribution and allocation problems in manufacturing operations.

sync circuits—Refers to the circuits in radar and television which control the movements of the scope beam.

synch—Signal use; to identify the start of a block.

synchronization—In reference to the COBOL system the data alignment with respect to the left or right boundaries of machine words. (Compared with justification.)

synchronous computer—One in which each event or the performance of each operation starts as a result of a signal generated by a clock. (Contrasted with asynchronous computer, and clarified by clock frequency.)

syndetic—1. To have connections or interconnections. 2. Pertaining to a document or catalog with cross references.

synergetic—A combination of every unit of a system, but one which when combined or added, develops a total larger than their arithmetic sum. Also called synergistic.

synergic—The combination using every organ of a system, e.g., a coordinated system.

syntax—Sentence structure rules governing a language, or statement structure such as that of a compiler program.

syntax-directed compiler—A compiler based on the syntactic relationships of the character string.

synthesis—1. An act of combining parts in order to form a whole; e.g., to develop at a circuit, computer, or program from performance requirements. This can be contrasted with analysis of a given performance circuit or program. 2. A process for obtaining those operations desired in a new system.

synthetic address—One determined or generated by the instructions within the program which uses the address.

synthetic relationship—A relation existing between a concept that pertains to an empirical observation. Such relationships are not involved in defining concepts or terms, but in reporting the results of observations and experiments.

(SYSOPOs) system programmed operators—An important facility on some computers is the ability for user programs to directly access a set of "public" subroutines. These are not replicated for each user but are used in common. Such subroutines rapidly and conveniently perform many of the basic chores that all interactive and production programs must per form. Thus SYSOPOs enable users to create new application programs rather easily, given such a service framework. These systems supplied functions include: teletype input and output functions; I/O word and block output functions, characters string-manipulation functions; floating-point arithmetic; and system service calls of various types.

SYSPOP system programmed operators—A function making monitor mode service routines available to user mode programs without loss of system control or use of user memory space.

system—1. Usually concerns an assembly of components united by some form of regulated interaction to form an organized whole. 2. Refers to a collection of operations and procedures, men, and machines, by which business activity is carried on. 3. Any purposeful organization of resources or elements. 4. A collection of operations and procedures united to accomplish a specific objective. 5. A devised and designed regular or special method or plan of methodology or procedure. The organization of hardware, software, and people for cooperative operation to complete a set of tasks for desired purposes. 6. Any regular or special method or plan of procedure. Types: Accuracy-control, audio, back-up, biquinary, carrier, control, data processing, diagnostics, executive, executive control, error detecting, fail-safe, fail-soft, Fortran-compiler, geodetic, horizontal, information, information-feedback, information processing, integrated, job-processing, management information, multisequential, on-demand, open-ended, operating, peek-a-boo, pert/cost, polymorphic, post billing, prebilling, programming, quadruplex, real time, request-repeat, symplex, support, tandem, total, and utility.

system capacity—Quantitative system performance estimates relating to the expected efficiency and throughput of a given computer configuration.

system chart—A particular flow chart of an overall procedure or system showing the flow of information and/or documents.

system check—An overall performance check on the system, usually not made by built-in computer check circuits, e.g., control totals, hash totals, and record counts.

system, data processing—A network of machine components which are capable of accepting information, processing it according to a plan, and producing the

175

desired results.

system, data transmission—A series of circuits, models, or other devices which transfer or translate information from one site or location to another.

system (DOS), disk operating—A more powerful twin of TOS, this is a versatile operating system for IBM System 360 installations having direct-access storage devices. This operating system supports almost every peripheral device available for System 360.

system, duplex—Two computers used in special configuration, one is on-line while the other is standing by ready to be used if a malfunction of the on-line computer occurs. The stand-by computer is often used to complete off-line functions.

system, error-detection—A system employing an error-detecting code and so arranged that any signal detected as being in error is deleted from the data delivered to the data link (in some cases with an indication that such a deletion has taken place), or delivered to the data link, along with an indication that it has been detected as being in error.

system, executive file control—This file-control system has been designed to provide a user the highest possible degree of operational flexibility in storing and retrieving data, without requiring concern with the physical characteristics of the recording devices. Thus, most files are made insensitive to input/output media characteristics as the system adjusts the interface between the file and the device. The system invokes security measures to insure that files are not subject to unauthorized use or destruction. Full facilities are provided for rollback of files from mass-storage devices to magnetic tape, as well as the reconstruc-

tion of such files on the mass-storage devices when they are later referenced by the user; in general, the user need not be aware of the residence of his files.

system, fail-safe—Some real-time computing systems enable process variables to be locked into present values and saves some vital information before termination of operation in case of catastrophic failure, such as power failure.

system, file control—Many file control systems have been designed to provide users the highest possible degree of operational flexibility in storing and retrieving data, without requiring concern with the physical characteristics of the recording devices. Most files are made insensitive to input/output media characteristics, as the system adjusts the interface between the file and the device. The system invokes security measures to insure that files are not subject to unauthorized use or destruction. Full facilities are provided for rollback of files from mass storage devices to magnetic tape, as well as the reconstruction of such files on the mass-storage devices when they are later referenced by the user.

system, fixed-length record—When a system contains all records with the same number of characters, it is called a fixed-length record system. This is contrasted to systems which have a variable number of characters in a record.

system, FORTRAN compiler—The FORTRAN compiler system consists of two basic elements: a source language (FORTRAN IV) whose structure closely resembles the language of mathematics, and a compiler which translates the statements and formulas written in the source language into a machine-language program.

system, information processing—A system that receives and delivers information, changing the information in the process.

system input unit—A modem, unit, or device manufactured to be the source unit of an input job stream.

system, integrated—The combination of processes which results in the introduction of data which need not be repeated as further allied or related data is also entered. For example: shipment data may also be the basis for inventory inquiries, invoicing, marketing reports, etc.

system interface design—Applications for unique users, such as on-line installations, that require specialized input/output equipment. Liaison engineering staffs design the necessary interface units as part of the services to the customers. Then, the manufacturer will fabricate these units, at a normal product cost, for the particular system under close supervision by the same engineers that designed them. These engineers, who are naturally quite familiar with the logic and requirements are best qualified to do this important work.

system interrupts—These are programmed requests from a processing program to the control program for some action, such as initiation of an input/output operation.

system loader—It functions as a part of the monitor (control) system by loading system routines, object programs, and library subroutines. System routines are programs such as the FORTRAN II compiler or the ASIST assembler and utility programs. Each of these routines is uniquely defined with a name and entry. An object program is a binary main program with subprograms. Object programs are the compiler and assembler output of source-language programs. Library routines are those subroutines and input/output drivers that may be called by an object program in parts (primary, secondary and library) from a possible three separate devices. In this case the three parts combine to form a complete object program. The loader may be called on at any time during the system operation to load a system routine or object program. The loader is an absolute binary program in the master file (ASI).

system residence volume—A defined volume which contains the nucleus of the operating system and which has the highest level index of the catalog and which is a portion of a single unit of storage media, accessible to a single read/write mechanism.

systems analysis—1. The business activity analysis to determine precisely what must be accomplished and how to accomplish it. 2. The organized, step-by-step study and analysis of the detailed procedure for collection, manipulation, and evaluation of information about an organization with the goal of improving control over its total operation or segments of it. 3. The examination of an activity, procedure, method, technique, or a business to determine what must be accomplished and the best method of accomplishing the necessary operations.

systems analyst—1. A person who designs information-handling procedures which incorporate computer processing. The systems analyst is usually highly skilled in defining problems and developing algorithms for their solution. 2. Personnel who are primarily concerned with the planning of new applications. The general title "systems analyst" is normally used interchangeably with "systems designer" for most levels. There are occasionally more specific titles. The following list is arranged in ascending order for responsibility: Research Analyst, Forms Designer, Procedure Analyst, Methods Analyst and Systems Consultant.

systems, distributed computer—The arrangement of computers within an organization in which the organization's computer complex has many separate computing facilities all working in a cooperative manner, rather than the conventional single computer at a single location. Versatility of a computer system is often increased if small computers in geographically dispersed branches are used for simple tasks and a powerful central computer is available for larger tasks. Frequently an organization's central files are stored at the central computing facility, with the geographically dispersed smaller computers calling on the central files when they need them. Such an arrangement lessens the load on the central computer and reduces both the volume and cost of data transmission.

systems, dual—Special configurations which use two computers to receive identical inputs and execute the same routines, with the results of such parallel processing subject to comparison. Exceptionally high reliability requirements are usually involved.

systems flowchart—A visual representation of the system through which data provided by the source documents are converted into final documents.

systems programmer—The individual primarily concerned with writing either "operating systems" (computer internal control programs) or languages for computers. Systems programmers produce these control programs and/or monitors that operate central processors and peripheral equipment. They write test programs that detect errors and malfunctions. They design utility programs to control formats of output and do sorting and merging of files. It is they who are primarily responsible for efficiency of many computer systems.

systems programs—Those programs designed to implement system functions that may be requested from the user console. This is in contrast to system subroutines that may be called by system programs or other programs. System programs are normally provided by manufacturers, but they may be developed by the programmer. The programs contain a termination mode to return the communication link to the system program.

systems synthesis—Procedural planning to solve a problem. This involves analysis of the problem, preparation of a flow chart, detail preparation, testing developing of subroutines, allocation of storage locations, specification of input and output formats, and the incorporation of a computer run into a complete data processing system.

systems test—1. To check the whole system against test data. 2. A complete simulation of the actual running system for purposes of testing out the adequacy of the system. 3. A test of an entire interconnected set of components for the purpose of determining proper functioning and interconnection. 4. The running of the whole system runs making up a data processing application for test data.

system subroutines—Concerns various I/O

(input/output) format controls that provide for the various format statements used in the FORTRAN language. These subroutines are also available to other programs and may be called from the systems library tape.

system supervisor—The system supervisor is designed to allow an installation to proceed automatically from run to run with little or no computer time loss caused by setting up the "next program." It is also designed to accomplish as many of the setup and control functions as is possible prior to reading in the actual program. The system supervisor will also provide a step-by-step log of the day's operation. All this is accomplished without operator intervention.

System, Tape Operating (TOS)—A powerful and flexible operating system designed for System 360 computers having a minimum 16K of memory, at least four magnetic tapes, and no random-access storage devices.

System 360 operating (OS/360)—IBMs widely used and quite flexible operating system which spans a range from computers with sequential scheduling to large multiprogramming computers which can perform task multijobbing. For the very small computers in the 360 series, other types of operating systems are available.

* – * – *

tab—1. A label, marker or indicator, usually at either or both ends of a medium, as tapes, to permit quick awareness of its message. 2. A frequent slang or abbreviation for tabulating equipment.

table, input-output—A plotting device used to generate or to record one variable as a function of another variable.

table lookup (TLU)—1. The extracting process of a table of additional information associated with a particular field in the table. 2. To obtain a function value corresponding to an argument, stated or implied, from a table of function values stored in the computer. Also the operation of obtaining a value from a table.

table of contents, volume (VTOC)—1. Relates to an index record near the beginning of each volume, which records the name, location, and extent of every file or data set residing on that particular volume. Usually not found on magnetic tapes, but often required on all disk packs and drums. 2. A particular table related to and describing every set in a direct access volume.

TABSIM (TABulator SIMulator)—A simulator program to speed the conversion of tabulating-equipment tasks to computer processing. They are load-and-go type packages that permit users to run tab jobs on computers. (Honeywell)

TABSOL (TABular Systems Oriented Language)—A tabular structure language used for convenient solutions to problems involving multiple sequential decisions; particularly useful in manufacturing planning, engineering design, and inventory control. (General Electric)

tabular language—Composed of decision tables which become the problem-oriented language used in computation.

tabulate—The procedure of accumulating groups (families) of separate totals simultaneously. Each total is usually controlled by its individual key; as each key in turn changes, causing a total break, the total of this group is printed and added into the next higher level of totals.

tabulating equipment (electronic accounting machine)—The machines and equipment that use punched cards. This group of equipment is called tabulating equipment because the main function of punched card machines (for some 20 years before the introduction of the first automatic digital computer) was to produce tabulations of information resulting from sorting, listing, selecting, and totaling data on punched cards. This class of equipment is commonly called PCM (Punched-Card Machines) or tab equipment (similar to electrical accounting machine, and clarified by tabulator).

tag—1. An information unit whose composition differs from that of other members of the set so that it can be used as a marker or label. A tag bit is an instruction word that is also called a sentinel or a flag. 2. A specific identifier such as a label, an index, etc.

tandem system—A particular system configuration in which the data proceeds through one central processor into another processor. This is the system of multiplexors and master/slave arrangements.

tape—1. A linear medium used to store information that can be used as input or output to a computer, e.g., magnetic tape. 2. Magnetic, punched paper, sometimes other types of tape as paper loops, etc., used to control vertical formatting of printers, or plastic tapes used to control automatic typewriters. 3. A strip of material that may be punched, coated, or impregnated with magnetic or optically sensitive substances, and used for data input, storage, or output. The data is stored serially in several channels across the tape, transversely to the reading or writing motion.

tape alternation—A selection process, usually controlled automatically by a program, of first one tape unit and then another, normally during input or output operations, that permits successive reels of a file to be mounted and removed without interrupting the program.

tape character—Information composed of bits stored across the several longitudinal channels of a tape.

tape comparator—A unique machine whose function is to compare two tapes which are expected to be identical. The comparison is row by row and the machine stops when a discrepancy occurs.

tape deck—That special device or mechanism designed to control the movement of tape.

tape dump—Relates to the transfer of complete contents of information recorded on tape to the computer or another storage medium.

tape limited—1. The total processing speed time controlled or limited by the speed of the magnetic or paper tape units. 2. When the time required for tape reading and writing exceeds the calculating, the process is considered time limited; this concept is concerned only with computers that permit overlap or simultaneity of tape operations with computation (contrasted with input limited and output limited). 3. The description of a section of a program in which the time required, on buffered computers, to read or write tapes exceeds the time required for computation.

tape operating system (TOS)—A powerful and flexible operating system for System 360 computers having at least 16K of memory, at least four magnetic tapes, and no random-access storage devices.

tape parity—That particular parity application of checking codes or devices when transferring data to or from magnetic or paper tape.

tape-to-tape converter—A device used to change from one form of input/output medium or code to another; i.e., magnetic tape to paper tape (or vice versa), or eight-channel code to five-channel code, etc.

tape trailer—A special strip or tape length located at the end of tape reels usually containing a type of end-of-tape marker, i.e., a hole, long blank, special mag spots, etc.

tape unit—1. A device used to read data from magnetic tape or to write new data on tape. The device also rewinds completed tape. Some units read in either direction, although they write only in the forward direction. 2. The mechanism for reading or writing a magnetic tape. 3. A device consisting of a tape transport, controls, a set of reels, and a length of tape that is capable of recording and reading information on and from the tape at the request of the computer (clarified by tape, transport, magnetic-tape unit, and paper-tape unit).

target computer—One which is not designed to use a particular program but which must have another computer translate such a program for its ultimate use is called a target or object computer.

target configuration—The computer in which the target program is used is called the target or object computer. This is quite regularly also called a target (or object) configuration.

target language—The language into which some other language is to be translated.

target program—1. One that is the output of an automatic-coding system. Often this program is a machine-language program ready for execution, but it may well be in an intermediate language (synonymous with object routine and contrasted with source program). 2. That computer program which is written in the target or most desired language, i.e., the one which is either directly acceptable to the computer or indirectly so. The target program usually results from a generator, compiler, or translator and is thus eventually a machine language resulting from the source language after the compilation, translation or generation. The target program is the same as the target routine, object routine, and object program, i.e., the main program.

task dispatcher—A unique control routine or function which selects from the task queue or lists the next task to be processed and gives it control of the central processor.

task management—The set of functions of the control program or routine which controls the use of system resources other than the input/output devices by tasks.

task queue—That queue, line, or list, which contains all the task control blocks which are in the system at any one time.

taxonomy—The special science of classification, i.e., problems in taxonomy, are some of the most popular types which are solved by computer capability and usage.

technique flow charts—Detailed flow charts showing data and information requirements and the specific method and calculations for processing the information.

telecommunication—To transmit or receive signals, writing, sounds, or intelligence of any nature by wire, radio, light beam, or any other electromagnetic means.

TELEDATA—A device used to introduce parity bits and transmit over telegraph circuits data already punched in five-, six-, or eight-channel paper tape. The receiving unit at a distant point checks parity for code accuracy and reperforates the valid data onto paper tape.

telemetry—Remote sensing or metering of operating systems by a receiving instrument that converts transmitted electrial signals into units of data.

telephone trunk—A particular telephone line between two central offices that is used to provide communications between subscribers.

teleprinter—1. Used to describe telegraphic terminals. 2. Generally, an electric typewriter that can be operated manually or electrically by reading a reperforating paper tape. 3. The typewriter usually connected to a leased or dial-switched telegraphgrade circuit for transmitting text or data mesages in a readable form. 4. An input/output terminal device, normally used on lowspeed circuits, that includes at least a page printer.

teleprocessing—A term registered by IBM noting systems that transmit data from one point to another in the course of processing.

telereference—A procedure used to consult data at a remote location through the use of closed circuit television.

telesynd—Special remote control equipment that is synchronous in both speed and position, i.e., various types of telemetry equipment.

teletype code—The standard five-channel teletype writer code made up of a start inpulse and five character impulses, all of equal length, and a stop impulse whose length is 1.42 times all of the start impulse. Also known as the 1.42 unit code. The teletype code has been used by the telegraph industry for about 100 years.

telex (TEX)—A Western Union automatic teletype-exchange service extending into Canada via Canadian Pacific railroad facililties. Subscribers can dial each other for direct two-way telemeter communications.

temporary storage—Locations in internal-storage reserved for intermediate or partial results.

tens complement—The radix complement of a numeral whose radix is ten. The tens complement is found by subtracting each digit of a number from 9, and adding 1 to the least significant of the resultant number. For example, the tens complement of 2456 is 7544.

teracycle—A million megacycles per second (10^{12} cycles per second).

terminal—The point where information can enter or leave a communication network. An input-output device designed to receive data in an environment associated with the job to be performed, and capable of transmitting entries to, and obtaining output from, the system of which it is a part.

terminal trunk—A trunk circuit used to connect two or more terminals.

terminating symbol—A symbol on the tape designed to indicate the end of a block of information. (Related to gap.)

termination, loop—Loops can be terminated when reading data from cards, the cards can simply be let to run out, causing a "hang up" or stop. More commonly, however, in reading data, the last card contains some particular code number which may be tested and thus used to terminate the loop. Most often, the first card contains the number of data sets to be read, and this number is put into some counter "location," which is later tested for zero to end the loop.

terminator/initiator—A particular program which makes a job step ready to run in some computers and which also performs regular housekeeping tasks after a job has ended. Used in connection with job schedulers which select a job or job part waiting to be executed after allocating and clearing memory space of extraneous data.

ternary—1. This pertains to a characteristic or property involving a selection, choice, or condition in which there are three possibilities. 2. Pertaining to the number representation system with a radix of three. 3. Having the capability of assuming three distinct states.

ternary code—A code in which only three states are considered.

ternary notation—A numeration system designed with a radix of three, i.e., a positional notation arrangement restricted to three symbols: zero, one, and two.

test—An examination, particularly relative to a criterion; to determine the present arrangement of some element of computer hardware, e.g., a manually set switch.

test conditions-overflow (underflow)—Often tests are made for underflow and overflow conditions which occur when a result too large or too small for the arithmetic register has been generated, i.e., once an underflow or an overflow occurs, the appropriate indicator can remain "set" until it is tested. After the test, it is conventional for the overflow or underflow condition to be restored to normal.

test, diagnostic—The running of a machine program or routine for the purpose of discovering a failure or a potential failure of a machine element, and to also determine its location or its potential location.

testing, program—A procedure which is completed to discover whether the program is successful in meeting the defined systems requirements. Testing methods must be designed so that they thoroughly test the new system.

tetrad—A group of four, usually four pulses used to express a digit in the scale of 10 or 16.

theory, automatic—The theory development which relates the study of principles of operation and application of automatic devices to various behaviorist concepts and theories.

thin film—A unique ultrahigh-speed storage device consisting of a molecular deposit of material on a suitable plate, usually silicon or glass. Common sizes are 1/20th of an inch square that may contain entire etched circuits replacing thousands of transistors, etc.

third generation computer—Computers which use microcircuits and miniaturization of components to replace vacuum tubes, reduce costs, work faster, and increase reliability. The third generation of computers began in about 1964 and helped to foster the growth of time-sharing. There are "families" of third generation equipment, including IBM System 360, Honeywell's Series 200, NCR Century Series, GE's 400 and 600 lines, and RCA's Spectra 70. First generation computers used tubes (1954) and were made obsolete by second generation machines (1959-1960) which utilized transistors to increase speed and reliability and to decrease size and maintenance.

third-level address—Used in an indirect or

multilevel addressing system the third address sought in the attempt to arrive at the location of an operand, the machine interprets the contents of the first two storage locations as addresses rather than as operands.

thirty-nine feature code—One which is designed for punched cards to represent numerals only from 0 to 39 but with no more than two punches in any column.

THOR (Tape Handling Option Routine)—1. A set of general tape-handling and correction routines used to perform the functions of comparing and printing, locating, correcting and copying, and many others. 2. A Honeywell utility program that positions, copies, corrects or edits tape; it can also locate data on tape, compare the contents of two tapes for discrepancies, and perform general tape maintenance. Used with Honeywell 200, 800, and 1800 computers.

three address code—A machine instruction designed with reference to three address, for example, one each for the two addends and one for the sum.

three-addressed machines—Three-address machines will specify not only the address of the two operands, but also the address into which the result is automatically stored; also, variants are common, such as storing more than one instruction code per data word.

threshold—A logical operator that has the property that if P is a statement, Q is a statement, R is a statement . . . then the threshold of P, Q, R, . . . is true if and only if at least n statements are true, false if less than n statements are true, where n is a specified nonnegative integer called the threshold condition.

throughput—That productivity based on all facets of an operation, e.g., a computer with a capability of simultaneous operations of read/write/compute would have a high throughput rating.

throw-away characters—Found in tape transmitted over a telegraph channel where certain functions require more time than is allowed between successive characters in the transmission. Examples of these functions are from feedout, duplicating of card fields, etc. In order to prevent reception of an intelligence character while the machine is in the midst of performing such a function, a calculated number of "throw-away" characters must be inserted into the tape immediately following the function code and ahead of the next printing or function code. Letter codes are usually used as "throw-away" codes.

tie-line—A leased-communication channel or circuit between two or more PBX's.

time classifications—Includes serviceable time, with subheadings of effective and ineffective time, and out of service time, with subheadings of scheduled engineering time, divided between preventive maintenance time and fault time (or down time). Additions included in total time are also such classifications as debatable time, external delays, and unused time.

time, deceleration—1. The time which elapses between completion of reading or writing of a tape record, and the time when the tape stops moving (synonymous with stop time). 2. The time it takes to stop a tape after reading or recording the last piece of information from a record on that tape.

time, departure—The time at which control is returned to the Supervisory Program when a segment of an Application Program is completed.

time division—A process of communication in which several messages time-share a single transmission channel.

time, down—The period during which a computer is malfunctioning or not operating correctly because of machine failures (contrasted with available time, idle time, or standby time).

time frame—Relates to the limits of time needed for a particular situation or events.

time origin—A start of a pulse is defined as the time at which it first reaches some given fraction, i.e., 10%, of its full amplitude and this time is called the time origin, i.e., of all associated phenomena.

time sequencing—Signal switching generated by a program purely as a function of accurately measured elapsed time.

time sharing—1. The interleaved time use on a device—hence, a method of operation in which a computer facility is shared by several users concurrently. 2. The apportionment of intervals of time availability of various items of equipment to complete the performance of several tasks by interlacing (contrasted with multiprogramming). 3. The use of a device for two or more purposes during the same overall time interval, accomplished by interspersing the computer component actions in time. 4. A multiple communications control unit (MCCU) attached to the computer allows many consoles to "time-share" the central processing unit simultaneously during transmission and receiving periods. Time-sharing is a computing technique in which numerous terminal devices can utilize a central computer concurrently for input, processing, and output

functions.

time-sharing, demand processing—Complementing the batch-processing capabilities of the executive system are its time-sharing capabilities, i.e., the simultaneous accommodations by the executive systems of requests and demands from users at numerous remote inquiry terminals, operating in a demand (or conversational) mode. All facilities available to the batch-processing user are also available in the demand mode; the primary difference is that the executive system utilizes its knowledge of the existence of such demand devices to permit the user additional flexibility in the statement of and control of individual runs. The demand user may communicate directly with the Executive, a worker program, or he may communicate with a conversational processor.

time slice—The unit of time allocated by a time-shared computer system to perform a particular user's task.

time utilization—The arrangement of a program which allows processing to continue while records necessary for processing are being located in file and read into core and working storage.

timing error—Generated when a program is not able to keep pace with the tape-transfer rate, or a new motion or select command is issued before the previous command was completely executed.

TINT—A subset of JOVIAL designed for simplified time-sharing programs.

TIPTOP (tape input/output control)—The tape input/output control provides machine code, as directed by macro instructions, to perform the following functions: reading and writing tape records, opening and closing files, blocking and unblocking items within records, and detection of automatic correction of errors. (Honeywell)

TLU (table look up)—Obtaining of a function value corresponding to an argument, stated or implied, from a table of function values stored in the computer. Also, the operation of obtaining a value from a table.

top-down method—A compiling technique using a template-matching method; prototypes for a statement of unknown nature are assumed one-by-one, until one prototype is found which matches.

TOS (Tape Operating System)—IBMs design of a powerful and flexible operating system for System 360 computers having at least 16K of memory, at least four magnetic tapes, and no random-access storage devices.

total system—Many times called the integrated system, it is a plan to place all important and significant operational components of an organization under the complete or partial control of computers. Real-time system configurations, and their immediacy of data collection, processing, and generation are convenient to this total-system concept.

touchtone—An input achievement of great significance to the data communications industry, developed by the American Telegraph and Telephone Company. With this service, the conventional telephone dial is replaced by a panel of buttons, which when pushed generate a tone which operates switching equipment at the telephone exchange. These tones can be used to provide input to a computer, and it's expected that touchtone equipment will soon be able to incorporate a full alphabet in addition to the ten digits.

TRAC—A procedure describing language

for the reactive typewriter written by C. N. Mooers.

trace—A diagnostic technique, interpretive in nature, that provides an analysis of each executed instruction and writes it on an output device as each instruction is executed.

trace program—A special type of diagnostic program designed for the performance of checks on other programs or for demonstrating such operations. The output of a trace program may include instructions of the program which is being checked and intermediate results of those instructions arranged in the order in which the instructions are executed.

track—1. A location or sequence of binary cells arranged so that data may be read or written from one cell at a time in serial fashion; for example, a track on a magnetic drum in a path one-bit wide around the circumference of the drum. 2. The portion of a moving-storage medium, such as a drum, tape, disc, that is accessible to a given reading station.

tracking cross—A specific crosslike array of bright dots on a display unit used for locating points and lines or for drawing curves.

traffic control—A method of optimizing the flow of work through a factory communication system or operation by means of a computer.

trailer—1. A special or distinct record that follows a group of detail records and gives information about a group not present in the detail records. 2. A record that follows a header.

trailer record—An information record that follows a group of records and contains pertinent data related to the group of records.

training mode—The training of terminal

186

operators and the testing of a system in which normal operations are defined and carried on by the operator and in which he is encouraged to enter all types of transactions from normal to exceptional. The randomness and inventiveness of the input operator is used to check the formal test input and any inconsistencies are resolved.

transaction—A collection or specific group of several related actions entered by a terminal operator as in an airline reservation system where the sale of a space on one flight is an action, and the sale of an itinerary or schedule, including several alternate flights for the same passenger, would be a transaction.

transaction record—Specific information of applications which modify information in a file.

transceiver—1. A unit of equipment for card-to-card transmission by way of telephone or telegraph wires. 2. A device that transmits and receives data from a punched card to a punched card. It is essentially a conversion device which at the sending end reads the card and transmits the data over the wire. At the receiving end it punches the data into a card.

transcriber—Relates to the specific equipment associated with a computer for the purpose of transferring the input or output data from a record of information in a given language to the computer medium and language, or from a computer to a record of information.

transducer—A specific device which is used to convert energy from one form to another; e.g., a quartz crystal imbedded in mercury can change electrical energy to sound energy as is done on sonic delay lines in computer-storage systems.

transfer—1. The ability to transfer control by means of an instruction or signal that specifies the location of the next instruction and directs the computer to that instruction; to jump. A transfer is used to alter the normal sequence control of the computer. 2. To transfer data; to copy, exchange, read, record, store, transmit, transport, or write data. 3. To terminate one sequence of instructions and begin another sequence. Types: interpreter, parallel, radial, and unconditional.

transfer instruction—An instruction to a computer designed to enable the programmer to instruct the computer to choose between alternative subprograms depending upon the conditions determined by the computer during the execution of the program.

transfer medium—Refers to the material which enables the transfer of ink during printing, i.e., sheets, ribbons, plastic film.

transfer vector—Relates to a specific table that contains a list of transfer instructions of all the programs that are in core which enable transfers of control to be made from one program to another program.

transfer table—See transfer vector.

transition card—1. A specific control card, used in the loading of a deck of program cards, that causes the termination of loading and initiates the execution of the program (synonymous with transfer-of-control card and transfer card). 2. A card that signals the computer that the reading in of a program has ended and the carrying out of the program has started.

translate—To translate means to change information from one language to another without significantly affecting the meaning, e.g., changing problem statements in pseudocode into machine language.

translater, language—1. A program which converts a language to equivalent statements in another computer language, usually for a different computer. 2. A routine which aids in the performance of natural language translations such as French to English. 3. Any assembler or compiling program which brings forth same or equivalent output from human-readable statements.

transliterate—A procedure to represent the characters or words of one language by corresponding characters or words of another language.

transmission system codes—Specific methods for using a character parity check as well as a block check to detect errors.

transportation, linear programming—When given a large number of warehouses with limited capacities and a large number of distributers with known demands, linear programming procedure enables the problem design of a shipping schedule which will minimize total costs.

transport unit—One of many specific pieces of peripheral equipment or media handling devices such as a card feed.

transverse check—A unique system of error control based on some preset rules for the formation of characters.

trapped-program interrupt—Normally, any condition that causes an interrupt should be identified as soon as possible. However, in some cases it may be more convenient to ignore this condition. To allow for this possibility, the interrupt traps may be armed or disarmed by program control. An interrupt trap is associated with each interrupt event; an interrupt may occur only if its corresponding trap is armed. Any trap may be individually armed or disarmed and its condition may be stored in memory or tested under program control. The seven events that may cause an interrupt to occur are: (1) add overflow, (2) operator-interrupt switch, (3) memory-parity fall, (4) power fail, (5) programmed input/output channel, (6) nonpriority external device, and (7) priority external device.

trapping—A feature of some computers whereby an unscheduled (nonprogrammed) jump is made to a predetermined location in response to a machine condition (e.g., a tagged instruction, or an abnormal arithmetic situtation). Such a feature is commonly used by monitor routines to provide automatic checking for error causes or for communication between input-output routines and their programs.

tree—A specific term often used for some types of decoders because their diagrammatic representation can resemble the branches and trunk of a tree, i.e., a decision tree.

true complement—The complement for a given notation system. The binary-true complement is called the 2's complement, and the decimal-true complement is called the 10's complement. See two's complement.

truncate—1. A procedure which causes the reduction of precision by dropping one or several of the least significant digits; contrasted with rounding off. 2. To drop digits of a number of terms in a series, thus lessening precision; e.g., the number 3.14159265 is truncated to five figures in 3.1415, whereas one may round off to 3.1416. 3. To terminate a computational process in accordance with some rule.

trunk—1. One or more conductors of an electronics station used for distributing

188

a-c signals or power from one or more sources to one or more destinations (synonymous with bus). 2. A path for the transfer of data or signals.

truth table—A Boolean representation of a switching function, or truth function, in which every possible configuration of argument values 0-1, or true-false is listed, and beside each is given the associated function value 0-1 or true-false. The number of configurations is 2^n, where "n" is the number of arguments, unless the function is incompletely specified, i.e., don't care conditions. An example of a Boolean truth table for the AND-function and the OR-function (inclusive) is:

Variable		AND Function	OR
A	B	AB	A+B
0	0	0	0
0	1	0	1
1	0	0	1
1	1	1	1

TSC—An abbreviation for transmitter start code. A specific bell system term sequence that is sent to an outlying teletypewriter terminal which automatically polls its tape transmitter or keyboard. Related to ITS.

TSS/360, time-sharing system—An operating system for large-scale 360 configurations having time-sharing features.

T Test—A comparison test of two units of quantitative data for the determination of their inequality, i.e., a determination of which quantity is the greater.

TTY—Abbreviation for Teletypewriter equipment.

tub file—A type of open account file which provides ready accessibility to punched cards or other computer storage documents.

tube—A tube in EDP (electronic data-processing) systems usually refers to a cathode-ray tube that has the capability to display data.

Turing machine—A unique and useful mathematical abstraction of a device that operates to read from, write on, and move an infinite tape, thereby providing a model for computerlike procedures. The behavior of a Turing machine is specified by listing an alphabet; i.e., collection of symbols read and written, a set of internal states, and a mapping of an alphabet and internal states which determines what the symbol written and tape motion will be, and also what internal state will follow when the machine is in a given internal state and reads a given symbol.

turnaround time—The particular measurement of the amount of time that is required for a computation task to get from the programmer to the computer, onto the machine for a test or production run, and back to the programmer in the form of the desired results. Important problems occur when the turnaround time is excessive, especially in scientific installations.

tutor, electronic—A teaching machine which makes use of programmed instructions in the computer to help each student achieve his educational goals. Each student communicates with the computer via his own terminal. The computer will be programmed to adjust its teaching style automatically to the needs of each student, and each student will progress at his own best pace independently of others. Bright students will move from topic to topic rapidly, while slower students will be carefully tutored

189

and given extra practice to raise them to the desired achievement levels.

twelve edge—The upper most edge of an 80 column Hollerith card. Interpreting equipment requires a twelve edge feed first.

twelve punch—1. A specific punch in the top row of a Hollerith card. 2. Relates to punch position 12 of an 80-column card. It is often used for additional control or selection, or to indicate a positive number as if it were a plus sign. (Synonymous with Y punch.)

twenty-nine feature code—A specific code which is designed for punched cards to represent numerals only from 0 to 29 but with no more than two punches in any one column.

twin check—A redundancy or continuous duplication check achieved by the duplication of hardware and/or an automatic comparison of data.

twin-drum (sorting)—In a multidrum computer configuration, this term represents the use of two drums for storing a file of data. The elapsed time required to sort is significantly reduced by alternating the moving of one drum head with the reading and writing of data from another drum.

two-addressed machines—In contrast to single-address (operand) machines, two-address machines are designed to store the result of the binary operation in some assigned register or at the location of one of the operands, as well as specifying two operand addresses.

two-pass assembler—An assembler designed to require scanning of the source program twice. The first pass constructs a symbol table. The second pass does the translation.

two's complement—A value derived by subtracting an original number from the base number (or a power of the base number) from the numbering system of the original number. For binary numbers, the twos complement; for decimal numbers, the two's complement would be the tens complement.

two-state variable—A variable which is used to assume values in a set containing exactly two elements, often symbolized as 0 and 1. This is often confused with double-value variable, i.e., $y = \pm\sqrt{x}$. (Synonymous with binary variable.)

two-wire channel—A circuit or channel for transmission in only one direction at a time.

type-font—The entire character set for a particular type size, e.g., 12 pts.

type statements—A series of statements in FORTRAN used to override the normal mode of assigning variable names and also to reserve arrays.

* – * – *

UA—An abbreviation for user area, i.e., the area on a disk where semipermanent data or programs may be stored. This is contrasted to reserve areas that contain compilers, tracks and sector information, etc.

UDC—Abbreviation for Universal Decimal Classification.

ultrasonics—The field of audio science devoted to frequencies of sound above the human-audio range.

umbral—A distinct heading which is distinctly and totally relevant to the data being sought.

unbalanced error—Those distinct or specific errors or sets of error values in which the maximum and minimum are not opposite in sign and equal in magnitude,

190

as contrasted to balanced errors, i.e., the average of all the error values is not zero.

unblind (blind)—The selective procedure for controlling of a transmission printer or reperforator. Used, for example, to prevent prices from typing on a receiving teletypewriter.

UNCOL—An abbreviation for Universal Computer Oriented Language.

unconditional branch—A specific operational instruction of basic importance that develops a deviation from the program-execution sequence despite existing conditions.

unconditional jump—A basic operational instruction that switches the sequence of control to a specified location (synonymous with unconditional branch and unconditional transfer of control).

unconditional transfer—An instruction jump which is made to occur under all possible conditions.

underflow—1. In an arithmetical operation, this term relates to the generation of a quantity too small to be stored by the register or location that is to receive the result. 2. The generation of a quantity smaller than the accepted minimum, e.g., floating-point underflow.

underpunch—A locational punch in one of the lower rows, 1-9, of an 80-column 12-row punch card.

UNICOMP—Universal Compiler, FORTRAN compatible.

uniformly accessible storage—A particular type of storage which is designed to reduce the effect of variation of access time for an arbitrary sequence of addresses.

unitary code—A specific code which has only one digit; the number of times it is repeated determines the quantity it represents.

unit-distance code—A specific code design in which the characters of a character set are represented by some or all of the different words of n bits arranged in a sequence such that the signal distance between consecutive words in the sequence is 1.

unit element—A specific alphabetic-signal element having a duration equal to the unit interval of time, i.e., a quantum.

uniterm indexing—1. Single terms are used to define and describe the contents of a document with some measure of distinctness. Mortimer Taube labeled the terms, uniterms. This process is used primarily for information or document retrieval. 2. A system of coordinate indexing that utilizes single terms to define a document uniquely (related to uniterm system).

unit record—1. A single card containing one complete record; currently, the punched card. 2. A printed line with a maximum of 120 characters; a punched card with a maximum of 72 characters, a BCD (binary-coded decimal) tape record with a maximum of 120 characters.

unit separator—A specific character developed for the demarcation of the logical boundary between items of data that are referred to as separate and distinct units.

universal button box—A programmer coined term for a set of push buttons whose functions are determined by the computer program.

universal decimal classification—Refers to an expansion of the Dewey decimal classification started by P. Otlet in Brussels; sometimes referred to as the Brussels system.

unmodified instruction—An instruction which is designed to be modified in some prescribed way by means of a store program computer available for a particular purpose, to produce the complete executable instruction.

uptime—1. The measured time during which equipment is either producing work or is available for productive work (contrasted with downtime). 2. Uptime includes production, program development, incidentals, delay, idle, or even unused time, and is generally the same as serviceable time.

USASCII—An abbreviation for USA Standard Code for Information Interchange.

USA Standard Code for Information Interchange—A code which uses eight bits per character (one being a parity bit), the character set consisting of graphic characters and control characters, used for the interchange of information between data processing systems and communications systems, and between the equipment associated with systems of both types.

usec—An abbreviation for microsecond, 1/1,000,000 of a second.

user area (UA)—A specific area on a magnetic disk where semipermanent data is stored. This area is often used to store programs, subprograms and subroutines. This area is contrasted with reserved areas that contain compilers, track and sector information, etc., which may not be written into.

user-oriented languages, time sharing—Languages used at remote terminals are more critical than in batch-mode systems. Time-sharing increases the accessibility of computers to nonprogramming types of problem solvers. Higher percentages of lay users use time-shared systems. Language forms, syntax, and special words are tailored to these users lacking in computer expertise.

user programs—A group of specific programs, subprograms or subroutines that have been written by the user as contrasted to manufacturer supplied programs.

utility functions—Relates to auxiliary operations such as tape searching, tape-file copying, media conversion, and dynamic memory and tape dumps.

utility system—A system or program or set of programs which are developed to perform miscellaneous utility functions such as card-to-tape, tape-to-printer, and other peripheral operations or suboperations.

utilization ratio—That particular measurement which is the ratio of effective time to serviceable time.

* — * — *

validity check—1. A specific check related to the accuracy of character representation. 2. A checking technique based on known reasonable limits on data or computed results. For instance: a man cannot work 400 hours in one week, a month does not have 32 days, an hourly classified man very seldom has a net pay greater than $250.00 per week, etc. Also called a reasonableness check.

variable—1. A symbol whose numeric value changes from one repetition of a program to the next, or changes within each repetition of a program. 2. In COBOL, a data item in storage that assumes different values during execution of the object program. Types: Boolean, dependent, fixed, independent, integer, logical and real.

variable address—An address that is to be modified or which has been modified by an index register or similar device.

variable, dependent—A variable whose

192

value is determined by some function of another quantity or representation, i.e., the standard expression is y = f(x), where y is considered the dependent variable because its value is determined by the value of x and the nature of the function to be performed.

variable field length—A data field that may have a changing number of characters requiring item separators to indicate the end of each item.

variable length—Relates to the actual number of characters which may be available in a particular storage location or data element. Since it is variable, the programmer has discretion, and it is possible that each successive block may have different or varying numbers of words, but the word packing density usually remains constant.

variable name—An alphanumeric title selected by a programmer to represent a specific program variable. Rules for naming variables vary between compilers (FORTRAN, BASIC) and computing equipment.

variable point—Relates to a number system in which the location of the point is indicated by a special character at that location.

variance analysis—Relates to the estimate of probability relatedness by comparison of between-columns variance with within-columns variance.

varioplex—An electronic device, used in conjunction with a time-sharing multiplex system, that enables the multiplexed channels to be distributed between the users in a variable manner, according to the number of users who are transmitting at a given time.

variplotter—A large, high-accuracy graphic recording device which plots curves on either a 30" x 30" or a 45" x 60" surface. Single- and dual-arm models are available for use as horizontal table units or as mounted-vertical units. The plotters feature solid-state circuitry, backlighted plotting surface, vacuum-paper holddown, continuously variable scale factor and parallax controls. (ESI)

VATE (Versatile Automatic Test Equipment—VATE is a project that presents a new concept for computer-controlled checkout of complex instrumentation systems. The overall system consists of equipment, test programs, and trained people. VATE tests Air Force inertial-guidance systems, including those on the Titan and Minuteman missiles. The latter system is put on a platform, and flying conditions are simulated during test. The operator at the VATE console receives instructions on each step in the testing procedure by means of a 35-millimeter slide viewed. The computer-controlled random-access slide viewer forms the upper portion of the operator's console and displays a succession of instructions to the operator. When a fault is discovered, an illustration of the malfunction is displayed. Then, as VATE isolates the fault, the exact location of it is shown.

vector—A mathematical or geometric line denoting magnitude and direction, as contrasted with a scalar denoting magnitude only.

venn diagram—A logic diagram in which sets are represented by closed regions.

verb—In COBOL, an instruction word that specifies one or more operations to be performed by a data processor.

verify—1. A process of checking, usually with an automatic machine, one typing or recording of data against another in order to minimize the number of human errors or mistakes in the data transcription. 2. In preparing data for a computer, to make certain that the data prepared is correct. 3. To check a data transfer or transcription, especially those involving manual processes.

vertical format—Pertaining to the vertical arrangement of data, as viewed by an observer of a document.

vertical redundance—A specific error condition that exists when a character fails a parity check; i.e., has an even number of bits in an odd parity system, or vice versa.

vertical tabulation character—A specific control character which was developed to cause the printing or display position to be moved a measured number of lines at right angles to the line of printing.

video-data interrogator—A specific terminal unit that is comprised of a keyboard and separable associated display, providing a terminal facility for conventional communications lines.

violation subroutines—Often times, when the input does not conform to pre-set criteria or limits, a violation subroutine takes over.

VIP—An abbreviation for: Variable Information Processing, a generalized proprietary program for information storage and retrieval system, for small nonformalized files, and which provides for retrieval techniques without programming effort, i.e., it is organized by file, using mnemonic codes or abbreviations and plain text language, with no limits on characters.

virgin coil—A paper or plastic tape completely devoid of punches.

virtual address—The immediate address or a specific real-time address.

virtual address, effective—The virtual address is a specific value developed after only indirect addressing and/or indexing modifications have been accomplished, but before memory mapping is performed.

virtual memory pointer—As an aid for storage efficiency some computers are designed so that parts of programs and data may be scattered through main memory and auxiliary storage. Various pointers or lists of pointers automatically keep track of the location of these program portions. The user of computers so designed may be unaware of this scattering procedure and most often operates computing procedures as though he were using normal memory.

VLF—An abbreviation for Very-Low Frequency. Frequencies below 30,000 hertz.

vocabulary—1. A specific list of operating codes or instructions, available to the programmer, used to write the program for a given problem on a specific computer. 2. A group of characters occupying one storage location. This unit of information is treated and transported by the computer circuits as an entity; it is treated by the control unit as an instruction, and by the arithmetic unit as a quantity.

volatile dynamic storage—A specific unit for a storage medium which depends only on the external supply of power for the maintenance of stored information.

volatile memory—A storage medium of the type in which information can be destroyed when power is removed from the system.

volume—Relates to a single unit of external storage, all of which can be read or written by a single access mechanism or

I/O device.

volume statistics—Distinct groups of various pertinent facts in relation to the nature and level of operations of an area under consideration expressed in numbers (e.g., number of sellers, number of different items, orders, purchases, etc.), plus, or including, subclassifications of these data to obtain a clear understanding of the pattern of the operations.

volume table of contents (VTOC)—1. An index record near the beginning of each volume, which records the name, location, and extent of every file or data set residing on that particular volume. Usually not found on magnetic tapes, but often required on all disk packs and drums. 2. A particular table related to and describing every specified set in a direct access volume.

volume test—The processing of a volume of actual data specifically to check for program malfunctions.

(VTOC) Volume Table of Contents—Concerns a specific index record near the beginning of each volume, which records the name, location, and extent of every file or data set residing on that particular volume. Usually not found on magnetic tapes, but often required on all disk packs and drums.

VU—An abbreviation for voice unit.

* _ * _ *

wait—The condition a time-sharing or real-time program meets when it requires information from a file-storage unit and is forced to "wait" until the required-file record is accessed and brought into the main memory. File-oriented systems have this characteristic that leads to multi-programmed approaches by interleaving and overlapping "wait" times for one program to achieve process time for another program.

wait condition—A circumstance or condition related to a task in such a way that transition into the ready state depends on the occurrence of one or more events.

waiting lines (queuing theory)—When a flow of goods (or customers) is bottlenecked at a particular servicing point, losses accumulate in the form of lost business, idle equipment, and unused labor. Minimizing such costs involved in waiting lines, or queues, is the object of queuing theory, an O/R (operations research) technique for the most efficient handling of a waiting line at a particular service point.

warning, end of tape—A visible magnetic strip on magnetic tape which indicates that the few feet, often five feet, of the tape remains available.

waste instruction—An artificial instruction or address designed to be inserted in a list to serve a purpose other than the execution as an instruction. (Related to constant instruction.)

WATS—An abbreviation for wide area telephone service.

WDPC (Western Data Processing Center)—Established in November 1956, it is the first and one of the largest university-computing centers specifically oriented to business applications.

whirleybird—The slang reference or expression to designate some types of disc pack equipment.

who are you?—An inquiry character.

wide-area telephone service (WATS)—This is similar to WADC (wide area data service). A service which provides a special line allowing the customer to call a certain zone(s) or band(s), on a direct-distance dialing basis, for a flat monthly charge. The continental United States is divided into six bands for the purpose of rates.

wired-program computer—The operations of these specialized computers are performed or their sequence is controlled by the placement and interconnection of wires, as on a plugboard.

WIZ—This algebraic compiler, further down the scale, is a very fast algebraic compiler. Unlike most scientific compilers which require two or three passes, WIZ requires only one—and its language is considerably easier to learn. Used primarily for engineering, scientific, and other complex mathematical problems, this coding system accepts a program written in easily-understood algebraic format and translates it—in one pass—into a program of machine instructions, punched on cards or paper tape, and ready to run.

WIZ permits engineers and mathematicians to write their own programs in a language familiar to them. As with GECOM, the WIZ user need not be concerned with the complex details of the computer—he can state his problem in its own element. (GE)

word—1. A designated set of characters that occupies one storage location and is treated by the computer circuits as a unit and transported as such. Ordinarily, a word is treated by the control unit as an instruction, and by the arithmetic unit as a quantity. Word lengths are fixed or variable, depending on the particular computer. 2. A unit of data or a set of characters that may be of any length but which occupies one storage location. A word is usually treated as a unit by a data processing machine. Quantities, dollar amounts and names are examples of words. 3. In telegraphy, 5 characters plus 1 space, or 6 key-strokes. Types: alphabetic, banner, data, halt, and machine.

word capacity—1. Relates to the selection of one of the word lengths of the equipment as a datum and thus to classify different operations as partial or multiples of these lengths for working. 2. The number of characters in a machine word. In a given computer, the number may be constant or variable.

word length—1. The number of bits or characters specified as a physical unit by a programmer. 2. The size of a field. 3. The number of bits or other characters in a word.

word-mark—An indicator to signal the beginning or end of a word.

word-oriented—Usually refers to the type of memory system used in early computers. The memory system divided into sections called "words", each of which had a location number and contained enough bits of binary digits to hold about 10 numeric positions.

word-select, memory section—Many of the significant features of the computer are a result of its fast memory which has been designed to provide a total memory-cycle time of microseconds. This fast memory speed is mainly the result of the word-select with diode steering technique that is used for memory addressing. This replaces the more conventional method of X and Y axis half-read and half-write currents which is much slower. Another design consideration is the non-destructive readout with a positive, automatic restoration feature that prevents an accidental loss of memory information.

word time—1. That measured time required to transfer a machine word from one storage position to another. 2. In reference to words stored serially, the time required to transport one word from one storage device to another. Related to access time.

working memory—The internal memory which stores information for processing and releases it after usage for the entry of new data.

worst case—The circumstance or case in which the maximum stress is placed on a system, as in making it purposely error-prone, or inefficient for testing.

wow and flutter—Electronic terms used to describe changes in signal output frequency caused by tape speed variations occurring at relatively low and relatively high rates, respectively.

wrap-around storage—Concerns an arrangement of core storage in which the lowest numbered storage location is the successor of the highest numbered one.

write time interval—The determination of the interval during machine operation when output data is available for an output operation, i.e., the net time exclusive of transmission which it takes to perform an output operation such as printing or writing on tapes.

WS—An abbreviation for working storage, that specific area on a disk used to hold dynamic or working data. This area is contrasted to reserved area containing permanent information such as compilers, track and sector information, etc., and user area for semipermanent storage.

* _ * _ *

xerography—A patented (Xerox) dry copying process involving the photo-electric discharge of an electrostatic charge on the plate. The copy is made by tumbling a resinous powder over the plate; the remaining electrostatic charge is discharged, and the resin is transferred to paper or an offset printing master.

x-off—Transmitter off.

x-on—Transmitter on.

x punch—1. A punch in the X or 11 row (2nd) of an 80-column card. 2. A punch in position 11 of a column. The X punch is often used to control or select, or to indicate a negative number as if it were a minus sign.

xs-3—Abbreviation for excess three (code).

X-Y (plotting board) recorder—A recorder that makes a record of any one voltage with respect to another.

* _ * _ *

zata code indexing—1. A unique library system of indexing individual documents by descriptors of equal rank, so that a library can be searched for a combination of one or more descriptors. 2. An indexing technique where the interrelations of terms are shown by coupling individual words. 3. An indexing scheme by which descriptors may be correlated or combined to show any interrelationships desired for purposes of more precise information retrieval.

zero access—Relates to the ability to obtain data from or place data in a storage device or register directly, without serial delay due to other units of data, and usually in a relatively short period of time.

zero kill—A specific feature of some sorters to offer a capability to determine that only zeros remain in the high order positions of documents while the documents are being sorted in lower order positions, i.e., this permits the machine operator to remove documents that are fully sequenced earlier in the sorting operation.

zero-level address—An instruction address in which the address part of the instruction is the operand.

zero suppression—A process to cause the elimination of insignificant zeros (those to the left of a quantity in a field or word) during a printing operation.

zone—1. The 12, 11, or 0 punches in a Hollerith card-code. 2. That portion of a character code that is used with the numeric codings to represent non-numeric information. 3. In some processors, two bits are used in conjunction with four numeric bits to represent alphanumeric characters. The zone bits therefore may be used separately to represent signs, to identify index registers, and for other purposes. 4. For punched cards, the 11 and 12 punches are used with numeric punches 0 and 9 to represent alphabetic and special symbols. Zone punches may be used independently and for special control purposes. 5. A portion of internal storage allocated for a particular purpose.

ZOOM—1. An assembler or compiler routine [part of GAP (General Assembly Program)], that writes statements (called macro statements) which can be translated into more than one machine instruction—or, you can write single GAP mnemonics. In other words, ZOOM statements that will generate several machine instructions can be combined with those which generate only one instruction, forming a highly-workable "shorthand" coding system. This allows a high degree of flexibility and provides near-optimum coding. For the experienced programmer, ZOOM provides a condensed and readable input and near-optimum output. (General Electric) 2. A highly-workable "shorthand" coding system for the experienced programmer. ZOOM provides a condensed and readable input and near-optimum output, thus aiding the programmer in gaining a highly-efficient and flexible program.

APPENDIX A

IMPACT OF COMPUTERS
ON STUDENTS AND TEACHERS

IMPACT OF COMPUTERS ON STUDENTS
AND TEACHERS

The Impact of Computers on Education, the Professions, and the Public
The basic parts of this appendix concern the widespread applications of computers in four distinct and most significant areas which quite specifically affect both students and teachers. The purpose is to relate the approaching all-pervasive nature of computer applications in practically every area of man's endeavor. Each of the four areas described below will be segmented into very broad categories and topics to develop the overall impact and to stress the specificity and range of computer capability and versatility throughout the various worlds of science, the professions, finance, the communication media, the American government and culture.

However, before this analysis is read, and for the benefit of those students and teachers and other readers who are not fully aware of the fundamental concepts related to the definition and structure of the computer, it is suggested that a few minutes be devoted to the basic analysis of a computer system, its functional components, and their utilization in the computing process. This brief summary begins on page 213.

For the purpose of clarity and brevity a discussion of computer applications and impact is divided into four basic sections, although certainly many other areas importantly also pertain.

I. Computer Systems Control of Finance and Credit.

II. Computers Are Now a Requisite Assistant in All Professions: Medical, Education, Engineering, Libraries, and Law.

III. Computers Become Vital Operating Tools in Insurance, Public Utilities, Communications and Transportation.

IV. Widespread Computer Applications Are Basis For New Media, Evolution, and a Resultant Computer Culture.

Although each of these topics will be subdivided into specific and brief analysis of distinct application areas and although the range may appear to be quite extensive, a great many other far-reaching areas of computer utilization are equally significant but space prohibits their discussion and analysis in this text. More than 5,000 distinct computer applications have been developed in listings of the computer versatility by other authors and writers surveying the computer applications extensive range of utilization. The areas of discussion in this appendix are designed to alert the reader to the impact of computer applications in order that he may realize both the scope and importance of the many professional and vocational areas in which he is challenged to prepare himself for computer related operations and knowledge if he has determined any of the specific endeavors analyzed to be his goal or future means of livelihood.

I. COMPUTER SYSTEMS CONTROL OF FINANCE AND CREDIT

Automated Banking Rapidly Leading to Total Financial Control Systems

Perhaps the greatest and quickest impact of computer applications affecting the largest segment of the American population was the pioneering developments of computer applications in the banking profession. The basic attempt to solve the problem of efficiently recording funds of millions of people in the daily activities of transferring their money were through the use of bank demand checks, which contain computer-readable magnetically coded identification numbers. Through the processing of billions of checks, credit instruments, and other documents, the computer has created a total upheaval in the banking and credit industry. Significant progress has been developed and the fundamental concepts and experimental programs have been established which will bring forward a "checkless-cashless society". Credit cards are expected to soon become "money cards" containing a magnetically encoded amount in dollars and cents. This amount will increase by the amount of his weekly or monthly wage as the individual presents his card to his company's payroll office and will decrease as he presents his "money card" to various retail and service institutions when he purchases products or services. The Point-of-Sale (POS) computer terminals at these establishments automatically deduct the amount of purchase from the balance on his money card. On-line computer teller terminals are becoming automated to such an extent that the number of human beings involved in customer transactions has been significantly reduced, and in many cases, the existing systems are designed for total elimination through the use of the "money card".

Smaller banks have already become part of large communications networks to tie into the elaborate systems of large banking institutions for computerized clearing of checks and credit instruments. Obviously, the elimination of the transfer of the paper itself will be accomplished by substituting direct computer inter-bank communications for daily balancing. This will be completed by computer controlled and verified money transfers. Banks have traditionally been one of the most important customers for the computer mainframe and peripheral equipment companies, software, consultant, and service companies. Banks are expanding the use of their computer systems to provide complete financial, payables, and receivables accounting, inventory control, and automated purchasing for the majority of their clients. Computers have become the central and dominating influence of the major operations completed by savings and loan companies, credit unions, and finance companies. Students and teachers are well aware of most of these developments, but perhaps have not fully considered or analyzed the deep and penetrating conquest by computer control of banking, finance, and credit.

Computers are Becoming the Conquerors of Accounting and Auditing

Following the lead of banking institutions and the use of their computer systems to provide accounting and auditing services in ever increasing range and variety to their customers, accountants and auditors face significant and portentious competition from these institutions as well as from the larger accounting firms and computer service companies that now offer total financial systems control through the utilization of extensive, complex, but extremely rapid and accurate computer control accounting. The majority of the largest wholesale, retail, and manufacturing companies have installed computers to achieve efficiency and cost reduction in record keeping, systems control, and information acquisition and dispersion. Inventory control systems and management reporting and analysis, as represented by specifically designed computer programs, are now central for large hotel and restaurant operations, as well as many other service and entertainment companies. The majority of accountants now realize that the computer has become a mainstay as regards computation and control of the myriad types of state, federal, local, excise and other taxes. The use of computers for accounting procedures in medical institutions has become an emphatic necessity. It certainly requires no further elaboration to establish that computers are indeed becoming synonymous with accounting.

Computer Service Companies Information Utilities Provide Effective Competition to Banks, Accounting, and Financial Companies

Computer companies for years have offered accounting services, total facilities management, and both in-house and outside consultant capabilities to business, engineering, and professional clients with consistent progress and innovative capability. The professional literature of computer science stresses the capability of such companies to create: (a) Information utilities with instantaneous retrieval of facts and data from large, but specific, topic designed data banks, (b) Credit utilities designed for providing "approval/denial" of personal credit within seconds of inquiry from any individual by practically any institution—and soon on a nationwide basis, (c) Accounting-service utilities as the next steps toward goals of direct transfer of transaction data between seller and purchaser and between customer and client through expanding direct communications systems and devices. Although the reader may be personally aware of these services, very few students and teachers fully realize the rapidity and range of operations demonstrated by the large and expanding computer services industry or the impact relating to the growth of computer information, financial, and accounting utilities.

The Computerized Stock Market Operations and Automated Portfolio Evaluation and Projections

Students and teachers of money, banking, and finance are aware of computer controlled reporting of all stock and bond transactions on all stock exchanges and the vital role computers are playing in "backroom" accounting and transfer of stock equity, certificates, and records. Computers are used to evaluate the performance of various stocks and to project price movements as developed by highly intricate forecast models. Just as insurance companies analyze individual requirements for protection and types of savings based on the needs and desires of customers, so also computer programs have been developed to analyze and evaluate stock portfolios of individual clients and companies with designs for conservation of funds, stability of income, or diversity of investments. The computer is becoming the essential tool of forecast and analysis for the majority of commodity transactions. The use of the computer for the development of econometrics, Input-Output, and other information and decision making models related to Macroeconomics and the Gross National Product (GNP) has expanded rapidly and importantly for government, institutional, and individual firm financial planning and forecasting. The impact of the computer in the financial world has just begun to be felt by students and teachers in these areas who should become diligent in developing knowledge of computer systems and software for use in these specialized but significantly important areas of planning, forecasting, and information retrieval.

II. COMPUTERS ARE NOW A REQUISITE ASSISTANT IN ALL PROFESSIONS: MEDICAL, EDUCATION, ENGINEERING, LIBRARIES, AND LAW

Major Changes in Medical and Health Sciences Due to Computer Systems Advances

The space program and heavy television emphasis on the physical and mental condition of astronauts and cosmonauts clearly demonstrated the importance and success of computer controlled monitoring devices. All major hospitals use computer instrumentation, usually attached to various portions of human bodies, for monitoring and control systems in the intensive care wards to alert physicians and nurses of changes or dangerous patient conditions. Computer on-line patient monitoring has rapidly progressed so that remote warning signals are now flashed to doctors from devices which patients wear while performing their normal routines or special activities. The computer has also become invaluable for efficient, rapid, and low-cost automated laboratory testing for an endless variety of patient examinations, such as bloods, liquids, respiratory and circulatory systems, etc. Indeed, computer cathode-ray tube (television-like) interrogation and display are receiving phenomenal acceptance as substitutes for routine physical examinations. The patient responds directly to the questions displayed on the screen, and the computer program is developed so that answers to certain questions automatically trigger the new inquiries, with deeper penetration in specific areas, to thus provide a significantly more thorough analysis of the individual's physical state, medical history, and psychological make-up. Most physicians who have researched, studied, and/or used automated diagnosis by computer experimentally have guarded but abundant praise for the truly remarkable results and accomplishments. The computer's giant memory and millionth-of-a-second response have allowed scientists to develop techniques for correlation, specific analyses, and searching historical verifications to provide unusually accurate diagnoses and recommended physical and drug therapy to aid the physician in questions, new discovery, or confirmation of his judgments.

All major medical research institutions, projects, and personnel are performing near miracles through the use of computers in discovering new cures or causes for diseases, as well as results of experimental use of a myriad of drugs and medical prognosis, therapy, analyses, and treatment. Practically 80% of the hospitals in the United States now are using computers almost completely for hospital accounting and administration, or very soon will install such systems, due basically to the pressing need for efficient and thorough control of the total hospital system. The impact of computers on medical and health sciences ranges much further than the above brief description and is causing a much needed and desired revolution in this most vital area of protection and preservation of life itself.

The Campus and the Computer — Problems and Progress

Surveys conducted recently have developed data showing that computers now are being widely used for multidiscipline educational purposes on the majority of campuses in the United States. Several hundred high schools have also taken advantage of special price-concession offers by computer mainframe manufacturers and the new low prices of small computer systems and minicomputers to begin computer education at the secondary level. Hundreds of private schools heavily promote the availability of scores of computer courses for convenient "crash" sessions or for evening or correspondence study. The popularity to students of the wide range of computer courses, coupled with the student and faculty acceptance of computer science as a profession and the rapid establishment of data processing and computer curriculum for undergraduate, advanced, or graduate study programs, all have worked in almost modular or building-block fashion to firmly establish computer science as one of the largest and most expansive areas of student and teacher goal drives for professional careers. The impact on education can only be considered as astounding. Data processing and computer science in high schools, junior colleges, and major universities have become the "IN" vocation and "seek" profession for today's typical future-minded student as he gropes for direction in his pursuit for gratification of challenges in today's complex society.

The computer itself as a teaching device, after a decade of concentrated and expensive widespread research, is now considered by most experts to portend radical changes in the architecture, geographical location, and internal structure of practically all educational institutions. Computer-Aided Instruction (CAI) has had phenomenal success and acceptance as the procedure which develops greater efficiency, better retention, low-cost instructions, and guided information (lessons) acquisition to individual students with only minimal direction by teachers and professors. Continuing two and four-year advanced education research projects have brought further analytical reports with comments that suggest that the colleges and universities as we know them today (i.e., as centralized groups of buildings), are already going through their evolutionary process of disappearance. Computer programmed courses, with each student in direct contact with huge remote computers and interconnected automated libraries, do not require the presence of students at lectures or in university buildings for the majority of their time. The introduction of hundreds of computer communications devices and media will allow students to use their homes as classrooms, and the computer terminal "genius" in their bedrooms acts as the vast store house of every type of knowledge especially including searching depths of penetration in selected topics. It also prods and gives references, just as do most friendly teachers and leaders.

Industry has also had phenomenal success through the use of computer terminals and programmed courses in great varieties, quickly and almost painlessly introducing or updating their workers to new procedures, policies, techniques, or specialized training. Although the computer does not totally replace the teacher and/or professor, it does permit the student to operate at his own pace, to probe deeply into areas beyond the knowledge and experience of human teachers, and to check his capabilities and progress as he himself chooses or desires. Primarily, the teacher and professor are relieved of the administration, testing, and extensive questions and reference tasks that formerly occupied a great portion of their valuable time. Teachers and professors now become the true leaders, innovators, and challengers; they provide counsel, guidance, motivation, and discussion leadership for students in smaller groups on individual bases as they help to plan and develop their students' individual skills, interests, and goals. Although most of the above still remains in the formative and experimental stage, practically no educational leader denies the capability of the computer to function as the most significant tool for the mental development of the youngsters in elementary, secondary, or higher level education pursuits. Only the rate of progress, i.e., the time required to break down well based educational tradition and bureaucracy, remains in doubt.

Although the use of computers in research is perhaps the largest and widest ranging area of computer applications, time and space does not permit the elaboration of the detail that this immense topic encompasses. It is, perhaps, sufficient to say here and now that, as regards the world of educational research, practically no professor who continues to pursue higher degrees or research honors can remain unaware of or refuse to accept the undeniable necessity of the use of computer systems in research activities. The range is so extensive that computer research applications apply from Archeology and Anthropology through practically all known disciplines and areas of academic pursuit, including Art, Music, and all areas of Social Science. Certainly, the Physical Sciences, the professions, and the commercial or administrative education areas utilize computers as central to the achievement of their ends. The student and teacher are therefore, willing or not, faced with an imperative demand that they use this servant and tool on an almost continuous basis as they thread their way through educational or life experiences.

Computers and Engineering Approach the Stage of Being Almost Synonymous

Engineering programs, whether they are civil, mechanical, industrial, chemical, or electronics, are beginning to appear as mirror images of computer science programs. Computer-driven automated plotters complete mechanical drawings with unyielding accuracy and miraculous speed. Few engineering students would attempt to solve any problem with a significant degree of complexity and precision without using computers. By the same token, few engineering students will acquire a degree in college without completing several courses relating to a thorough analysis of the internal construction of computing and communication instruments of all basic types. Automated production and process control has become the central area of instruction for industrial engineers. Computer-Aided Design (CAD) has become almost basic to architects, civil and mechanical engineers, and its mastery is of prime necessity to them. Computer-controlled devices of all types provide the challenging inquiry and solution procedure for design and utilization of communications, measurements, and fabricating tools and apparatus. Students and teachers of engineering classifications are perhaps receiving the heaviest impact of computers of any profession at this stage of the Computer Era.

Automated Laboratories and Libraries and Clinical, Psychological, and Social Experimentation Gain Rapid Prominence

Research and implementation of computer-controlled instruments and devices are significant tools for solving the problems of Pollution

Control and Conservation Simulations. Computer applications in weather and seismology studies are producing much sought after results. Space exploration and military science progress would be impossible without the continuing innovation of computer controlled systems. Automated laboratories are commonplace at all educational and research levels. Management science and management information systems, using computers to solve the intricate models, are progressing rapidly to new types of controls for greater efficiency in decision-making and information acquisition and dispersion. Library scientists now consider the computer as the core of their total operations from book purchasing and record keeping through all measures of information circulation and communicative abilities. Automated document retrieval systems and procedures are either now being implemented through library networks or are in the design stages for future utilization. Computers and information are now becoming synonymous terms and students and teachers are learning that these two major concepts are really one.

III. COMPUTERS BECOME VITAL OPERATING TOOLS IN INSURANCE, PUBLIC UTILITIES, COMMUNICATIONS AND TRANSPORTATION

Centralized Computer Systems in Life and Casualty Insurance

Insurance companies without computers simply do not exist in today's world. Computer programmed systems, information storage and retrieval data bases, and computerized actuarial research and calculations are mainstays and vital necessities for the vast insurance bureaucracies. The most alert insurance companies complete premium planning and personnel requirement calculations, as well as billing and analysis, using computer-controlled remote printing and communications. Computations and analyses of dividends, customer collection procedures, and rate changes of almost endless variety distinctly require computer precision and speed. Processing of claims, claim adjustments, and claim evaluation and verification are now developed into efficient systems through computer techniques. Many innovative and forward-looking insurance firms now provide highly individualized policy formulation, content printing, and direct issuance from computer printers and remote agency terminals. Due to the above listed computer operations, most insurance companies also complete agency and commissions accounting and scores of other automated office procedures by computers. Students aspiring to become members of the insurance community are strongly advised to become thoroughly motivated for education in computer procedures and systems.

Computer Systems and Public Utilities Provide Emulative Models for System Planning

Public utilities, including gas and oil combines, provide excellent examples of far-reaching versatility in computer applications. Gas and oil field data correlation and analysis combined with well exploration and distribution networks demonstrate thorough and explicit use of computer power and versatility. Pipeline design, construction, and distribution calculations, as well as seismic tests, evaluations, and projections are developed by the utility computer specialists and engineers on several sizes, types, and models of computers. Power plant production scheduling, operations stability and control, water reservoir management and other routines make up significant sections of computer systems developed by computer center directors for both large and small utilities. It would be difficult to find any sizable public utility which does not fully utilize the computer capability: for utility load flow computations; for information and data collection; and for meter readings and communication switching networks. Because of the tremendous number of employees in the various offices of most utilities, practically all currently possible aspects regarding office automation have been inaugurated. Some of the best examples of the value and efficiency of computer systems are the total control systems for complete oil refinery operations, network simulations, and maintenance schedules. Computers are also valuable as decision-making tools for the scores of investment analysts employed by public utilities to determine values and timing regarding leases, investment management, design systems and stock portfolio selections, evaluations, and analyses. Many of the public utilities also use computers for worldwide communications and expansion plans, projections, and cost analyses.

Computerized Communications — The Real Pioneers of Systems Utilization

The telephone companies have a history of computer use switching networks for more than two decades. Microwave systems and branch switching centers have used computers very efficiently to reduce the ever-increasing need for human employees. Had this not been done the number of telephone employees providing the high quality service of today's communication-mad world would now number almost half the population of this country. The major telephone companies, some years ago, provided significant blocks to improvement of nationwide data processing communications. However, they are now joining the computer device manufacturing leaders to provide for near miraculous speeds and capabilities required to process the huge volume of intercomputer communications now developed. The telephone companies have had good experience in audio response computers and have aided significantly in establishing the communications components necessary to complete governmental and educational computer networks, as well as hospital and medical inter-building information systems. Data communications for airlines and railroads are completed through direct visual communications devices with the computer as the centralized control and switching device. Many computer experts provide data and information to develop strong and confident cases that the communication devices will supersede the computer itself in importance and total utilization. Many feel that the computer, in decades hence, will be significant only as a component of information processing communications networks for instant intelligence acquisition and dispersal. It is felt that the computer will, thereby, disappear as an entity of individualized dominance and importance.

Computers Provide Solutions to Most Mass Transportation Enigmas

All major American railroads and, most major trucking firms now employ central computer systems to remain competitive in routing and scheduling efficiency and cost control. They use computer operations research programs and techniques to solve the majority of their operations problems, inventory of rolling stock as regards maintenance and location control, and complete routinized equipment maintenance. Highly significant and successful computerized auto traffic control systems have been developed in a score of major American, Canadian, and European cities to scientifically operate traffic signals which control flows and unclog monumental jams by alerting motorists in sufficient time to use alternate routes. Airlines use computers in almost every phase of their total operations. Computerized testing devices, equipment maintenance routines, reservation systems, weather analyses, accounting procedures and equipment scheduling are just a few of the operations which make the airline industry almost completely dependent upon the skill and expertise of computer applications and the quality of computer personnel and components. Computer systems also provide for automobile registration in almost every state. Police cars, in the larger and more alert traffic and criminal divisions of many cities, are equipped with computer terminals for instantaneous "suspect" information acquisition and retrieval. Students and teachers of transportation will certainly require thorough knowledge of computer equipment and system operation to move forward in the executive ranks of communications, transportation, utility and insurance companies.

IV. WIDESPREAD COMPUTER APPLICATIONS ARE BASED FOR NEW MEDIA EVOLUTION AND RESULTANT COMPUTER CULTURE

Automated Media and Publishing for the Seventies

Computer-automated photo composition has already developed systems which produce complete and finished books from rough manuscripts without people through all stages except final proofing. Magazine and book publishers use computers for subscription and other fulfillment, circulation control, promotion analyses, and automated ad copy production. The standardized accounting procedures are also computer controlled, such as information retrieval, records management, departmental operations, and corporate budgeting. RCA has done this original pioneering work for the development of individually customized televised newspapers. The customer simply dials various codes on his television set to request immediate new coverage in his specific areas of interest. He receives instantaneous hard copy printouts of those topics, in the depth and range he chooses, from the computer memory of up-to-the-minute worldwide events already analyzed and pre-digested. He may also request video tapes to be played on any of tens of thousands of subjects, events, or hobby or scholastic areas.

Computer Terminals for the Family at Home

The home has become the center of computer operations for amateurs and professionals alike. "Touch Tone" telephones and CRTs (Cathode-Ray Tubes) are the computer terminals of students completing home work, make inquiries to libraries and laboratories and completing CAI (Computer-Aided Instructions) courses at their own pace, convenience, and depth of penetration. Huge apartment buildings provide computerized shopping for customers through TV sets. Computers are a necessity for many aspects of the sporting world, for developing plays, selecting personnel, reworking strategies, and determining probabilities and betting odds.

The Computer Impact on Culture and Urban Society

Authors, editors, artists, music composers and conductors are all delighted and amazed concerning the revolutionary utilization of computers to bring forth magnificent examples of both current and modern art, full motion pictures, and original scores of popular and classical music, as well as an endless variety of computer-produced tone ranges and qualities.

The science fiction writers are most enthusiastic about SOMs — Self-Organizing Machines. These "adaptive" computers not only correct themselves, repair themselves, expand themselves, but have the human-like intelligence characteristics of associative, self-learning capabilities. When SOMs are combined with photoelectric and television eyes and maneuverable arms and legs they become extremely efficient robots. More than 8,000 of such computer-created and controlled "man-like" machines are now serving industry in many ways.

Computers are now providing automated research and reporting for state legislatures, as well as the House of Representatives in Washington. The various government bureaus and departments have already purchased more than 8,000 computer systems. Computers are significant and valuable aids for police as they fight crime and develop crime prevention programs and techniques. All space and military activities now seem to be centrally based on computerized planning, communications, logistics, and tactical control. Many civic leaders are justifiably alarmed concerning the threat of invasion of individual privacy and the quite evident depersonalization consequences of too much automation. Labor unions fear loss of jobs as more computers prove their efficiency, speed, and much lower costs in completing thousands of tasks formerly performed by humans. Yet, these same leaders must also recognize that a total new industry has evolved with best estimates suggesting employment in excess of 2,000,000 Americans. Certainly, the computerized society will quicken the pace to the obvious arrival of the three day work week within the next generation.

Many more applications could obviously be discussed and projected. The foregoing, however, should be the challenge to the student and teacher to become quickly aware of computer capability and proficient in the utilization of its power. Modern computer systems demonstrate rapid and steady progress designed to release the minds and hands of mankind for more creative, higher level aspirations. Computers can thus help achieve goals for greater equality, fraternity, love and respect of human beings for each other.

APPENDIX B

BASIC PRINCIPLES OF COMPUTER SYSTEMS

Basic Principles of Computer Systems

As technology progresses and the mountain of resulting data grows higher, more and more people are forced to acknowledge the incalculable value of this strange machine which has the power to store and retrieve information, make decisions, and control inventories, machines, or even the operations of whole plants. The list of applications seems almost endless and yet grows longer day by day. Not only must people acknowledge the value of the computer, but they are now finding themselves compelled to gain a much better understanding of it.

How does the computer solve problems? How does it store and retrieve information? How does it follow instructions, perform checks on itself, and correct its own errors? Fundamentally, it performs these processes much the same as a human being does. The digital computer has five basic functions: (1) input, (2) storage, (3) control, (4) processing, and (5) output. These functions of the computer (Figure 1) may be compared quite closely to the functions of the human brain as it processes information. Let us examine these analogies.

(1) INPUT. This is the process of obtaining and assembling the facts so they can be accessed. The brain receives basic information through its senses. This is accomplished on a computer by feeding in data punched into cards, tapes, etc., or relayed from remote terminals, through a direct manual keyboard, etc.

(2) STORAGE. After input, the pertinent data must be kept readily available for use in working a problem. Like the human brain, the computer also possesses a memory capability for storing information. It is similar to the human memory in that it may be randomly and immediately accessible. Computer storage devices include such items as tapes, discs, drums, cores, and punched cards.

(3) CONTROL. In order to solve a problem, a step-by-step procedure must be followed. These steps must be executed in the proper sequence to arrive at a valid solution, and the control function is the means by which this is accomplished. A human goes through this same process many times each day, although the sequencing of the steps may be carried out subconsciously so that he is unaware of its step-wise occurrence. The control function on a computer is

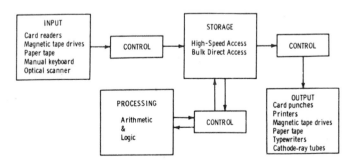

Figure 1. Computer sequence.

215

accomplished through the use of control programs which direct the CPU, or Central Processing Unit, in sequencing the various operations of the computer.

(4) PROCESSING. Processing is the actual calculating, or arithmetic manipulation, performed to arrive at a solution. Once a person is taught how to add numbers together, he performs calculations quite easily. The same is true of a computer, where the CPU is the switching device which performs the processing function, using an "on-off" or binary number code manipulation.

(5) OUTPUT. After the necessary facts are gathered and stored and the necessary calculations are performed, a solution is obtained. The output function is the delivery of this solution in one of many different forms. Human output may take the form of a spoken or written answer, an overt action, or merely a facial expression. The output of a computer can be in many media types. Generally, it will be printed, punched on cards or tape, stored in memory, displayed on a Cathode-Ray Tube (CRT), or communicated to other remote devices, such as Voice Answer Back (VAB).

PROGRAMMING

A computer is completely helpless in solving any kind of problem until it has been given a detailed set of instructions. The computer is incapable of any reasoning to solve a problem. All it can do is subserviently follow directions step-by-step until the job is completed. This applies to any problem in which the computer is used to attempt its solution, whether it's the simple addition of two numbers or the complex equations involved in guiding a missile through space. These detailed instructions are called the computer program.

In order to write a program, the problem to be solved must be carefully defined and understood. Next, it must be analyzed and broken down into its basic components and sequence steps.

The most common method of accomplishing this is to construct a flowchart of the problem. The flowchart is a diagram, using lines and symbols, which depicts each problem-solving step in its logical sequence from start to solution of the problem. And it shows how all the parts of the problem fit together to form the whole. A sample flowchart is shown in Figure 2.

Once the flowchart is completed, it must be converted into short, distinct instructions which are usable by the specific computer used. This, in essence, is the computer program. Each part of the flowchart must be broken down into simple instructions, and one part of the flowchart must require 20 or more individual steps in the computer.

The basic concept behind the computer's decision-making ability is illustrated in the sample flowchart (Figure 2). It is based upon the idea of using a question which can be answered with a simple "yes" or "no." By this method the computer can be directed either to skip or to execute a specific set of instructions. This action of skipping part of the program, or of choosing which of two sets of instructions to follow, is called branching. In branching, the computer decides which of two sets of instructions to follow simply by making a "yes-no" decision.

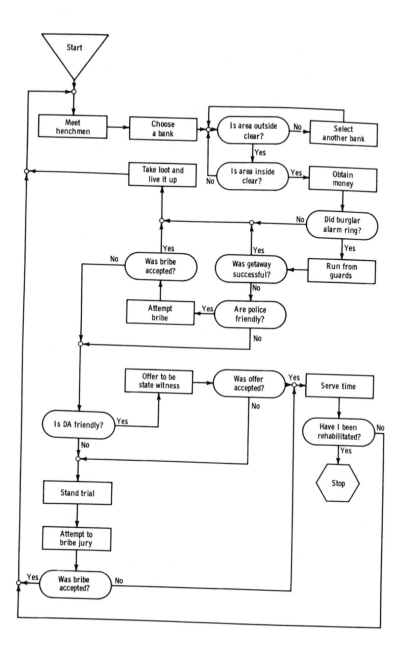

Figure 2. A sample flowchart.

217

The computer is said to have a logical capability because it can make decisions. But, in doing so, it simply follows instructions. It is the person writing the program who decides when a decision is needed, and what factors will determine which choice is taken.

After the problem has been diagrammed in a flowchart and broken down into individual simple operations, the actual program, or instructions which tell the computer how to handle each operation, must be written. But the computer doesn't understand English. So, the instructions must be written in a language, or code, that the computer understands.

SYMBOLIC LANGUAGES

Binary code is the computer's language, and one must understand binary before he can learn how a computer really works. However, thanks to short-cut methods, known as symbolic languages and other modern computer languages, binary coding is completed by the computer itself.

A symbolic language is simply an artificial language which is, in many cases, very similar to common English. The symbolic languages, however, have been formalized to avoid the ambiguities and logical inadequacies of the natural languages such as English.

Through the use of symbolic languages, almost anyone can quickly learn to write programs for a computer. Languages, such as FORTRAN, COBOL, ALGOL, and BASIC, make it easy for businessmen, scientists, and engineers to write programs using words and symbols already familiar to them. The program written in symbolic language is automatically translated into binary code, or "machine language," by computer techniques. The computer has this capability because somebody previously had written a special program, called an "assembler," or a compiler that converts other people's symbolic programs into machine language. Once the symbolic program or source program has been converted to binary, it can move as "flip-flop" electronic impulses into the computer's CPU and memory.

COMPUTER MEMORY

When information has been translated by the computer into binary language, the computer is ready to store it in its memory. There are many kinds of memory devices used in computers, but most of today's high-speed machines use magnetic or semiconductor cores. Magnetic cores are tiny little "doughnuts" the size of pinheads which are made of a special ferromagnetic ceramic material. Each core can be magnetized at any time in either of two directions. One direction stands for a binary 0, the other direction for a binary 1.

By arranging these cores in a column, any binary number can be stored. Each one of the columns is assigned an address and can store either one fact or one instruction. If the computer is told to read the contents of address 105, it will read each of the cores in the column designated 105, moving the bits of information in the form of electronic pulses to whatever location designated, such as to the arithmetic unit.

218

Thousands of these tiny ferrite doughnuts are strung on criss-crossed wires inside a frame. The frames are stacked one on top of the other to make a basic memory unit, and one unit can store over 150,000 bits of information. Other types of memory devices can store billions of bits in very small areas.

COMPUTER INPUT DEVICES

PUNCHED CARDS. Punched cards have many uses, such as college registration cards, electricity bills, and payroll data. They are low-cost and versatile. The standard punched card is called a Hollerith card after Dr. Herman Hollerith who, as head of the U.S. Census Bureau's tabulating section, invented punched cards to help with the 1890 census. The 1880 census had taken seven years to complete and Dr. Hollerith feared that, due to the growing population, the 1890 census might not be finished in time to start the next census in 1900. Because of his work and designs of punched cards and card tabulating machines (not computers), the 1890 census was completed in less than three years.

The familiar and standard punched card has 80 vertical columns and can hold 80 characters of information (letters, numbers, or punctuation). Using the Hollerith punching system, one punch in a single column (number row) can represent any number from 0 to 9. Above the nine number rows are three zone rows: 0, 11 and 12. By making two punches in a single column—one in a zone row and the other in a number row, it is possible to represent any letter of the alphabet or various other symbols. Certain special characters can be represented by three punches in a single column. A period is represented by a 12 punch, a 3 punch and an 8 punch. A dollar sign is represented by an 11 punch, a 3 punch and an 8 punch. The typical card contains punches for the alphabet followed by punches for numbers 0 through 9. The Hollerith symbolic language must be translated (it's done automatically) into binary to be used by a computer.

PUNCHED PAPER TAPE. Punched tape is low-cost and easily stored in rolls. Some kinds of business machines, including typewriters and cash registers, can be equipped to automatically punch paper tape as they are used in normal business. The resulting records can be easily fed into computers for further processing.

MAGNETIC TAPE. Two major advantages make magnetic tape the principal recording medium for computer data. Tape can hold huge quantities of data—a single 10-1/2 inch reel of tape can hold the contents of 250,000 punched cards, and magnetic tape can be read with very great speed. Some computers can read up to 240,000 characters a second from magnetic tape, compared with only 1,200 characters a second from punched cards.

Rolls of magnetic tape serve as one type of a computer's external memory, just as books serve as a person's external memory. Both provide information as needed. In working many problems, computers require both fresh data and stored data. In doing a payroll, for example, the fresh information probably would be fed into the computer from punched cards or paper tape. In addition, the computer would need certain basic facts, such as employee's rate of pay, income tax deductions and so forth. This information would be stored on magnetic tape or a magnetic disc to be fed into the computer's internal memory as needed.

The magnetic tape used in a computer system is similar to the kind used in a home recorder. It is a plastic ribbon with an iron oxide coating that can be magnetized. A tiny area of oxide is magnetized to indicate a 1 in binary code; a blank area in the pattern stands for zero. A pattern of symbols is arranged in vertical columns on the tape, just as holes are punched on a paper tape. One advantage of magnetic tape is that its pattern of symbols almost always is in "pure binary" and can be read directly by the computer. The code punched into paper tape may be punched in binary. But, it may also use a special code of its own, as is the case with some telegraph punching equipment. Like tape used on a home recorder, computer magnetic tape can be easily erased and reused.

MAGNETIC DISCS. An alternative to external memory units which use magnetic tape, or sequential storage, some computer systems use magnetic discs, or random access units. The discs, which look something like big phonograph records, can make information available to the computer substantially faster than tape, because there is usually a read-write head positioned immediately above each track on the disc.

MAGNETIC INK. Documents printed with magnetic ink are "read" in much the same way magnetic tape is read. The additional advantage of magnetic ink characters, which were developed by General Electric, is that they can be read by people, as well as by computers. Today, every bank makes wide use of magnetic ink characters, particularly on checks.

OPTICAL SCANNERS. If all numbers and words, not just those printed in magnetic ink, could be read by computers, it would save much of the bother of translating information into special codes for computer input. The computer industry has now achieved this kind of versatility. An optical scanner or reader (OCR) has a set of electronic patterns in its memory and a photoelectric cell that scans material to be read, converting characters into electronic pulses. The scanner can "read" any character that matches the patterns stored in its memory, including hand-written documents, sketches and diagrams.

HIGH-SPEED PRINTING. This is the most important medium for getting information out of the computer. A high-speed printer whips out information at as much as 6000 lines a single minute. An individual typing 6000 lines at a speed of 60 words a minute on a fast, electric typewriter, would take forty hours. Types of information turned out by these fast printers include accounting forms, checks, and department store bills.

TYPEWRITER. As part of their input-output or terminal units, most computers use electric teletypewriters. Human operators can conveniently enter information directly into the computer. Also, operators can receive short answers to problems worked by the computer through the typewriter terminal.

If there is a programming error, the computer may diagnose it and type out information that will enable the human operator to make a correction immediately.

DISPLAY LIGHTS. Some computers have sections of lights on the control console that can instantly show what information is in the control, memory and the arithmetic sections. The display often is in binary; if a light is on, it is a 1; if it is off, it is a 0.

CATHODE-RAY TUBE. Some types of scientific problems completed by computers have answers that are in curves, patterns, or other lines. While these answers can be printed, it is sometimes more convenient to translate the information into an image that is flashed on a cathode-ray tube, similar to a TV screen. The human operator may learn what he needs for alteration or further development by simply looking at the image. Or, for future reference, he may photograph the pattern. CRTs also have input typewriters, "light pens" and function selector keys for data and information manipulation on-line (direct) to the computer.

BATCH PROCESSING

Before the development of direct communications to a central computer (on-line communications), the majority of computer operations were performed by bulk processing, or the grouping of data into batches. These data were collected in volumes to match or calculate the amount of computer time required for processing. Data was forwarded for processing in the form of original documents or copies, or punched into cards or paper tape. Once at the processing center, additional handling was necessary to convert source data into cards or tape, as well as to add supplementary data to the pre-punched cards. Further off-line sorting was also necessary to arrange the file data in the required order for processing. The cut-off dates for processing were controlled by setting them on a regular basis, such as weekly or monthly.

The cumulative process associated with the establishment of each batch, in conjunction with the fixed cut-off, resulted in peak load requirements. This often resulted in around-the-clock operations to obtain the necessary results and special reports. These peak processing periods frequently lead to the installation of oversized systems to absorb the peak volume at costs far in excess of the overall productivity realized.

As the utilization of electronic data processing was expanded for multi-plant or multi-office operations, data collection problems grew more complex. Attempts to deal with this problem led to the multi-system approach, where systems of different sizes and capabilities were located in the various departments, divisions, and offices. Output data from these systems were then sent to the main processing center for organization-wide processing and analysis. This method was worked in some instances, but serious data collection problems still persisted.

By now it was obvious that the physical collection and transfer of data by mail or similar means slowed down the computer operations considerably. The logical solution seemed to be the use of public telephone and telegraph facilities. The combination of semi-automatic electrical data communication with the multi-system approach yielded a partial solution to the problem of data collection and processing. However, the actual processing of data continued to be performed on a batch basis, which meant that transactions were transmitted only periodically. This resulted in historic reports for management rather than current ones. The solution lay in the ability to operate upon transactions immediately.

To more fully understand the problem created by batch processing, assume that a remotely located sales office receives an order from a customer. As the initial step, the clerk consults the inventory listings. If the listings indicate that the required items are available, the order is taken, and the customer is informed when delivery will be made. This arrangement, however, contains one important flaw. The inventory listings used by the sales office may not reflect the current inventory status at the time the order is placed. This situation results from the fact that the inventory listings are updated on a periodic basis and are, therefore, correct only on the date they are processed. Between updatings, orders may be placed for items that are not actually available. These items later have to be back-ordered and the promised delivery date cannot be met.

PROGRESS TO ON-LINE, REAL-TIME (OLRT)

To close this time gap between actual transactions and master file updating, UNIVAC and other manufacturers pioneered the concept of real-time processing. The real-time system combines data processing with communications. This unique method of operation involves direct communication of transaction data between remote office locations and the central computer, thus allowing the data to be processed almost simultaneously with transmission.

In order to gain a better appreciation of the capabilities and implications of a real-time system, let us refer to the previously mentioned sales application. The remote sales office would be equipped with an inquiry-response device capable of communicating directly with the computer itself. To place an order, the necessary information is entered into the system through the input device. Since the device has a direct connection with the computer, complete information concerning the inventory status of the items ordered is confirmed in seconds. If the items are available, the invoice is printed automatically, along with associated shipping information, at the sales office. This indicates to the salesman that the order has been filled as requested. If any particular item of the order depleted the inventory to the reorder point, the computer automatically sends a message to the reorder source, warehouse, or factory directly connected to the computer, requesting an updating inventory. All of these operations are executed in a matter of seconds.

The phenomenal success of real-time systems can be directly attributed to the total systems concept. This concept is found not only in the equipment, but in the software and operating programs as well. The success of OLRT is a result of the skill with which these elements have been combined into a total system.

Real-time systems place remote inquiry-response devices in offices, plants, laboratories, and warehouses—all connected through communications lines or microwave relays to the central computer. These units allow simple and instant input of data, and answers can be returned almost immediately. Thus, hundreds of people have access to live storage by being on-line to a large, sophisticated computer for random access "real-time" information.

REAL-TIME APPLICATIONS

Since real-time generally pertains to a technique of processing data so fast that there is virtually no passage of time between inquiry and result, each of many varying inquiries may be communicated to the system separately and the results received immediately. Batch processing could be improved by immediate collection of data at the source, but processing would still be deferred until batches have been accumulated. Real-time is a mode of operation in which data, necessary to the control and/or execution of a transaction, can be processed in time for that specific transaction to be affected by the results of the processing. Thus, time is of the essence . . . great speed, concurrency, simultaneity.

Real-time is basically the refinement of integrating data processing with communications. It eliminates the slow information-gathering discussed above which resulted in dated reporting techniques and lax communications. It insures that data within the system are as current as the decisions which they must support. Answers are provided when needed; data is delivered instantly; incoming information is edited, updated, and made available on demand. Imminent problems are automatically detected by "exception principle" reporting, and management is notified in time for corrective action. The split-second input-reply principle was pioneered for military real-time systems which were employed to guide and track missiles in flight. And computer manufacturers soon realized that many types of businesses, laboratories, and colleges also needed constant control, updating, and reporting.

Airline real-time systems must be capable of simultaneously receiving inputs from agents, sending output messages to the remote terminals, receiving and sending urgent teletype messages and initiating requests. This eliminates underbooking and overbooking in reservations, lost profits, and disgruntled customers.

Real-time computing is vital for certain types of production automation. In industrial process-control applications many rapidly changing variables must be monitored, analyzed, and controlled continuously to make corrective actions and instigate exception report programming for continuous operation and optimum results.

Real-time processing for decision-making based on requirements for immediate information retrieval are examples of complex, rapidly changing systems. Some cases might be "flash" credit-approval requests, or decisions on orders based on exact current inventory and its location. Other examples of necessity for fast analysis of completely current information are banks, libraries, hospitals, automobile-traffic control, police-information networks, etc.

Even in medium-sized businesses, real-time permits rapid fill-ins and reorders or warnings to buyers and section managers about imminent stock shortages. Information is immediate concerning stock location, quantities on hand at remote warehouses, instant price changes, and delivery priorities. This instant knowledge provides for improved service, more satisfied customers, and lower operating costs through more efficient use of time, space, and personnel.

For manufacturers, the quantity of raw materials available in stock or from teletype-tied suppliers, or the status of finished or semi-finished products might be all-important to deliveries and profits. Costly management decisions for multiplant manufacturers would no longer be affected by delayed action or guesswork since reserve and forward stocks are always known exactly, and delivery schedules can be adjusted to fit actual conditions in the plants, warehouses, or schedules—with no loss in time, efficiency, or customer satisfaction.

Thus, the speed and sophistication of real-time hardware and software enables the military, business, industry, scientific research, etc., to make rapid responses to unanticipated fluctuations in process variables far better than is possible by simple human supervision. The real-time computer can instantly correlate the behavior of numerous production factors. It can integrate the relationships among similar, diverse, or remote data for better quality control, increased safety, and lowered costs for greater efficiency and competence of managers of all types. The combination of real-time and time-sharing provides for the most optimum use of real-time systems. From the point of real-time, each terminal in the multiconsole system may be using different programs and may actually share the central processor sequentially. Inquiries, however, are measured in seconds, while the CPU computes hundreds of thousands of times faster, i.e., in microseconds and nanoseconds (millionths and billionths of seconds). Thus, the high speed of the machine and the slowness of human reactions give each user the equivalent of an entire computer at his immediate command. Even medium-sized time-sharing systems have the capability of computing in microseconds and transmitting data back (to a bank teller, for example) at rates of thousands of numbers or characters per second. The answers achieved by the computer must be buffered (temporarily held) because the communications are too slow relative to computer processing speeds. Yet, the human would have great difficulty accepting information as fast as communications devices can furnish it despite their sluggishness compared to the CPU computing speeds.

The reader is warned, however, that the apparent magic of real-time is not without difficulties in at least three primary areas: (1) the regimentation, organization, and maintenance of records and data; (2) the background systems necessary to properly develop and use the information which must be made available in proper form, format, and content; and (3) the software or programming necessary for storage and retrieval including addressing, segmenting, and memory protection. The observer who watches the valuable and timely information appear on the video display or on the sheets of the teletypewriter is usually unaware of its complexity.

Of basic importance at the outset is the segmenting of information between noncritical general activity, which is to be more economically batch processed, and the segregated activity, which pertains to information which is more dynamic and of immediate need to operate the business on an hour-to-hour basis. Most often the general activity (batch or background) systems are employed at night or in between the time-shared real-time processing.

Generally the systems use controlling programs called monitors, executives, operating systems (OS), allocators, etc., as supervisory communicating controllers such that each inquiry request from remote stations is assigned priority as originally designed and/or subsequently altered as business conditions and requirements dictate.

APPENDIX C

SUMMARY OF MODERN COMPUTER LANGUAGES

SUMMARY OF MODERN COMPUTER LANGUAGES

Introduction

Two basic functions must be performed by a computer program: data "handling" and data "processing." The function of processing includes calculating, changing recorded entries, and creating information for new file records or report items. The function of handling—the lion's share of the programming effort—includes all the time-consuming detail of editing and selecting pertinent information, sorting records, arranging information in files, positioning information for reports, providing for beginning and ending procedures, providing continuity between processing operations, etc. The details of "handling" normally comprise more than 75% of business programming tasks. Usually manufacturers offer software packages or compilers which aid immeasurably in reducing this "handling" chore. They are especially important when changes are necessary in programs for some modifications which would require hundreds or even thousands of coded instructions—a task perhaps too time-consuming to be feasible. Operating on newer more economical equipment, the necessary modifications of programs usually require complete rewriting of most of the programs in the libraries. Using "emulators" or special software packages prevent these costly reprogramming tasks—or keep them down to economic workability (e.g., GE's GECOM, Honeywell's FACT, etc.). Documentation is vital to insure understandability among experts (specialists) of equal capability. If a programmer leaves or is reassigned, his programs cannot be understood without adequate documentation.

The detailed sequence of instructions (algorithm) used in solving a problem requires strict attention to the individuality of each instruction to attain the correct answer. Nonmathematical problems, with little or no algebra, are now quite often expressed as algorithms such as commercial and scheduling (PERT) problems in order to prepare them for computer input. Algorithms are the basis for procedure-oriented languages or are at least segments of these programs to be examined element by element. ALGOL and COBOL are examples of algorithmic languages—ALGOL for mathematical problems, COBOL for English-language commercial problems. These programs written in these and other compiler languages (FORTRAN, QUIKTRAN, PL/1, MAD, JOVIAL, ETC.) may contain hundreds of instructions, and these hundreds actually represent thousands or hundreds of thousands, even millions, of steps that will be executed by the computer in carrying out the instructions.

Types of Languages—Criteria for Selection

Only a few of the many languages available are discussed in this appendix. The general classes are as follows: machine or binary languages; symbolic assembly or mnemonic languages; algebraic compiler languages (as FORTRAN, ALGOL, etc.); report program generator languages; business-oriented compiler languages (as COBOL); or communications languages as QUIKTRAN, BASIC. There are also hundreds of specialized languages as "Prudential" (Insurance Co.) COBOL. These types are subsets designed for unique applications and for limited objectives. Emphasis is put on those characteristics which are important to the individual user. Many users thus have become increasingly interested in developing their own support software which can be more easily and quickly learned by their employees than the software furnished by suppliers. They can also be uniquely designed to use less memory and consume less computer time. Software companies are more than anxious to provide such services.

However, the determination of which language to use is sometimes quite a difficult decision. Criteria can include: knowledge of staff; number and type of jobs expected in the future; ease and speed of operating; costs as related to speed of operation and compilation; availability of other software packages; debugging aids; meshing of equipment on hand or contemplated purchase of new units. Other aspects of planning should include: decisions as to the rules and methods (and enforcement) for use of special symbols, input/output routines, registers, and standard routines. To avoid confusion, special programming tricks are usually not allowed. Complete documentation by a programmer is considered by most data processing managers as the most important elements of his work.

Comparisons of programming languages cannot be justified nor accurate because there are no standards for languages, compilers, operating systems or user's requirements. For example, various non-programmer scientific users prefer algebraic types as ALGOL, JOVIAL, FORTRAN, etc. Others prefer subsets of specific definition and operation. The design of the program usually will aid in determining the most efficient or easiest language to use.

Fundamental Algorithmic and Procedural Languages

FORTRAN. FORTRAN was developed by IBM as an aid to programming scientific problems and processes. The name was derived from FORmula TRANslator and is widely accepted as a convenient and practical language. FORTRAN IV has superseded FORTRAN II and contains many more powerful features which include greater versatility in input-output statements and specific functions. It is fundamentally a language and a processor (compiler) designed to be written in a mathematics-type language format. It is machine independent and procedure oriented. Because FORTRAN is based on mathematical concepts, instructions must explicitly and exactly follow the rules of grammar, symbols, and syntax. FORTRAN instructions relate to five function areas: input-output, arithmetic, control, looping (recursive or repeated execution of program steps or segments), and specifications. After a problem has been defined, analyzed, and flowcharted, it is programmed, frequently on special FORTRAN 72-column code paper, and then tested and debugged on the computer. On-line debugging can be accomplished using a time-sharing mode directly at the terminal.

FORTRAN is designed to permit expressions, algebraic operations (including three levels of subscripts, exponents, and Boolean operations), hierarchies, subroutines, and extensive input-output capability. All FORTRAN-type languages provide for commands that evaluate expressions and substitute results representing current values of variables. In most FORTRAN languages variable names begin with: I, J, K, L, M, or N for integer values, while all other variables are considered floating point or real variables and may take on any value—specifically, fractional values.

One basic logical decision command concerns the IF statement which causes expressions to be evaluated and control to be transferred to one of three statements, the branching depending upon the result of a calculation being either less than, equal to, or greater than zero. The more extensive FORTRAN compilers permit the use of overlay techniques called "chaining" for greater operation efficiency. Contrasted to several other languages, since every program in a job does not necessarily communicate with every other program, complete jobs need not reside in the same memory at the same time. Jobs may be divided into independent segments which may occupy various memory segments at different times.

COBOL. COBOL was developed by the Conference Of DAta SYstems Languages (CODASYL) in 1959. COBOL has been expanded, revised, and improved many times since then. COBOL 65, for example, has added many new streamlined capabilities and reduced many burdensome attributes of the former COBOL system. Since the word COBOL is an acronym for COmmon Business Oriented Language, the COBOL compiler is a processor specifically designed in sentences and structure for commercial use and application. The object program, after being compiled, can run on digital computers because it has been reduced to binary instructions and routines. The translation procedure (compiling) is accomplished by and within the computer itself. The compiler program (processor) reads, analyzes, and translates the source program which is then defined as the object program. The object program then processes data and instructions, the results of which are transferred to some external medium as:

cards, tapes, disks, drums, or Cathode-Ray Tube (CRT) terminals.

The COBOL language has specific key words, symbols and rules for its use. Generally, each key word and symbol specifies a definite set of machine operations, i.e., many series of prefabricated portions of object programs readily available. The COBOL language program brings together these groups of machine instructions. The rules for writing COBOL are considerably simpler than those for writing machine code or machine language. The programmer can use English words and conventional arithmetic symbols to complete the instructions required for his particular desired result.

COBOL programs are precise, distinct, and readily understood by nontechnical people. They can be run on practically all types of computers with simplified testing procedures. COBOL documentation is quite standardized, complete, and easily understood by programmers and many business managers.

The programmer generally requires: the length of each kind of data; the location of the decimal point; name or names of data requiring identification; the organization of each type of data with respect to other data (groupings and relationship among groups); and the value of constants, specifically the actual value of names, numbers, special characters, etc. to be stored in the computer for future processing. Each type of data or information must be described in accordance with clearly defined rules and constraints. The Data Division is the part of the program reserved for this purpose and certain portions of it are related to specific machine characteristics.

COBOL has four structural divisions. The Identification Division identifies the program and states the various ways computers may accept and handle alphabetical information. The Environment Division states which equipment is to be used. The Data Division relegates the formats of input-output data by defining the manner in which input-output information appears. The Procedure Division defines the actual operations to be performed. COBOL also contains many important file organization features and can deal conveniently with variable data lengths. The strong points of COBOL are variability of input-output procedures and development of report generators.

PROGRAMMING LANGUAGE/1 (PL/1). PL/1 is a multipurpose programming language developed by IBM for the Models 360 and 370 Systems. The language is designed to be suitable for solving business and scientific problems and contains many of the advantages of both COBOL and FORTRAN. The language statements are as simple and concise as FORTRAN statements, and the flexibility in manipulation of input-output records or files is similar to to the advantages of COBOL.

All PL/1 statements are separated only by semicolons. Large sets of reserved words are available and comments can be of any length and inserted at practically any point in the program. Prior to using the program, various declarations can be made concerning arithmetic, strings, number characteristics, and quantities of digits and characters. Character strings can be joined to form longer strings by the use of a special linking operator. Data can be handled during input-output operations either as records, separate data, or items, and can be interrupted by higher priority or special conditions. Also, flexible procedures are available which identify items in arrays, for subscripting and sequencing. PL/1 is, therefore, very convenient for time-sharing and real-time operations. The primary advantage of PL/1 is that statements may be written as blocks and brought into storage only as needed, thus providing economic utilization of storage capacity. The overall effect of the versatility of PL/1 is that beginning programmers can turn out productive work quite quickly. The use of "labels" represents procedures in which the language adapts to various levels of detail and readability.

ALGOL. ALGOL stands for ALGOrithmic Language. It resulted from international cooperation to obtain a standardized algorithmic language, and IAL, International Algebraic Language, is the forerunner of ALGOL. ALGOL was devised in 1958 and revised in 1960. It is a strong language, used more widely in Europe than in the United States and is most often used in the programming of scientific problems or as a reference and publication language. It is also used as a guide for the development of new artificial languages or mathematical structures. It has become internationally accepted for designing mathematical, engineering and scientific problems. Briefly, ALGOL provides (1) precise in instructional statements, (2) a problem-solving procedure, (3) a translator or compiler. In many ways it is very similar to FORTRAN and COBOL. It has rules of grammar, syntax, format, and special characteristics. None of the three languages can be executed directly without first being compiled (processed, translated) into machine language.

After the formulation of the problem, it has to be structured for solution. The allocation of storage and the selection for the incorporation of the various library, housekeeping, or special mathematical routines must be made. The last step is the machine coding, and the run.

The ALGOL program closely resembles the detailed problem definition required for machine language, but the language and the problem definition format have been standardized. Not only does the computer itself produce the machine language program and the processing, but the program definition must be complete, unambiguous and expressed in an acceptable form with adherence to the rules and terminology.

The ALGOL language incorporates (1) arithmetical expressions, (2) Boolean expressions, (3) standard functions, (4) operational statements, (5) blocks and declarations (switch and array), (6) coding sections (procedure headings) and (7) loops. Almost all ALGOL manuals of various computer manufacturers state their specific lists of standard functions, limitations, and restrictions as well as reserved words. ALGOL 60 is currently most popular, and a time-sharing version called "Dartmouth ALGOL" is available.

JOVIAL. JOVIAL is an acronym for Jules Own Version of the International Algorithmic Language developed by Jules Schwartz of the Systems Development Corporation, Santa Monica, California. It is mostly used in programmed command and control procedures. The JOVIAL language is translated (compiled) by a program called a compiler. The compiler interprets, analyzes, and translates the program statements and the inputs and outputs from the source program to an object program on which the particular computer can operate. The major deviation from ALGOL is that jovial supplies the power the control data on the "byte" and even the "bit" level when desired. JOVIAL has extensive capabilities for developing software applications, utility and compiling-type programs. JOVIAL was apparently created quite specifically for government agency applications. It is used in real-time programs, commercial time-sharing applications and software design for other computers.

JOVIAL has extensive command and retrieve language rules but the basic structure of the program is relatively simple. The JOVIAL program fundamentally consists of procedure definitions and language statements. There are language statements which define and initialize data while others manipulate and test data.

CAL. CAL is an acronym for Conversational Algebraic Language. CAL, like BASIC, JOSS, QUIKTRAN, etc., is a time-sharing, real-time language for use by many remote simultaneous terminals. The CAL language is designed for higher-level time-sharing purposes and was developed at the University of California, Berkeley. It has been adopted quite widely throughout the United States for medium-sized time-sharing systems.

CAL programs consist of a series of steps; the programs can be saved or destroyed, errors are identified and error messages provide examples to illustrate the correct format required. CAL also provides for all types of arithmetic operations, editing capabilities, manipulation of data files, conditional expressions, etc. Numbers are expressed as integers or scientific notation or floating-point form and variables can be subscripted on an unlimited number of levels. CAL also allows statements to be deleted or added, thus making debugging a relatively simple task at the console.

Programming in CAL requires each step to have a statement number and the beginning statement to be indicated. CAL can handle programs of complexity as regards to arithmetic, but programmers are advised to use FORTRAN or ALGOL for major and large scientific programs.

JOSS. JOSS is an acronym for Jonniac Open Shop System. The Rand Corporation developed it for quick calculations too complex for calculators. It can serve more than 100 consoles simultaneously and can handle concurrent use by hundreds of people, each accessing the computer through his own console typewriter. Although many people seem to be using the computer simultaneously, the computer actually handles each user in sequence. It solves each problem or basic part of each problem so quickly that it "only appears" to the user that he alone has full use and control of the computer. Thus JOSS is a real-time language and is productive for solving many types of immediate calculations and problems. JOSS was designed for small and medium sized programs. It is not considered a general-purpose language in interactive environments. Even though it is similar to other languages, it has distinct and powerful features usually not found elsewhere. Arithmetic in JOSS is performed on numbers inputted in scientific notation using integer magnitudes and decimal exponents.

Time-Sharing Languages

When terminals function as computer consoles the user is concerned with the various subsets of FORTRAN (or other languages) which can be QUIKTRAN, CAL, BASIC, JOSS, etc. Users may solve problems immediately or may compose partial or complete programs. Diagnostic and debugging information are expressed entirely in the source language. Interpretive execution permits retention of all information contained in the user's original source statements. The combination of interpretive execution and multiprogramming makes the conversational mode a real-time, man-machine communication system highly efficient and feasible. Programs are constructed, tested and debugged statement by statement and on-line because of easy, direct, and sustained access to the computer. Large programs can be segmented; the user is unaware of other time-sharers; human errors are reduced due to immediacy of diagnostics and thought-continuity; exploratory, experimental and simulation efforts are enhanced, permitting users to exercise rapid judgment and evaluation in the formulation and testing of programs.

QUIKTRAN. QUIKTRAN is a language, compiler, and a data processing system. Checks or execution of each statement according to instructions from the sending location are done by the compiler. QUIKTRAN is a FORTRAN-like time-sharing language which handles lengthy jobs that must be processed in their entirety rather than statement by statement, by placing them temporarily in disk storage until the computer is free to do them. QUIKTRAN continuously monitors all incoming time-shared programming statements from each line to the computer. The communication system which has a typewriter keyboard is used as the terminal device at the user's location, and each terminal, together with its various peripheral equipment, is linked by telephone lines to a communications control system at the computer center or main computer.

QUIKTRAN uses FORTRAN-like language and includes built-in functions augmented by powerful and versatile operating statements permitting the user to operate upon and maintain complete control over his program. For easy parameter insertion and changes special codes are used, such as assigning new values to variables. The language has the facility of starting execution at any point and provides for easy insertion, deletion, or replacement of program statements. Other capabilities are cross-reference listing of program statement names and labels, detection of incomplete executions, and selective output. More than thirty control statements are used for programming.

QUIKTRAN subsystems—The computer system is divided into subsystems as follows: The scheduler controls operations maintaining consistent response times at all terminals; the translator is designed to transform the source language into an efficient equivalent internal form; the interpreter is designed to perform the execution; the process control program coordinates the translator and interpreter activities; the input/output control system performs all I/O functions; the exchange program controls the communications control system. A disk storage is available for user-library storage; a drum storage acts as a temporary working storage for the user's programs, and a magnetic-tape unit is used for logging transactions and for maintaining normal computer capabilities.

BASIC. BASIC is an acronym for Beginners Algebraic Symbol Interpreter Compiler. It was originally developed by Professors J. G. Kemeny and T. E. Kurtz at Dartmouth College under a grant by the National Science Foundation. BASIC is a language and a compiler that was originally designed for the GE-234 computer and the GE Datanet 30, a stored program data communications processor. It is very similar to CAL. Each line of BASIC begins with a line number which identifies it and specifies the order in which the statements are performed. The computer sorts out the program before running it and, therefore, statements need not be input in any specific order. It is not as powerful or versatile as ALGOL or FORTRAN but is considered more than adequate for most of the commercial and business problems that can be processed in a time-sharing mode.

Various conventions at specific computer centers or time-sharing installations allow the initial command to be either "HELLO" or "HOW DO YOU DO." BASIC permits conversational statements, free-style input (72 characters per line), segmenting of complex statements, accuracy of six significant digits, easy and safe program modification, editing functions allowing combinations of two or more programs into one, and it permits selection from a library of stored program or functions, such as procedures for solving simultaneous equations, curve fitting and statistical analysis. BASIC responds rapidly enough for debugging at the keyboard. In one pass it compiles computer instructions in fractions of seconds.

List-Processing Languages

These languages are designed for digital computers for the convenience and manipulation of data, especially non-numerical data whose length and structure change considerably during the calculation of a problem solution. They are referred to as symbol manipulation and non-numerical data processing languages. IPL (Information Process Language) was developed in 1957 by Newell, Shaw, and Simon. Others are LISP, SLIP, COMIT, FORMAC, FLPL and DYSTAL. Most list-processing languages are used as research tools rather than production-line programs. The basic research areas which have gained from the use of list processing are (a) pattern recognition, (b) algebraic manipulation, (c) simulation of human problem solving, (d) information retrieval, (e) machine translation of numerical languages. List-processing routines are oriented more toward techniques of programming rather than toward particular applications, except perhaps in the areas of information retrieval, algebraic manipulation, and language translation.

Some characteristics of lists are (a) variable length, subject principally to gross machine limitations, (b) different types of items may appear on lists including numbers, alphanumeric symbols and sublists, (c) items can be added at the beginning, end or middle, (d) any number of distinct lists can be created, (e) reference ability of lists by the program. The process used when elements of lists may themselves be lists is recursion. There are many levels of subsidiary lists, or sublists. Recursion is ordinarily mechanized through the use of a push-down stack, in which the temporary storage contents required by a subroutine are stored as the subroutine is entered. As the execution of the subroutine is completed, the temporary storage is restored from the stack and the space that is occupied is again made available. The ability to vary storage allocation during run time is called dynamic storage allocation. Recursion and dynamic storage allocation are useful program requirements and both are requirements of list-processing languages.

237

LISP. LISP stands for LISt Processing. It is radically different from traditional gramming. The instructions of an IPL-V routine pertain to: (1) the name, (2) the sequence of characters formed according to distinct rules, or internally as a set of computer words interlinked in a specific way. Atomic symbols may be either numeric or non-numeric, and the external representation of a non-numeric atomic symbol is a string of letters and digits starting with a letter, such as AB5Y, or a Greek letter. LISP also allows the use of special characters such as asterisks, minus signs, etc. Numeric atoms or atomic symbols can be decimal, octal or floating-point numbers.

IPL-V. IPL-V was developed by Newell, Simon and Shaw. The language is more machine-oriented than LISP and a program in IPL-V consists of sequences of instructions quite like the ordinary machine instructions. Generally, however, the programmer has more control over the calculations. Some programmers prefer IPL-V over LISP due to the similarity of IPL-V to normal machine programming. The instructions of an IPL routine pertain to: (1) the name, (2) the symbol, (3) the prefixes and (4) the length. The name part labels the entire routine and specific label points for transfer of control internally. The IPL-V data are in the form of a symbol list; each symbol can itself stand for a list. The prefixes are 3-bit numbers indicating the meaning of the symbol part, as well as the levels of indirect addressing. Thus, an instruction can be used in storing an input, recovering an output, performing an additional transfer, or calling a routine. The specific choice depends upon the first prefix. Routines may be either standard IPL-V processes or ones which the programmer himself defines. IPL-V differs from LISP because the programmer must communicate his arguments to routine explicitly. The communication cell is the procedure used and is actually a special-purpose push-down stack. Various prefixes cause a data unit to be either removed from or replaced into the communication cell. The erasure method is used in IPL-V to maintain storage for lists.

SLIP. SLIP is an extension to FORTRAN and not really a stand-alone system. SLIP increases the freedom for manipulating lists and also increases the amount of storage required for them. SLIP is a form of a set of special list processing FORTRAN functions. These functions are used to accomplish the operations a programmer normally does in list processing: (1) the creation and erasure of lists, (2) traversal of lists, (3) specific recursive communication of arguments, (4) translation of list structures between internal and external representations. SLIP programs are FORTRAN programs which use SLIP functions. SLIP programs resemble LISP programs because they consist of nestings of function calls. FORTRAN IF statements are used instead of conditional expressions and a special "VISIT" function aids automatic recursion and must be called explicitly by the programmer.

Two words, rather than one, are necessary for each element of a list; the first contains a two-address field called the right and left lengths (the left length points to the previous word on the list and the right length to the following word). This makes it easy to traverse a list backward and forward, a procedure different from LISP and IPL-V. The second word holds the list element itself. Each list has a header with pointers to both the beginning and end of a list; the list name is a pointer with its header. Readers are available to make the traversal of lists quick and easy. The mathematics of SLIP is the same as that of FORTRAN, though more efficient. In dealing with problems which involve large amount of numerical calculations and list processing, SLIP has a major advantage. BALGOL is the SLIP version of ALGOL.

COMIT. COMIT is basically used in studies of mechanical translation of human language. It is oriented and designed for lists in which the list elements are not lists themselves but are closer to strings. The manipulation of strings in COMIT is quite easy but somewhat awkward for both trees and recursion. COMIT programs operate by manipulation of a data depository called "work space." The work space holds a string composed of a sequence of constituents; the string could be a sentence and the constituents would represent words of the sentence, or even individual characters including spaces and punctuation marks. String constituents might also be subscripts and subscript values attached to them. COMIT provides sequences of shelves for temporary storage which may be replaced in their entirety by new data. Adding of new data can be done at the head of the shelf while preserving the rest in a manner similar to the LISP function append. A COMIT program is formed by sequence of rules. Each rule specifies a string transformation and has a right half and a left half. From left to right the work space is searched until a sequence of constituents matching the last half is found. Such a sequence is then replaced by the sequence of constituents corresponding to the right half. In the execution of a rule, no sequence of constituents in the work space may match the left half. Rules can be used to move data and the work space and to modify and test subscripts and their values.

SNOBOL. SNOBOL is an acronym for StriNg-Oriented symBOLic language. It was developed by D. J. Farber, R. E. Griswold, and I. P. Polonsky at the Bell Telephone Laboratories. In program compilation and generation of symbolic equations it has significant applications. It provides complete facilities for the manipulation of strings of characters. SNOBOL is especially applicable for programs dealing with text editing, linguistics, compiling, and symbolic manipulation of algebraic expressions. SNOBOL statements consist of a rule which operates on symbolically-named strings. The fundamental operations are: string manipulation, pattern matching, and replacement. There are procedures for integer arithmetic, indirect referencing, and input-output. The SNOBOL basic concepts begin with strings and string names and may be numbers or characters, while the strings may be any symbol.

FLPL and **DYSTAL**. Other list-processing languages include FLPL, an acronym for FORTRAN List Processing Language. It was developed for use in a program for proving theorems in geometry. It is much like LISP but has no provision for recursion. Another FORTRAN-based system is DYSTAL, which stands for DYnamic STorage ALlocation. Constructive storage locations are used to keep the elements of a list when using DYSTAL so they can be integer-indexed. Programmers can then find the "nth" item of a list by simple table lookup. Programmers are freed from some of the constraints of FORTRAN by DYSTAL but it lacks the extensive flexibility in construction of a list which other list-processing languages contain. The integer-indexing ability, however, is unique.

Simulation and Simulation Languages

Simulation is defined as follows: (1) The representation of physical systems and phenomena by computers, models or other equipment; e.g., an imitative type of data processing in which an automatic computer is used as a model of some entity. When information enters the computer to represent the factors of process, the computer produces information that represents the results of the process, and the processing done by the computer represents the process itself. (2) In computer programming, a model of the technique of setting up a routine for one computer to make it operative as nearly as possible like some other computer.

A model is a system representation in which the processes or transactions bear a close resemblance or relationship to those of the specific system being simulated or studied. Therefore, models that are used in simulation are seldom highly abstract or strictly mathematical. Manipulation of a simulation system concerns the acceptance of inputs and the generation of outputs similar or analogous to those of the system represented.

In a simulation system the activity is dependent on the time framework and can be stable or unstable. It can be studied as a static or steady-in-state system or as regards the transient behavior of a dynamic system. The components are processes of a physical entity, such as hardware, which are precisely defined in physical simulation. The process which includes physiological or sociological

240

behavior of individuals or groups is called behavioral simulation. Operational simulation incorporates processes which include human beings, such as when they are involved in automobile traffic, highway analyses, etc.

There are several specific languages well suited for simulation applications and to make simulation systems easier to manipulate, more accurate in results, and more universal in acceptance. The analog computer is used for simulation of continuous systems, but the special languages relate to general simulation which provides a variety of services and eases the job of translating a conceptual model of a system to develop useful statistical outputs. These languages contain status descriptors, which define the essential elements of a system or model. They also have procedures which modify models for controlling the dynamic performance or observations of model behavior. Most simulation languages develop data structures, transformations, sequencing of transformations, and output routines. Extensive error checking is available for preventing misuse of the language or in hand coding or key punching mistakes. Routines for debugging models and locating logical errors are most useful.

SIMSCRIPT. SIMSCRIPT, a general-purpose digital simulation system is based on the idea that the system can be described in terms of "entities," which are the specific objects or things of which a system is composed, "attributes," which are those properties associated with the entities, and "sets," which are which are groups of entities. The major prerequisites in the development of a simulation model are a complete list of explicit entities, their attributes, and the possible set memberships. The state of a system once described is changed by the occurrence of an event which is a user-defined subroutine written with either SIMSCRIPT or FORTRAN statements. Entities can be created or destroyed; set memberships of individual entities can be altered, and numeral values of attirbutes can be changed. Because entities and attributes must be individually located, much of the SIMSCRIPT language is devoted to providing convenient and flexible methods for performing storage and retrieval functions. Input to the SIMSCRIPT translator usually is developed on sets of cards containing definition, initialization, and subprograms.

General-Purpose System Simulator (GPSS)

GPSS has three basic components: blocks, transactions and equipment. By using the terms in block diagrams it develops simulation models. Block diagrams are graphic devices which delineate the logical and physical flow of transactions and moved from one block to another. There are eight parameters simulation block diagram are very specific from which models are built.

Punched cards or other entry program segments define the properties of each block in the model. Within the model, temporary GPSS elements are formed into transactions and moved from one block to another. There are eight parameters which are associated with each transaction and also eight possible priority levels (all Priority 3 transactions are serviced before Priority 2, etc.). As transactions enter blocks, various subroutines associated with those particular block types are interpretively executed causing a modification of one or more status descriptors.

Equipment elements are provided in GPSS with a fixed number of each of three types: storages, facilities, and logic switches. Equipment or logical concepts are represented by them. Transactions are processed by the equipment on a first-come, first-served basis within each priority class. There are ten types of elements in GPSS, each referenced by one or more of the block types. Blocks and transactions are what make up block elements. Equipment elements include facilities, storage and logic switches. Statistical elements are queues and distribution tables. Reference elements are savexes—for data storage. Arithmetic variables and functions are computational elements. A subset of fifteen attributes are associated with these types and are called standard system variables. Their values can be addressed by name and index number in a simulation model.

A GPSS model is made up of a set of definition cards and each card defines a block, function, table, arithmetic variable, or storage capacity. The GPSS program operates upon the model definition in essentially an interpretive fashion, providing considerable flexibility for handling multiple runs on the same or similar models.

DYNAMO. DYNAMO is used for continuous closed-loop information feed-back systems. Linearity or stability is not required in the system concerned. Therefore, a very broad class of systems can be developed or represented by the DYNAMO language. The definition of a continuous system is one in which all basic variables are continuous and possess a first derivative with respect to time; i.e., the state of the system is given by the levels of continuous variables at any point in time without the conception of any discrete changes to this state. It is also adequate for dealing with more discrete phenomena pertaining to aggregate levels of behavior; i.e., an aggregate inventory level in a manufacturing environment may be considered a continuous variable even though it has a descrete delayed composition. For example, at any instant in time the level of a variable is a distinct single numeric value.

An information feed-back system is defined as one in which information relating to the state of the system at a given time is what determines the future state of the system. Variables are introduced for the purpose of dealing specifically with the flow of information. Time delays are of major importance because they establish the dynamic performance of such systems and also determine the lag between the time in which a change in one variable occurs and the time at which this change is reflected in some other variable; i.e., an increase in one level of inventory may lead to a reduction in the level of orders for inventory.

A closed-loop system is defined as one in which successive states of the system depend upon variables outside the system. The internal structure of the system and the manner in which the basic variables interact is of primary interest. It is not necessary that the system be completely closed. A limited set of external inputs can be provided, although these are intended to serve only as independent stimuli to the systems being manipulated and analyzed.

Also available are provisions and procedures for modifying the state and controlling the dynamic performance of DYNAMO models. DYNAMO simulation model output is generated in the form of time series for any desired variables; i.e., level, rate, or output. The output variable is determined by the level or the rate variables at each output time. DYNAMO programs operate in five phases: (1) Input; cards are read and internal tables are constructed for each equation. From the PRINT and PLOT cards, output specifications are established. (2) Generation; machine coding is developed from skeleton instructions for each type of equation. (3) Running; the concerned equation types having initialization are solved to provide starting values for all variables requiring them at the beginning of a run. (4) Printing/Plotting; such phases convert the output data into specific output format. (5) Rerun; extra or additional cards modify the values of defined constants or other output requirements are read in. The program then returns to the running phase.

Numerical Control

Numerical control pertains to the control of machine tools, drafting machines, etc., by punched paper or magnetic tapes suitably encoded with directive information. Numerically controlled devices rely on their input tapes for detailed and explicit guidance because they have very limited logical or arithmetic capability to keep costs low. This may mean 8 bits for every .001 of motion or a great amount of data on the tape. Using information presented in a more manageable and concise form, it is common for a computer to prepare the control tapes. An example is the automatically programmed tools (APT) system developed by aerospace industry combine. Using APT, the designer describes his tool and the desired part in a high-level geometrically-oriented language. A preprocessor program accepts the high-level language and processes it into a simpler, more formalized internal representation. The tool independent central program converts the material, tool, and geometrical information into tool motion commands. A postprocessor program prepares the tool motion information in a format suitable for the particular control mechanism being used. A simultaneous output for a numerical control drafting machine permits preparation of detail blueprints while the robot tool is making the part, if desired.

APT. APT (Automatically Programmed Tools) is a program specifically designed through the cooperation of the computer industry with substantial assistance of the Univac Division of Sperry Rand, for the ease and convenience of computer controlled machine tools. The machine produces the desired part or product by following the numerically-coded instructions written by the programmer. The program must be very precise and intricate, so it is fundamentally a mathematical operation. The computer automatically controls the function of the machine to produce a part or component when the programmer defines the geometric dimensions of the part he wishes to create. To reference the intersections of these various components with instructions to the cutting tool, the statements are of English-language type. Such instructions are produced on punched paper tape for input to the controlled machine.

Even though APT cut only straight lines, their use is not restricted. These straight lines may be as short as 1/1000 of an inch, so that any conceivable shape can be cut. Because the machine has to be told by the computer to cut each of the tiny segments, this demonstrates the tediousness of programming the operation of the tool. After this is accomplished, with no added instructions, there can be endless repetition of the procedure, and the tape can be stored for later use. APT has made the great step forward by performing many tasks better than can be done with a human operator.

APT III is a UNIVAC system used in computer-assisted programming of machine tools, numerically controlled flame cutters, drafting machines, and other similar equipment. It was written to be production-oriented by simplifying the effort, time, and money needed, taking full advantage of numerically controlled techniques in engineering and manufacturing. Besides being able to provide machine-tool programming capabilities, which are virtually impossible by manual methods, APT system enhances most of the usual advantages found in numerical control: reduced lead time; greater design flexibility and freedom; greater accuracy; lower direct costs; lower tooling costs; improved production forecasting; better engineering control of the manufacturing process; and simplified introduction of changes. The APT III program represents over a century of development and testing man-hours.

STRESS. STRESS is an acronym for STRuctural Engineering System Solver. By using a problem-oriented input language it is designed to solve structural engineering problems. After a minimum study of the manual and without any prior programming experience a structural engineer could use STRESS. STRESS can be used to analyze structures with prismatic members in two or three dimensions, with either rigid or pinned joints, and subjected to distributed or concentrated loads, support motions, or temperature effects. A STRESS user will describe his problem by writing a series of statements specifying size and type of structure, physical dimensions, the loads, and the desired solution. The solution then supplies such information needed as member forces at the member ends, joint displacements, reactions, and support displacements. Employed by STRESS are the recently developed techniques in structural analysis, such as matrix and network formulations. In order to describe all the members and joints of a three-dimensional structure it is necessary to have a common reference system. STRESS employs a right-handed orthogonal cartesian coordinate system. The location of the system's origin can be found at any arbitrary point in the structure; e.g., one of the support joints. Described in terms of joint coordinates with respect to the origin of the coordinate system, are all joint data; and all computed joint reactions and displacements are similarly given in the same system.

COGO. First developed by Professor C. L. Miller and his associates at the Massachusetts Institute of Technology in association with the Puerto Rico Department of Public Works, is COGO, a civil engineering oriented language. Based on the technology of civil engineers, the COGO programming language or system is also applied in other areas. Also available is a special time-sharing version called QUIKTRAN/COGO. The engineer quickly and easily can write a problem using the COGO vocabulary and feed it to the computer for automatic computation. No intermediate programming is required.

The system, based on a coordinate table, and the problem, expressed in terms of angles given in degrees, minutes and seconds, are also the intersection (X, Y axes) points. COGO commands are based from such points formed on the coordinate table. Each point is given an identification number and is referenced by that number. The computer may be instructed to compute distances between points 1 and 2, to dump all coordinates, to locate and calculate bearings from known points, develop parallel lines, compute angles, calculate new points, etc., by a single word or short phrase command of COGO. For qualified engineers who require only a short time to learn its techniques and special power, COGO is a very versatile tool.